CD-ROM F

A Directory And Practi

For Media Specialists

CD-ROM FOR SCHOOLS

A Directory And Practical Handbook For Media Specialists

Pam Berger
Susan Kinnell

EIGHT BIT BOOKS

Wilton, CT
1994

ISBN 0-910965-13-7

**Dedicated with love to Bill and Bob.
They made it all possible.**

CONTENTS

ACKNOWLEDGMENTS

We would like to acknowledge many people whose help and assistance during all phases of this project was absolutely invaluable, including the producers who sent us titles to review; Mainstay in Camarillo, California for the donation of Capture software; colleagues and associates such as Debby Baker, Hugh Jones of IBM, Betty Kotcher of National Geographic, Nancy Larkin and her second-grade students at Malcolm S. Mackay Elementary School in Tenafly, New Jersey, Ann Lathrop, Scott Quimby, Helen Renevitz, Linda Singer, Sheryl Troy-Palladino, and Louise Wollman. The support of the administration and staff at Byram Hills High School (BHHS) and most especially the feedback from the wonderful students at BHHS was enormously helpful. And of course we owe a huge debt of gratitude to our steadfast editor, Nancy Garman, Adam Pemberton, for his invaluable assistance with the hardware chapter, Jeff and Jenny Pemberton, for their vision and encouragement, and the wonderful staff at Pemberton Press and Online, Inc. in Wilton, Connecticut. And, above all, the help and support we got from Chris Berger, Matt Fineman, and especially Kathryn Berger ensured that the project finally got finished.

Thank you one and all!

Pam Berger and Susan Kinnell
August 1994

PREFACE

"Please Touch the Paintings" was a recent headline in the Sunday section of the *New York Times Book Review*, March 6, 1994. It is not unusual for the *New York Times* to devote space to reviewing a work about art. What *is* unusual is that this particular work was not a print item, but a CD-ROM product. The CD-ROM contained more than 2,000 digitized pictures in full color from the collection of the National Gallery in London, England. The reviewer, Bernard Sharratt, described how this product allows users to explore this splendid collection at their own pace, studying authoritative biographies, history, commentary and glossary, as and when needed. He also indicated that the format has particular appeal for the young. It allows users to teach themselves, to proceed at their own pace, and to take responsibility for their own learning. Granted, the CD-ROM is no substitute for an authoritative book on the collection, but it is an alternative approach with enormous opportunities for individual learning.

CD-ROM has become the resource format of choice in schools for just these reasons. Resources in schools must reflect what is available, practical and suitable for fulfilling the school's mission—educating students to become independent, competent individuals. Although schools claim they collect only the best resources, technological developments and ongoing school reform efforts demand reconceptualization of what *best* means.

SHIFTING CHALLENGES

The exploding nature of information availability means that students must be able to learn with new technologies as they develop. Students must have the opportunity to identify and use resources in many formats, as appropriate for their particular questions and problems. School reform efforts reinforce this. Educational philosophy and practice has shifted from an assembly-line model that viewed students as raw material to be acted upon, to one that accepts the growing realization that different techniques and materials are needed for different individuals. The constant in the educational process remains the curriculum. It acts as the driving force for resource decisions.

As resource access is redefined in an increasingly electronic world, the school library media center's need for new types of materials becomes a high priority. The growing paradigm for library services of all types, in all settings, stresses that the uniqueness of users must be the central focus for collection development and information access decisions. The goal is to match resources to a myriad of identifiable characteristics of users, including age-appropriate subject materials. The school library media center must be prepared to house materials, or suggest pathways to access, that range from in-house storage of multiple formats to external connections to the virtual library.

Traditionally, collections in schools have been composed of materials evaluated by experts for quality and suitability to support the curriculum. This is not a new concept in librarianship, but there are some new wrinkles in the storage and retrieval process. New formats, such as CD-ROM, have extended the power of users to locate, select, and apply relevant information, ideas and resources to the solution of problems. Identifying these resources for possible purchase and logically planning for their inclusion in the collection has been a key concern for practitioners with limited time to search and test what is available!

This directory and handbook is a welcome addition to the collection development literature. It calls attention to CD-ROM as a powerful and growing access mode and suggests how to plan for its inclusion based on local curriculum assessment and the needs of your community of users. Specific selection tools and evaluative criteria are included, as well as individual titles that have been examined for their applications in schools.

Berger and Kinnell are a logical team to address this rapidly growing electronic medium. They have been working with and writing about electronic access for more than five years. They pioneered the successful DATABASES IN SCHOOLS conference (now MULTI-MEDIA SCHOOLS), and Berger launched the first newsletter dedicated to news of the online world as it related to schools and school curriculum concerns. This handbook provides another opportunity for school library media specialists to let experts lead the way.

Jacqueline C. Mancall
Professor of Information Studies
Drexel University
College of Information Studies
Philadelphia, PA

PROLOGUE

Allison walks into the study off the family room, tossing her coat and books on the sofa. In the afternoon, Allison and her brother, Jason, frequently use the study as a convenient place to do their homework, especially since her mother is a computer enthusiast and buys all the latest equipment. Today, Allison has, among other things, a report to do for her advanced placement class in U.S. history. She is working on a joint project with three other classmates on the effect of U.S. foreign policy in Japan. Her first task is to find background information about Japan and the history of U.S.-Japanese relations since World War II.

She sits at her mother's desk to use the Macintosh IIci computer there. It has a CD-ROM drive attached to it. The Mac IIci has a Seiko Trinitron monitor with good color and high resolution. The IIci has 8MB of RAM and a 240MB hard drive—lots of room to work with a CD-ROM and plenty of room to store her report without crowding anyone else's files. The CD-ROM drive is an Apple CD 150, almost two years old. Her mother and father have been talking about buying a new one because the transfer speed is 150KB/sec, and the newer models have double or even triple that speed. It would be nice for the multimedia discs, like the New Grolier Multimedia Encyclopedia, to have that faster speed available.

The drive is connected to the back of the computer via the 50-pin SCSI connector and has an additional SCSI connector so that other devices can be daisychained with it. Right now, the scanner is connected to it so that both devices can be operated without switching cables every time.

There's a power cord from the drive to the outlet. The two small amplified speakers on the floor under the desk are connected to the dual RCA jacks on the back of the drive. A small pair of headphones hang from a hook on the bookcase over the computer in case other people working in the study don't want to hear the sounds from the CD-ROM. The headphones plug into a jack on the front of the drive, making it very accessible and easy to use.

To the right of the computer is the printer, a nice laser printer that makes Allison's homework look really good. It sure beats the old IBM typewriter her father still insists on using sometimes!

Above the printer and the computer is a bookcase crammed full of manuals, how-to books, paper and supplies, and some CD-ROMs. Taking only about five inches of shelf space, these discs contain clip art and fonts, a few good games and sports discs, and some of the best reference works possible. There's Webster's Ninth Collegiate Dictionary, the Grolier Encyclopedia, the Guinness Disc of Records, the World Almanac and Book of Facts, the Project Gutenberg disc that has the text of hundreds of books, and her brother's space discs, as she calls them. Jason wants to be an astronaut, and he is very interested in the new discs that have photographs and information about space travel. Space Shuttle, Murmurs of Earth, Small Blue Planet, and The View From Earth are his current favorites; and Allison is sure Jason will prove the experts wrong by completely wearing these discs out!

Allison selects the encyclopedia and the almanac as a starting place. She adjusts her mother's chair (she's taller than her mother and needs to lower her seat a little) and reaches over to turn on the CD-ROM drive. She has finally remembered that you have to turn it on first, before the computer, or the computer won't be able to recognize the drive's presence. The green light on the front of the drive comes on, and she hits the keyboard power-on key for the IIci. While the IIci is warming up, she takes the disc out of its jewel case and puts it in the disc caddy to insert in the drive.

The printer is turned on and she looks at her notebook to double-check what she has to do. When the computer is up and running, she inserts the disc caddy into the front-loading drive. The green light on the drive flickers back and forth from green to yellow indicating that the drive is reading the disc. The icon for the CD-ROM drive comes up at the right side of the screen. Allison double-clicks on the icon to launch the program on the disc. Too late she remembers that this is a disc that must be launched from the hard drive. The software to search the disc is on the disc itself, but it was copied to the hard drive when they first got the disc. To run the encyclopedia, she must click on the software icon on the hard drive so the computer can do all the hard work, while the drive just has to access images, sounds, and video segments.

An hour and a half later, Allison stretches and yawns, leans back in her chair and waits for the printer to print her notes. She has found some interesting statistics on U.S.-Japanese relations, the melody of the Japanese national anthem (that's recorded on her own disk), the Japanese flag, the text of the treaty signed after World War II, and the current issues about trade between the two nations. There's a ton of information out there, and she's only just begun to find it all.

The tricky part will be choosing which source is the best for which kind of material. Some will be straight facts, some will be background information. Other sources will provide current data on congressmen and laws. She remembers that Mrs. Berger, her high school librarian, was talking about a new disc that gave all of the Senators' and Representatives' voting records. She'll have to ask Mrs. Berger tomorrow which disc that is and see if she can find some more information on....The front door crashes into the wall as her brother arrives home from band practice. Hurriedly, Allison gathers up her notes and materials so she can get out of Jason's way and not have to listen to him any more than she has to. Besides, it isn't yet too late to call Laura Beth and find out what she is wearing to school tomorrow, and just casually ask when her brother, Ted, is coming home from college....

SCENE 2

As Allison walked into her school library the next morning, she saw Mrs. Berger behind the circulation desk. There weren't too many people around yet; classes didn't start for twenty minutes and most students weren't early birds as she was. The two library aides were in the back of the library unlocking windows, putting out newspapers, and turning on the machines—getting ready for the new day. "Hi, Mrs. Berger," said Allison as she walked around the desk, heading for the computers behind it.

"Good morning, Allison. What brings you here so early?" Mrs. Berger smiled at the girl.

"I am working on two reports—one for my AP history class, and I need some Congressional voting records. But I can wait for that one I think. What I really need now is some help for Mr. Charleston's government class. I have to do a paper on cultures in conflict. Which CD-ROM should I use to get some good ideas for a topic? I can't decide between Northern Ireland and the Arab-Israeli conflict."

Mrs. Berger nodded, and said, "Go sit down and I'll see what I can find." Allison walked to the last computer in the semi-circle behind the circulation desk. It was her favorite workstation and always seemed to work well for her. Besides, it was the one 486 machine that Mrs. Berger had set up to be able to drop off the network and run the multimedia CD-ROMs as if it were a standalone machine. That was still a necessity these days because full-motion video just didn't run on the network. So, if the disc had really good video on it, it was better to look at it on a standalone machine and not one that was on the network. Because of that, there was always something good on that machine, and it wasn't easy to find it free. At lunch time and during free periods, it was always busy. She dropped her books on the table area beside the computer and reached over to touch the space bar and turn off the screen saver. The familiar menu with the bright blue background came on, and she typed in her ID and password, then selected Byram Hills High School Library from the list.

Mrs. Berger walked over with a CD-ROM jewel case in her hand, looking at the cover and muttering to herself. She looked at Allison and said, "I think this one would be the place to start. It has a lot of information on groups in different countries, and you can download the records to your disk. It's called CNN Newsroom. When you're finished with that one, you might try some of the indexes like Readers' Guide, and also some of the newspaper titles. Ethnic NewsWatch is on the network now, and it has some really good articles from Middle East newspapers, Irish papers, and others. If you don't know which group or conflict to look at, this would be a good place to start. Then you can compare some of the reporting of the same incidents by looking at the New York Times and see how they're different. And don't forget that DIALOG has that new CD-ROM with the full text of five major newspapers. Let me know if you want to look at it. Are you here during first period?"

Allison nodded and thanked her for the disc. She loaded CNN Newsroom in the caddy and pushed it into the computer. This computer had an internal CD-ROM drive, not like the external, separate one on the computer at home. Allison spent about 30 minutes looking through CNN Newsroom and finding some good material for the background for her report. She downloaded the good sections to her own disk that she had already put into the A: drive. Usually she saved the information she was collecting to her own file on the server, rather than to a floppy disk. Then, when she had quite a bit, she moved it all onto her floppy disk. It saved a lot of time and effort that way, especially if her disk was full or she had forgotten to bring it that day.

More kids had come in and some were working on the computers around her. William was looking through SIRS to find a good topic for his science project. He was always a little bit behind the rest of the class, Allison thought. He was still looking for a topic, and the rest of the class was already hard at work on their projects. Linda, beyond William, was writing a story for the school paper and laying it out in PageMaker. Miss Williston, an English teacher, was writing up some notes in WordPerfect on the conference she had just attended in Georgia. At the end of the row, she could see Jeanette sending an e-mail message to her computer-pal in Montana via the Internet. They were probably talking about their joint project on the movie City Slickers. Allison could see the CD-ROM, Cinemania, next to Jeanette's computer.

Allison leaned back in her chair and stretched, thinking again as she had many times before that this was a nice room to work in. There were big windows and lots of natural light. There were bright "ALA—Read" posters on the wall (she particularly liked the one of Alec Baldwin) and racks and racks of colorful books on wooden shelves. Last December, there had been a beautiful pine tree in the middle of the library, decorated with CD-ROMs! There always seemed to be things going on—it was as though the library were the center of the school. If you wanted to know what was happening, this was definitely the place to be. Although, now that the whole school was networked, she could access the same information from her classroom. What a fabulous opportunity that was! Now the library with all its information was accessible everywhere—it really was a room without walls these days.

She was soon reabsorbed in her task. When the bell sounded for the end of first period, she looked up in surprise. She quickly finished her downloading, ended the program and gathered her belongings. She stopped at the desk, handed the disc in its plastic box to Mrs. Hunter and said, "Thank Mrs. Berger for me, would you? This was great. Just what I needed. I'll come back on my next free period and check it out so I can look at it at home tonight." She smiled again and hurried to her next class.

CHAPTER 1

INTRODUCTION

T
wo years ago when we began work on this book, the CD-ROM industry was just beginning to blossom. CD-ROM was routinely included in conferences and workshops about information for schools and businesses, and computer hardware and software companies were developing better equipment and more titles for all markets.

Then sometime in 1993, the "blossoms" became veritable jungles filled with new titles and equipment; and how-to books, new periodicals, and conferences flourished. Multimedia became the hottest buzzword in computerland and beyond, and predictions for the inclusion of multimedia in everything from classroom tools to home shopping to business presentations were rampant. After years of languishing behind the scenes, CD-ROM was the hottest topic around and the fastest-selling peripheral ever.

Numerous companies are producing countless new discs, and the educational community can only benefit from this proliferation. No longer is it a question of finding an appropriate disc for a specific need, but rather of selecting the best disc from several that are available. This is a much happier situation for schools and educators, for now CD-ROM is a task of evaluating and selecting, not just finding and purchasing.

Competition is a very good thing, and in the case of CD-ROM, competition has resulted in better and better discs. The color, sound, quality of images and animation, the depth and breadth of the information, and the design of interfaces have improved so dramatically that discs we considered excellent two years ago pale in comparison to newer releases. In the IBM-compatible world, the popularity of Windows has made a huge difference in the ease of installation, navigation tools, and interactivity of Windows-based discs. Macintosh computers and discs, with their ease of use and "plug-and-play" compatibility, provided an incentive for other manufacturers to develop similar capabilities in their hardware and products.

Now is an exciting time to consider the purchase of CD-ROM equipment and development of a CD-ROM collection. With this book, we hope to assist you—to give you the benefit of our research as we have looked at CD-ROM drives, discs, and literature over the past two years.

CD-ROM AND MULTIMEDIA

Exactly what is CD-ROM, anyway? In one sense, it is a storage medium. Using optical (laser) technology, a CD-ROM can contain up to 650 megabytes of data (all kinds of data) on one disc. That is the equivalent of 300,000 pages of text, or about 450 floppy disks, or an entire encyclopedia, 147 textbooks, or hundreds of pictures—all on a single, shiny, silver disc. Better yet, this material is all digital.

CD-ROM also offers a way of combining multiple types of information using a single machine. Multimedia is the hottest new word in educational technology these days, and CD-ROM is the rising star on this particular stage. Because of its huge storage capacity, CD-ROM can present all kinds of information about any topic or multiple topics. Text, illustrations (photographs, drawings, graphs, tables, etc.), video, sound, and animation can all be presented on one machine from a single disc. Rivaling arcade-type, computer games, CD-ROM can provide the most complete audio/visual/textual information for school use, giving new life and challenge to student learning and progress.

THE GROWTH OF CD-ROM IN SCHOOLS

At the end of 1992, there were approximately 3.5 million computers in schools from kindergarten through high school. This number continues to grow by leaps and bounds as school administrators, teachers, and parents see that information and technology will enhance students' learning experiences.

At the same time, the number of CD-ROM drives in schools is mushrooming. A growing number of low-priced, relevant, valuable educational titles has led to an awareness by schools' faculties and staffs that CD-ROM technology is not only priced right, but is pedagogically valid. Now students can explore for information, use Boolean searching, and find patterns and categories of information. When students search this way instead of just identifying and collecting data, they find new meanings in information, and when that happens, data becomes knowledge, and it becomes theirs. Students can take ownership of material in a way that previously seldom happened. It is an exciting and revealing process that will delight and reward everyone who participates.

In the past year and a half, several major U.S. textbook publishers have developed and released CD-ROMs. One such company is DC Heath, which produced a history textbook on disc called The Enduring Vision. This product replicates all of the text in its textbook counterpart, plus includes video, graphics and sound components that greatly enhance the understanding of history. The CD-ROM and the text version have similar prices, offering students and teachers a real choice between the two media. Primarily aimed at the academic market, it sends a clear signal to all educators—future textbooks will not be just paper, and future students stand to benefit from this creative and evolving industry.

At the same time, several state departments of education have recognized the growing role of CD-ROM technology in schools. Texas has committed to the adoption of textbooks that include CD-ROM and videodiscs; California has issued guidelines for textbook adoption that give the highest approval to materials in machine-readable format. California has also issued a list of "exemplary" and "desirable" CD-ROMs to help schools make buying decisions. In New York, a school library system won a competitive $87,000 federal grant under Title IIB to retrain school library media specialists in the new information technologies, including CD-ROM.

DINOSAURS

3-D Dinosaur
A World of Animals
Dinosaur Adventure
Dinosaur Discovery
Dinosaur Safari
Dinosaurs! The Multimedia Encyclopedia
Encyclopedia of Dinosaurs
Microsoft Dinosaurs
Prehistoria

List of CD-ROM titles about dinosaurs.

THE MEDIA CENTER AND CD-ROM

The impact of CD-ROM on the school library media center ranges from requiring a complete overhaul to a "What's that?" approach. Some media specialists have seen the future and have dedicated themselves to getting ready with purchases of equipment and peripherals, restructuring schedules and instruction times, and rearranging their furniture and their lives to provide access to multiple forms of information to students.

Other media specialists, especially ones who find the new technology daunting, will discover their students are ill-prepared to compete with others who can use various kinds of information with ease and who are conversant with different methods of accessing that information.

The objective of the library media program is to provide each student with the necessary skills to become information-literate—to know how to locate, access, analyze, organize and present information. That information may be printed text, animated computer programs, videos, sound recordings, or hyperlinked multimedia. Increasingly, information available to students will be of different, nonstandard kinds. It will be the job of the media specialists to provide all kinds of information, as well as the tools needed to access them. At the same time, the media specialist must remember that student learning comes first. The bottom line is that the school library media center programs must be curriculum-based, not technology-driven, even though some days it will feel otherwise!

CD-ROMS AVAILABLE TODAY

There are as many kinds of CD-ROMs today as there are types of print materials. It helps to think of CD-ROMs as just another kind of book—and develop your collection of CD-ROMs just the way you develop your book collection. What areas do you need to develop? What is your budget? How many ways can a resource be used? Where do you need more depth? More breadth? Is your school library media center more of a reference center? A teaching center? A research center? What titles do you need to enhance those strengths?

There are bibliographic and index CD-ROMs; there are games, storybooks, textbooks, and reference works (like almanacs, atlases, dictionaries, encyclopedias, and directories). Some discs concentrate on single topics in-depth, while others focus on broad subject areas (Whales & Dolphins, or Oceans Below). Some discs have giant public domain databases from government publications, and others are single titles from tiny companies just starting up.

The current issue of the TFPL *CD-ROM Directory* lists almost 4,000 titles currently available, and practically every publisher in the industry is expanding its publication goal for the coming year. There will be no dearth of titles for the school market in the foreseeable future! The problem, of course, will be choosing which titles are suitable for your school—that is what we hope to help you do by writing this book.

HOW TO USE THIS BOOK

We have collected more than 300 CD-ROM titles that are meant specifically for education. We have reviewed, read about, and discussed these titles with anyone who would stand still and listen. We have selected approximately 100 of the very best and most current ones and included them in a Core Collection, along with complete information and an evaluative description of each one (Chapter 6). Ten titles in the Core Collection carry our

TRAVEL

Adventures
America Adventure
Everywhere USA Travel Guide
Exotic Japan
From Alice to Ocean
Global Explorer
Great Cities of the World, Vol. 2
Great Cities of the World, Vol. 1
Great Wonders of the World, Vol. 2
Great Wonders of the World, Vol. 1
Let's Go 1993 California and Hawaii
Let's Go 1993 USA
National Parks: The Multimedia Family Guide
Oregon Trail

List of CD-ROM titles about travel.

very highest recommendation and are marked with a starred entry (see box on page 62). Chapter 7 lists more titles in a brief, directory-style format giving information about platform, producer, price, grade level and curriculum content, along with a very brief description. Chapter 8 covers the entire list of CD-ROM titles in the Core Collection and Supplementary List, sorted by curriculum area and grade level. For example, you can see at a glance which titles are suitable for Science at the Primary and Elementary levels, or which ones are good for Foreign Language at the Senior High School level.

The first five chapters of this book contain information you need to know about CD-ROM technology and use of CD-ROMs in schools. Chapter 2 is a complete overview of the hardware and software necessary to use CD-ROMs in your school. Use this chapter for reference as the need arises; do not attempt to read it like a novel (unless you have trouble getting to sleep at night!). Chapter 3 covers the management of CD-ROM technology in your school library media center and its relationship to the entire school. Evaluation and selection of CD-ROM titles is addressed in-depth in Chapter 4, and guidelines and an evaluation form are included. We encourage you to use and copy the form you'll find there. Chapter 5 discusses how to integrate CD-ROM into your curriculum and the instructional issues that are raised. Following the chapters that review and list CD-ROM titles, you'll find more helpful information including a list of producers and distributors. A glossary and an index complete the book.

We are solely responsible for the content of this book. Please let us know if you have any ideas for additions, changes, or corrections—we are always willing to look at new material or to reconsider old sources.

The next year or two will be great years for getting into CD-ROM. As the range and scope of information increases and the avenues to access that information grow into superhighways, school library media centers will be taking on new roles. The power of the information society will propel us all into the 21st century at warp speed. Fasten your seat belts—it's going to be a great ride!

Pam Berger
14 Hadden Road
Scarsdale, NY 10583
914/723-1995
pberger@bhhs.byram.k12.ny.us

Susan Kinnell
4891 Frances Street
Santa Barbara, CA 93111
805/964-2942
susan.c@bkstr.vcsb.edu

CHAPTER 2
CD-ROM HARDWARE, SOFTWARE AND NETWORKING

C D-ROM stands for Compact Disc-Read Only Memory and is an optical technology used to store large amounts of information on a plastic 12-centimeter disc. Information on a CD-ROM can be read and subsequently used many ways, but not altered on the disc in any way. (Newer technological developments are under way for discs that can be erased or rewritten.)

The capacity for storage on a CD-ROM is impressive—a disc can hold over 650 megabytes of data. That's the equivalent of 300,000 printed pages, one million library catalog cards, one hour of sound or 15,000 graphic images. Since the discs are small and relatively indestructible, they have become very practical for use in schools.

Optical discs, generically speaking, are discs that rely on laser beam technology for reading data from the disc. Optical discs fall into two broad categories, analog and digital. A videodisc (often called a Laserdisc, a trademarked term belonging to Pioneer) is an optical disc most often used to store video and photographic images. The data on the disc is not digital—the files can be accessed or shown by the computer, but not manipulated in any way. CD-ROM files are digital, meaning the data can be copied into a computer and used by word processing programs, spreadsheets, databases, photo-editing and other programs.

Both videodiscs and CD-ROMs are read-only discs; that is, the discs cannot be altered and additional material cannot be added. (As we write, CD recorders are dropping in cost, but the use of CD-R in school and educational environments is not likely in the near future. An exception is the Photo CD. See the section describing CD-ROM drives.)

The other kind of storage medium that we often use in the computer world is magnetic storage. Standard floppy disks and internal hard drives are both magnetic disks. The internal hard drive or disk is a metallic disk coated with a magnetic alloy approximately three-millionths of an inch thick, while the floppy disk is a mylar disk with a magnetic film on it. A read-write head rearranges (by magnetically polarizing) the molecules in the magnetic film to create a binary code which the computer can then read. Data on a magnetic disk, floppy or internal, can easily be added to, altered, erased, rewritten and changed.

THE CD-ROM

A CD-ROM is physically composed of three layers—a clear polycarbonate substrate layer, a metal layer and an acrylic layer. Polycarbonate is used for strength and rigidity (it is the same material used for bulletproofing). Aluminum is used for the metal layer, and a clear acrylic material is used for the top layer where the label and company information are printed.

The data on a disc is encoded and stored on a disc in the form of "pits" and "lands." Pits are depressions or hollows in the metal, and lands are perfectly flat areas. A laser beam reflects off the flat areas and is

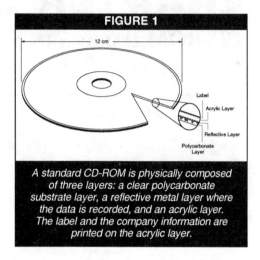

FIGURE 1

A standard CD-ROM is physically composed of three layers: a clear polycarbonate substrate layer, a reflective metal layer where the data is recorded, and an acrylic layer. The label and the company information are printed on the acrylic layer.

detected by the sensors in the drive. The light shining on the pits is deflected sideways or defused so that it cannot be detected by the sensors. This pattern of non-reflective and reflective areas on the disc is interpreted by the drive circuitry as a pattern of ones and zeros, and is thus translatable into machine language as binary code.

The focal plane of the laser is directly on the metal layer of the disc, so most scratches or marks on the polycarbonate layer will not interfere with the reading by the sensors. The pits and lands on a disc are on a single, spiral track less than one-hundredth the width of a human hair. If unwound, this track would be almost four miles long.

Magnetic disks spin at the *same* rate of speed or "revolutions per minute" (rpm). (When the rpm is constant, it is said that the disk spins at a "constant angular velocity," or CAV.) With magnetic disks, the tracks near the outer edge of the disk are moving faster past the read head than the tracks near the center. The concept of constant angular velocity is best explained by imagining yourself standing on a merry-go-round. It is spinning at a constant angular velocity. If you stand near the center, your linear speed is slower than if you stand at the outer edge. On the outer edge, you are traveling a much larger diameter circle in the same time (at the same rpm).

By contrast, CD-ROMs spin at a *varying* angular rate of speed, called constant linear velocity (CLV). The CD-ROM spindle motor is designed to vary the rpm of the disc (depending on the position of read head from center) to insure that the data moving by the read head always moves at the same linear speed. The sectors on an optical disc can all be of equal size, which permits many more sectors on any given disc. The trade-off is less storage and more speed (of access and transfer) on a magnetic disk, and more storage and less speed on an optical disc.

THE CD-ROM DRIVE

CD-ROM drives are small, compact and relatively simple-looking pieces of computer hardware. An internal CD-ROM drive is installed into the 5-1/4" drive bay of a computer. An external drive connects to the back of the computer by a cable (Figure 2).

The first thing to notice about a CD-ROM drive is the lack of front panel buttons, lights and LCD display. It is almost disconcerting not to see a lot of controls on such a modern, technologically advanced piece of equipment. On most CD-ROM drives, there is only a small power light that tells you when the drive is turned on and another light that indicates when the disc is being read. There is a push button to eject the disc caddy from the drive, a headphone jack and corresponding volume control. The disc open-

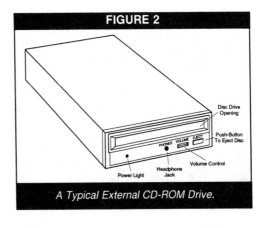

A Typical External CD-ROM Drive.

ing is about the size of a jewel box (the plastic case the disc comes in), and most drives have a dust-control door covering the opening. Although most CD-ROM drives utilize a plastic caddy into which the disc must be placed before insertion, some newer models are using the drawer-type mechanism similar to audio CD players.

So how is the drive controlled? How do you start it and stop it if there aren't any controls?

Unlike the standard audio CD player, which has a collection of start, stop, pause and seek buttons, the CD-ROM drive and disc are controlled by software. This software may be on the compact disc itself and accessed by the computer, or it may be loaded on the hard disk or on a floppy disk. This software sends stop, start, search, play and other such commands to the drive. The software to read a CD-ROM may be as ordinary as HyperCard or LinkWay—or it may be proprietary and confined to a single disc or family of discs. (See the later section on Software.)

INTERNAL VERSUS EXTERNAL DRIVES

If you have a computer with internal room to hold an extra drive, you have the choice of buying an internal or an external CD-ROM drive. An internal drive actually fits inside the computer, much like a hard drive. An internal CD-ROM drive is cheaper than an external drive (because it does not have an external housing or power supply), but it needs to be installed inside your computer. That may mean an additional installation cost or some additional time for you or your technical support person to figure out how to do it yourselves.

In the Macintosh world, until the advent of the Macintosh IIvx and the Performa series, all Mac CD-ROM drives were external. Now, almost all new Macintosh computers (not the PowerBooks or Classics) can be fitted with an internal CD-ROM drive. Most new IBM-compatible machines also have enough internal space to hold a CD-ROM drive as well. The new acceptance of multimedia demands CD-ROM hardware, so hardware manufacturers are incorporating present and future CD-ROM capability into almost all machines. If your current system is older, you might consider buying a newer machine with an internal CD-ROM drive.

An external drive comes in a variety of configurations, from simple, single drives to drives that will hold multiple discs at once (sometimes called jukeboxes), and multiple drives in a single housing (sometimes called towers). Each of these kinds of drives connects to the computer via an external port. On the Macintosh, the port is a SCSI (pronounced "scuzzy") port. A SCSI port provides a high-speed standardized interface for any number of peripheral devices, including a CD-ROM drive. On a PC, the CD-ROM drive connects to either a proprietary interface card (that comes with the CD-ROM drive) or a SCSI host adapter card (available from Adaptec, Future Domain, or any number of vendors). SCSI adapters are even available on PCMCIA cards for use in laptops! The choice of a proprietary or SCSI interface depends on the CD-ROM drive you purchase. Check your computer manual and your CD-ROM drive manual to make sure the ports you want to use are compatible.

CD-ROM drives can also be connected to the serial port of a computer, instead of to a proprietary or SCSI port. These drives are usually less expensive and come with an internal proprietary card to enable them to run on the computer. You will find that such drives are usually slower, but the main disadvantage is that devices using the serial port cannot be daisychained with other peripheral devices as they can be with a SCSI port. A new interface in the CD-ROM world that is just becoming available is IDE (this is how most magnetic hard disks are controlled in PCs). The IDE CD-ROM drives may become an attractive way to add CD-ROM to your computer through the existing IDE controller.

An external drive also has an external power cable for the drive itself (an internal drive uses the computer's power supply). Once the CD-ROM drive is connected to the computer and plugged in, you must load software on the computer so that the computer will recognize that there is a CD-ROM drive attached to its port. Typically, the CD-ROM "driver" software comes with the drive or with the SCSI host adapter. Now you're ready to go!

MECHANICS OF A CD-ROM DRIVE

There isn't a whole lot to know about the mechanical workings of a CD-ROM drive. In fact, there is very little that is mechanical about these drives. The little door over the opening, the eject mechanism and the motor that spins the disc are about all there is. The rest of the drive runs with electro-optical components. That is, they don't have any moving parts—which means that there is relatively little about a drive that can "break."

The components and circuits that control the disc in the drive are:

- A small servo-motor that spins the disc (at varying speeds)
- A laser that projects a beam of light onto the disc
- A prism that deflects the reflected light onto a light-sensing diode
- A circuit that reads the voltages generated by the diode

When the disc is spinning in the drive, a unit containing the detector moves to the part of the disc being read. The motor spins the disc at a constant linear velocity (CLV), so that no matter which part of the disc is being read, the pits and lands are moving at exactly the same

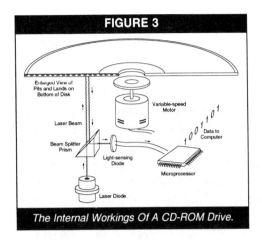

FIGURE 3

The Internal Workings Of A CD-ROM Drive.

rate over the detector. The detector contains a laser diode to project the beam, a prism to deflect the reflected beam of light, and a light-sensing diode.

The reflected light from the lands (and the absence of reflected light from the pits) is deflected by the prism onto the light-sensing diode. Each bit of light generates a tiny electrical current in the diode, and this pattern of electrical pulses is then passed to the computer as a data stream of zeros and ones. This is a binary code that the computer can understand.

SPEED OF A DRIVE

When a CD-ROM is in the drive, the user looks for something on the disc by typing a search query, clicking on a button on the screen or typing a word. Then there is a wait while the light on the drive goes on, the motor hums, and finally the response to the query appears on the computer screen.

Access Speed

Part of the search speed is determined by how fast the drive finds the requested information and gets to its exact location on the disc. That's called *access* time or, sometimes, *seek* time. Speed of access is an important criterion for a CD-ROM drive. The access time for today's new drives ranges between 200 and 380 milliseconds. For this measure, the *smaller* number is better—that is, the fewer number of milliseconds it takes to access the data, the better. (CD-ROM drives are not fast by other standards in the computer world. A hard disk drive accesses information in 15 to 30 milliseconds.)

Transfer Rate

The other measure of search speed is *transfer* rate. The transfer rate is the amount of time it takes for the accessed information to be transferred into the computer (and onto the screen). Transfer rate is measured differently from access speed on a CD-ROM drive. It is measured by how many kilobytes of information are passed from the disc to the computer per second (kilobytes per second or KB/sec). The transfer rate of a drive is directly related to the speed at which the drive motor spins the disc. The faster the disc spins, the more data travels past the read head, and the faster it goes into the computer.

The industry norm for years was 150KB/sec, but in late 1992 and early 1993, many new drives were introduced that were rated at 300 or more KB/sec. Continuing this trend, NEC released the first triple speed drive in late 1993. The transfer rate of this drive is 450KB/sec, or three times the normal rate of 150KB/sec. Quad speed (600KB/sec) drives are also now available, but the cost is typically $1000 or more. Most major drive manufacturers have announced plans to deliver lower cost ($500-$600) quad-speed drives in late 1994 or early 1995.

For transfer speed, the *bigger* number is better—data gets passed from the disc to the computer faster. Remember, the transfer rate of CD-ROM drives is somewhat slow by other computer standards (the transfer rate of a hard drive is 600-2000KB/sec). In practical terms, transfer rate has the biggest impact on the quality of multimedia discs. The playback of motion video, audio and high-resolution scanned images demands higher transfer rate drives or the retrieval and playback is delayed and not smooth. If you expect to get good results with the latest multimedia titles, use at least a double speed (300KB/sec) or faster transfer rate drive.

The terms double-speed, triple-speed, quad-speed and MultiSpin (a NEC trademark for their faster spinning drives) also mean "dual-speed" drives, because the audio on any CD is designed to play back at the original 150KB/sec speed. So the data and graphics portions of the CD are transferred at 300KB/sec or faster, and the audio portion at 150KB/sec. This switching back and forth between the two is invisible to the user.

Caching Software

Caching software is available that improves CD-ROM drive performance. One example is CD-ROM Toolkit for the Macintosh. Toolkit is a high-performance driver for the SCSI device, a caching utility for CD-ROM drives and a desk accessory for playing CD-Audio discs. The software puts important file and folder information from a CD-ROM onto the hard disk so that file management functions can run at the speed of the hard disk, not the slower CD-ROM drive.

Caching, sometimes called *buffering*, is a term used in several different kinds of applications, including CD-ROM. It means that the data requested is transferred to a section of RAM (and sometimes the hard disk) and then transferred in sections to the monitor. By logically anticipating the next section of data to be requested, the caching utility can move data ahead of the actual request and have it ready to display. That's rather simply stated, but the principle is the same for all caching operations, just more complex. The logical choices made by the caching circuits are the only way to judge whether one caching system is better or worse than another.

KODAK PHOTO CD AND MULTISESSION CD-ROMS

During the latter part of 1992, Eastman Kodak unveiled its new Photo CD system. With this system, slide film is developed and the images placed on a compact disc called Photo CD using Kodak's proprietary process. A revolutionary aspect of this new process is its ability to store subsequent groups of images on the same disc. These discs, with multiple groups of images stored at various times, are called multisession discs.

The images on a Photo CD can then be viewed on a television monitor using a CD-I player or on a computer using any of the newer CD-ROM drives that are designated

"Photo CD-compatible." These drives are called CD-ROM XA—the XA stands for "eXtended Architecture."

While all such CD-ROM drives will read a Photo CD, some are rated for "single-session" compatibility and others for "multisession" compatibility. The difference is that multisession CD-ROM drives can read Photo CDs to which more than one group of slides have been added. The single-session drives can only read the first group of images on a Photo CD. Photo CD has a great deal of potential for long-term school use—such as school pictures, yearbooks, and the like.

CD-RECORDABLE

Thanks to recent hardware developments, it is now possible to make your own compact discs. Ranging in price from about $3000 to over $10,000, Compact Disc-Recordable (CD-R) systems are a very good way of putting large amounts of data on a lightweight disc. The data might be large archives, a prototype disc before an expensive multimedia production, preserving film, video, or audio recording for future use, or even a school yearbook! South Eugene High School in Eugene, Oregon created a Macintosh disc called The Electronic Eugenean that has photographs, maps, animation, images of the school staff and faculty, and some interactive features that make it a really outstanding yearbook.

Software accompanies a CD-R drive to allow the user to index and format the data to be recorded on the disc. Making a CD-R is not the easiest or the cheapest task to undertake, but developers are sure to keep working on all facets of a CD-R system so that prices will go down and user-friendliness will go up. If you have large amounts of data to be archived, by all means investigate the possibilities of recording your own compact disc.

STANDARDS

Late in 1985, a group of industry leaders met at the High Sierra Casino and Hotel in Lake Tahoe, California, to set standards for the structural organization of files and data on a CD-ROM. This became known as the High Sierra standard, and it was subsequently amended slightly and formalized by the International Standards Organization as ISO 9660. Virtually every disc manufactured since that time meets those standards and is thus playable and usable on nearly any CD-ROM drive.

The other CD-ROM format is HFS (Hierarchical File Structure) used by Macintosh computers. HFS is a description of the way the Macintosh reads and organizes files. CD-ROMs that are HFS-compatible are Mac-only; they can be used only with a Macintosh computer equipped with a CD-ROM drive. HFS discs are not limited in file-naming conventions like the ISO 9660 discs.

Almost every CD-ROM drive on the market today conforms to High Sierra, ISO 9660, or HFS for the Macintosh, so the standards of a drive are no longer of critical importance. You can purchase a drive without worrying about its compatibility with your hardware or future disc purchases.

PRICE

The final element to consider about a CD-ROM drive is price. The rule is to buy the best that you can afford. List the specifications that are essential to you, find the drives that have them and then buy the best-priced drive. The price range for drives today is $199 to well over $1000. Beware of the really low-priced drives and make sure that any drive you are considering has the minimum requirements for your situation. Street prices, of course, vary greatly, and the wise shopper looks many places before buying! Look for educational discounts and end-of-year sales.

Keep an eye out for good deals—bundles including a computer, drive, discs or any combination thereof. Some distributors and mail-order places sell a CD-ROM drive bundled with speakers, sound board, software and an assortment of discs. You can select the "bundle" that best suits your needs and get a good price as well. Beware, however, that sometimes bundles don't sport the top-of-the-line drives or other components, and some may include discs you will never use.

Features To Look For When You Buy A CD-ROM Drive

- **Transfer rate:** 300KB/sec or faster (bigger number)
- **Access speed:** 200-300 milliseconds or faster (smaller number). Sometimes called *seek time*.
- **Speed:** double speed, triple speed or "Multispin" (especially important for multimedia titles)
- **MTBF:** at least 15,000 (lots of hours before it "fails")
- **Port:** a SCSI drive, if possible (which may require SCSI host adapter on a PC)
- **Multisession:** Photo CD-compatible for additional sessions; also called CD-ROM XA

THE COMPUTER

The computer to which your CD-ROM drive is attached will determine to some extent the kind of CD-ROM usable in the drive and how fast its information can be accessed. If the computer is a vintage 8088 machine (the old PC XT model), the fastest CD-ROM drive on the market will not function at its best levels. If the computer monitor is not a high-resolution color monitor, a great deal of the visual excitement of CD-ROM will be lost. If there is no sound board in an IBM-compatible machine, then the audio files on the CD-ROM will be silent. If there is not enough RAM (working, temporary storage in the computer), then the computer may not even be able to handle a CD-ROM at all.

Mail-Order Sources For CD-ROM And Computer Equipment

Watch the advertisements in some of the major computer magazines like *PC World*, *Macworld*, *MacUser*, *Windows*, *PC Novice*, *PC Today*, and *Compute!*

The big mail-order houses run multipage ads in these magazines that offer competitive prices and quantities of information about new CD-ROM titles and new computer hardware. These informative ads are a comparison shopper's dream-come-true!

MPC Requirements

MPC Level 1 *minimum* **requirements are:**
- 386SX computer with 2MB RAM, 30MB hard drive, Windows 3.1 and DOS 3.1, MSCDEX 2.2 or later
- CD-ROM drive with 150KB/sec transfer rate
- sound board
- VGA or VGA Plus monitor
- Speakers or headphones
- Ports for MIDI input/output and a joystick

MPC Level 2 *minimum* **requirements are:**
- 486SX computer with 4MB RAM, 25MHz, 160MB hard drive, Windows 3.1 and DOS 5.0; MSCDEX 2.2 or later
- CD-ROM drive with 300KB/sec transfer rate, 400 milliseconds maximum average access time, CD-ROM XA ready, multisession capable
- sound board with 16-bit digital sound, 8-note synthesizer, and MIDI playback
- SVGA monitor
- Speakers or headphones
- Ports for MIDI input/output and a joystick

For more information about the Multimedia PC Level 1 and 2 Specifications, contact the Multimedia PC Marketing Council, 1730 M Street NW, Suite 707, Washington, DC 20036.

There are some minimum requirements for running certain kinds of discs. If the CD-ROM is a text-based disc, an older and slower machine without sound and color will be able to handle it. However, if there are graphics, video sequences, audio files or animation as well as text, then the computer behind the CD-ROM drive must have certain capabilities.

The Multimedia PC Marketing Council in Washington, DC has established a set of minimum hardware requirements for computers to be able to run a certain kind of multimedia disc. In May 1993, the council announced a second level of minimum requirements that extends the original list and also provides recommendations for maximum performance. Any CD-ROM that carries the label MPC, or MPC Level 2, will only run on machines that meet those minimum requirements.

Remember that all of this does not apply to the Macintosh family of computers. From the beginning, the Mac has supported sound and animation with its graphical interface. However, even with a Macintosh, you need enough speed, hard drive space, and RAM. Color is virtually essential for today's multimedia discs, and the new Macs are all offering color monitors. The minimum requirements to run a multimedia disc on a Macintosh would be:

- Mac II family or any of the newer models
- Color monitor
- 4MB RAM at least; 8MB RAM preferable
- External speakers to enjoy digital quality sound (built in on later model Macintoshes)
- 80MB hard drive or more
- System 6.07 or later; 7.1 preferable
- QuickTime

SOUND CARDS OR BOARDS

While some discs do not use sound, others would be almost useless without their audio component. If you are using an IBM-compatible computer, you must, therefore, consider adding sound capability to the machine.

Early personal computers had no need for sound and the capability to reproduce anything other than a tone or single beep was never added. Computers such as the Amiga, Atari and Macintosh were introduced in the early 1980s and had sound capability built into their operating systems. Considered only as toys or game machines in the beginning by "real computer users," these computers nevertheless pointed the way towards multimedia use. With the advent of CD-ROM and especially the multimedia discs, adding sound became important; and in the late 1980s, two companies introduced boards for IBM-compatible computers. The AdLib board and the SoundBlaster boards paved the way for good sound; and when Windows 3.0 was introduced for the IBM-compatible market, the days of the silent PC were definitely numbered.

A sound card works by converting sound waves (analog signals) into digital numbers. It receives tiny samples of the sound waves several thousand times per second and translates those into digital values. This sampling process is called Analog-to-Digital Conversion (ADC). The standard until now has been 8-bit sound, which means that the incoming sample of sound can be assigned any of 256 (2^8) separate values. Sixteen-bit sound means the sample can be assigned one of 65,536 values. For the near future, 32-bit sound is promised, and the assigned values will be that much greater again.

What does this mean? It means that the higher the number of values, the closer the precision in replicating the original sound on digital equipment. There are an infinite number of values in the sound of the human voice, or in music; and the more of those values that can be replicated by digital values, the closer the sound will be to its original source.

INSTALLING A SOUND BOARD

Installing a sound board inside your computer is not the easiest thing to do, but it is also not the world's toughest job. It involves removing the cover and seating the board in an empty expansion slot. Follow the installation instructions in the sound board manual carefully. The next step is to install the software drivers that come with the sound board and allows the operating system in your computer to recognize the sound capabilities of the board.

The final step is to attach speakers to the jacks on the board. Without speakers, the computer will recognize sound, but you won't be able to hear it! You can also attach amplified or self-powered speakers to a drive that has dual jacks on the back. This generates true stereo music with very high quality. This is the system configuration used by most Macintosh users, because the Mac already contains the sound capability that must be added with a card to the IBM-compatible computer.

In addition, most (if not all) external CD-ROM drives have a single headphone jack, usually on the front of the drive. This jack will suffice for headphones, which you may find useful in a multiuser environment.

When you have speakers connected to the CD-ROM drive or the internal sound card, you can also listen to CD-Audio discs. These CDs are the norm for recorded music nowadays. It's quite pleasant to be able to listen to music while working on your computer, and it will not interfere with the other tasks the computer is performing.

A discussion of CD-ROMs and sound is not complete without mentioning MIDI. An acronym that stands for Musical Instrument Digital Interface, MIDI is a standard for the exchange of musical information from computers to musical instruments, and back again. Music recorded on a CD-ROM in MIDI format can only be handled by a computer with a sound board that has MIDI capability.

THE VIDEO DISPLAY

The final piece of hardware to be considered for a CD-ROM system is the video display or monitor. Sometimes referred to as the terminal, tube or screen, the video display is the main source of information for the user. There are many fine distinctions and definitions for monitors; and while it may be next to impossible to understand all of them, it will help to know something about color, resolution, dot pitch and scan rates.

Color is almost essential today for running most software and it certainly enhances every operation. In the world of CD-ROM, the use of color can make a huge difference when running multimedia discs. Good resolution is also a requirement for programs that depend heavily on photographic images, fine drawings, animation or precise or highly-defined material.

Monitors fall into several categories that correspond to the development of better and better color and line resolution. The first color monitors were called CGA, for Color Graphics Adapter. The resolution was low and it offered 16 colors. Next in line was EGA, for Enhanced Graphics Adapter, (increased resolution and 64 colors) and then VGA, or Video Graphics Array. The current standard for IBM-compatible computers is SVGA, for Super VGA. Resolution for a VGA display is 640x480 pixels and 256 colors, the minimum required for an MPC Level 1 computer. A Super VGA monitor provides a higher resolution—up to 1024x768 pixels—and a lower dot pitch, which is the distance between the little phosphor dots on the screen. As a minimum standard, a good 17-inch monitor should provide a 0.31mm dot pitch, or about 80 dots to the inch. In general, the smaller the number associated with dot pitch, the sharper the image.

All Macintosh computers scan (draw their video pictures on the screen) at the same rate, so there is not a multiplicity of standards. Mac owners can choose any monitor designed for a Mac and it will work. With the advent of improved autosynchronous (or multisynchronous) monitors—that can work with a range of scan rates—Mac users can now choose from the wide variety of monitors that have long been available to PC users. There is still a problem with the cables necessary to connect these monitors so be sure and ask questions and read the manuals.

SYSTEM SOFTWARE FOR CD-ROM

The next element to consider when using a CD-ROM drive is the software that enables the CD-ROM and drive to communicate with the computer. If the drive is simply plugged into the computer's parallel or SCSI port (or, in some cases, to a serial port), the computer will have no internal instructions to help recognize the device or communicate with it. Those instructions are software files that are usually loaded with the other operating system software. On a Macintosh, the process requires copying four or five basic files to the System folder. The files that comprise this special Macintosh software include:

- Audio CD Access

- Foreign File Access

- High Sierra File Access

- ISO 9660 File Access

- A specific driver for your CD-ROM drive

If the machine is an IBM or compatible machine, then the enabling software is called MSCDEX, which stands for Microsoft Compact Disc Extensions. These are extension files for DOS, the internal disk operating system. For example, DOS can only recognize a file up to a certain size, and most CD-ROM files are considerably larger than that. In addition, a statement is added to both the AUTOEXEC.BAT and the CONFIG.SYS files so that the computer will look for and recognize the presence of the CD-ROM drive, just as it needs to recognize the presence of a printer, a modem or other peripheral device. There is also an application startup file, which is simply a file that tells the computer how to start the CD-ROM application.

SEARCH ENGINE OR RETRIEVAL SOFTWARE

Another kind of software enables the user to search the disc or access the programs, files or information on the disc. This software is supplied with each disc. Sometimes it is accessed straight from the disc, and sometimes it is recommended that the software be copied from the disc to the hard drive. This second approach lets the speed and power of the computer run the search software, so the CD-ROM drive only has to deal with accessing and transferring the information from the disc. Each disc will give you the necessary information about how to use the search and retrieval software to access the information on that particular disc. Examples of search and retrieval software are DiscPassage, TexWare and SmarTrieve.

If it is necessary, the retrieval software is copied to the hard disk when the CD-ROM is installed and is generally an invisible procedure. More than half of the discs reviewed for this book have retrieval software that is accessed from the disc itself. The remainder have software that must be copied to the hard disk or accessed from a floppy disk.

The software for accessing textual or bibliographic information takes a very different format from that used to access pictures or move through a database of varied material. A hypertext or hypermedia type of software is often used on discs with a mixture of types of information so that links can be made. HyperCard for the Macintosh and LinkWay for the IBM are two examples of hypertext software.

THE DATA ON THE DISC

The information encoded on the actual disc takes many forms—text, illustrations and pictures, audio, video and animation. How these different kinds of data are physically placed on the disc can affect the efficiency of the search software in finding the information on the disc. The capability to search the disc takes many forms:

- Single words may be searched.
- Lists of topics or subject headings may be browsed.
- Menus can be utilized.
- Words can be located in relationship to other words or in their contexts.
- Parts of words may be searched, with a variety of possibilities as a search result.

This whole process of deciding how the information will be organized occurs when the disc is first created or mastered. Databases of information, files of pictures or sounds, sequences of video or animation—whatever form the data takes—are loaded into an authoring system. This system organizes the information according to the ISO standards and creates indexes of all the words, their relationships and contexts. It filters out problems and misleading data and arranges the final files, folders, directories, lists, pointers, flags and tags—and everything else the authors can think of that will help the user locate information on the disc. Error detection and correction routines are run so that no mistakes will be encoded on the disc.

When the final version of the material has been settled and the master disc has been made, then it is replicated as many times as needed. Each disc is a perfect copy of the original data file and contains the exact material as authored and indexed.

NETWORKING CD-ROMS

One of the most exciting developments in the CD-ROM world is the ability to include CD-ROMs on a network. Although it is not feasible to network a full multimedia disc (full-motion video is not yet networkable except at very high cost), networking most CD-ROMs is both possible and desirable.

One of the main problems with any CD-ROM collection is the limited access to a particular product. For example, if the school library holds a 21-volume encyclopedia, it is possible for 21 different students to access that encyclopedia at the same time. (It is possible, but not likely, since some would be looking for similar information.) The same encyclopedia on a single CD-ROM would only allow access by one student at a time. But if that encyclopedia were available on a network with multiple workstations in various areas, many students could use it.

One problem in networking CD-ROMs is speed. Already we know that CD-ROMs are slow when compared, for example, to a hard disk. When one CD-ROM is accessed by more than one user at a time on a network, it is *very* slow.

Each network is different, and the problems depend on the number and location of the computers, as well as their age and capacity. Since every school is different, it is very difficult to describe and explain every possible network configuration. To understand the advantages and the disadvantages of putting CD-ROMs on a network, it is first necessary to understand a little about the physical characteristics of networks and how they are constructed.

A network consists of two or more computers connected with cabling. Each computer on the network is called a node. These computers contain hardware and software that enable them to share files, programs and peripheral devices, such as printers and CD-ROM drives. A group of computers networked in the same local area (usually a building), connected typically with no more than 1,000 feet of cabling, is called a local area network or LAN. Networks connected over longer distances are called MANs (metropolitan area networks) or WANs (wide area networks).

NETWORK HARDWARE

The way computers are physically arranged in a network is called the *architecture* (or topology) of the network and determines a lot about the way the network works. For example, the architecture determines the speed of the data being transmitted between workstations, as well as the method for passing data along a network.

Also included in this hardware category is a network interface card (NIC) that goes into every computer on the network. The interface card enables each computer or workstation to be recognized by the network. It also determines the kind of network, such as star, ring, tree, line, etc. Cables are attached to the card and link each computer to others in the network.

Some networks work with a series of computers attached sequentially by a cable. Others connect each computer individually to a central hub in a variety of wiring patterns. A serial connection of computers has what is called a bus topology (picture all the computers sitting in rows, one behind the other). This is the earliest form of network topology, similar to a string of Christmas tree lights. If one wire between two of the nodes broke, the whole network failed. A star or ring topology connects each computer to a separate wiring hub. If a wire breaks in this topology, only one node is affected and the rest of the network continues to function.

The Ethernet network was developed by Xerox PARC in the late 1970s and early 1980s and was standardized by the IEEE as 802.3. An Ethernet network has certain standards and protocols so that various equipment and software can be developed commercially for any such network. An Ethernet network transmits data at ten megabits per second (MB/sec), while a token ring network (802.5), the other major type of network, transmits data at either 4MB/sec or 16MB/sec.

About two-thirds of LANs in schools are Ethernet networks, while token ring networks (developed and heavily supported by IBM) account for about one-third. Ethernet networks

FIGURE 4

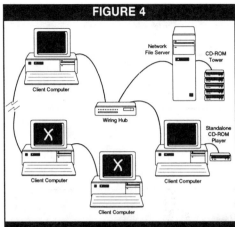

In an Ethernet network, computers may be "daisychained" together from the wiring hub. If a connection is broken somewhere in the chain, all computers beyond the break will be affected. In this illustration, the two end computers could not access a CD-ROM on the network server.

FIGURE 5

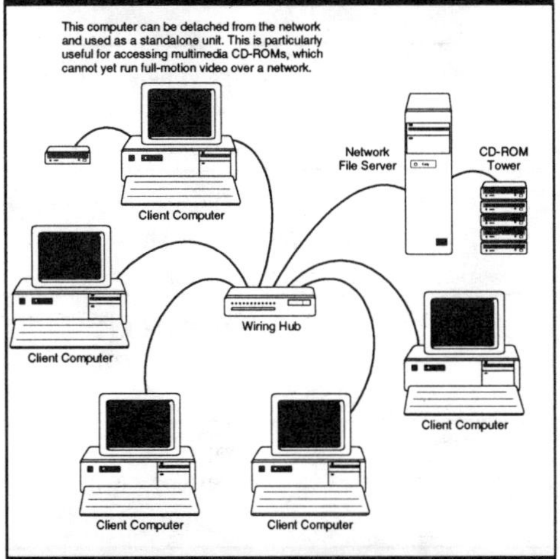

This computer can be detached from the network and used as a standalone unit. This is particularly useful for accessing multimedia CD-ROMs, which cannot yet run full-motion video over a network.

In a token ring network, each computer is connected to the network via the wiring hub. If a connection breaks in this configuration, only that one node is affected and the rest of the network continues to function.

are less expensive than token ring networks. For example, a single network interface card (NIC) for an Ethernet network is one-quarter to one-third the price of a token ring NIC. For multiple machines on a network, this can amount to a substantial savings.

There are two main types of networks—peer-to-peer and client-server. Most schools use a server-based network, as opposed to a peer-to-peer network. In the latter, the computers on the network are all equivalent in computing power and share data and peripheral devices, such as printers and tape drives.

In a server-based network, there is one large and more powerful computer that is the server, which provides the communications, printing, and file access and management functions for all of the other computers (clients) on the network. It has a very large hard drive (or multiple hard drives), usually a tape back-up drive, a printer and a CD-ROM drive or drives. It runs highly specialized multitasking software and monitors and manages the flow of information around the network.

The selection and installation of proper cabling for the computers on your network is very important. Different network specifications require different kinds of cabling. For example, a token ring network requires shielded twisted-pair wiring. And, since the cabling is generally installed in walls, floors or other hard-to-reach places, it is significantly more difficult to change the cabling for a network than it would be to remove or replace a computer on the network. Factors such as resistance to electrical interference, fire

CD-ROM Networking Products And Producers

Company Name and Address	Telephone	Product Name
Artisoft, Inc. 2202 N. Forbes Boulevard Tucson, AZ 85745	602/670-7000 602/670-7101 (fax)	LANtastic 6.0
CBIS, Inc. 5875 Peachtree Industrial Boulevard Building 100, Suite 170 P.O. Box 921206 Norcross, GA 30092	404/446-1332 404/446-9164 (fax)	CD Connection 2.22C
Corel Systems Corp. 1600 Carling Avenue Ottawa, Ontario, Canada K1Z 8R7	613/728-8200 613/728-9790 (fax)	Corel 4.0B
Digital Equipment Corp. 146 Main Street Maynard, MA 01754	508/493-4179 508/493-2500 (fax)	InfoServer
Logicraft, Inc. 22 Cotton Road Nashua, NH 03063	603/880-0300 603/880-7229 (fax)	LAN CD 2.2
Meridian Data, Inc. 5615 Scotts Valley Drive Scotts Valley, CA 95066	408/438-3100 408/438-6816 (fax)	CD Net
Micro Design International, Inc. 6985 University Boulevard Winter Park, FL 32792	407/677-8333 407/677-8365 (fax)	SCSI Express 1.4.1
Microtest, Inc. 4747 North 22nd Street Phoenix, AZ 85016	800/526-9675 602/952-6401	Discport 2.30A MapAssist 3.0Q
Novell, Inc. 122 East 1700 S Provo, UT 84606	800/453-1267 801-429-5155 (fax)	NetWare 3.12 NetWare 4.01
Online Computer Systems, Inc. 20251 Century Boulevard Germantown, MD 20874	800/922-9204 301/428-3700 301/428-2903 (fax)	OPTI-NET (NLM 2.0, DOS 2.1)
TAC Systems, Inc. P.O. Box 11370 Huntsville, AL 35814	205/828-6920 205/837-9807 (BBS) 205/721-0242 (fax)	SCSI Shuttle for Novell 1.16

resistance, adequate ventilation and distance between computers on the network must also be considered.

NETWORK SOFTWARE

The software required to run a network consists of a network operating system and CD-ROM networking software. The networking operating system works in conjunction with the computer's individual operating system to help it recognize the network and the individual protocols for sending and receiving data along the network. On a peer-to-peer network, each computer on the network has the same hardware and software. A very common networking operating system software for a peer-to-peer network is LANtastic.

CD-ROM network software allows individual computers on the network to recognize and use a shared CD-ROM drive, wherever it may be connected. The most common examples of this kind of software are OPTI-NET and CD Net. The nearby box on the left lists the names and producers of major CD-ROM networking products.

A client-server network also requires host or server software, separate software just for the big computer, which enables it to store and regulate the sharing of files, programs and peripheral devices by members (clients) on the network.

Novell is the company that produces NetWare, the hands-down favorite for networking operating system software. Since most school networks are equipped with NetWare, other devices and software should be "Novell-compatible." Version 3.12 of NetWare allows the integration of Macintosh and IBM-compatible computers on the same network, for up to five Macintoshes with no extra licensing costs and allows computers to recognize a networked CD-ROM drive (as a volume), thus eliminating the need for additional software like OPTI-NET or CD Net.

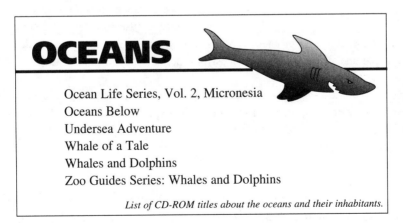

OCEANS

Ocean Life Series, Vol. 2, Micronesia
Oceans Below
Undersea Adventure
Whale of a Tale
Whales and Dolphins
Zoo Guides Series: Whales and Dolphins

List of CD-ROM titles about the oceans and their inhabitants.

NETWORKING CD-ROMS AND VENDOR SUPPORT

There are a variety of options for networking CD-ROM drives. There is a multidisc, single-drive CD-ROM player called a jukebox (or a mini-changer) that can store up to six

---

CD-ROM Networking Considerations And Issues*

Network Advantages
• Shared software
• Shared printers
• Quick and easy access
• Multistation access
• Workstation flexibility
• Increased communication
• Library without walls
• Server security

Network Disadvantages
• Dedicated equipment cost
• Maintenance and support
• Limited number of networkable CD-ROMs
• Server is down means the network is down

Networking Issues
• Planning
• Hardware
• Software
• Management and personnel
• Maintenance and support
• Curriculum
• Training
• Funding

Developed for the New Information Technology Workshop, Southern Westchester BOCES School Library System, Elmsford, New York.

---

discs. On a jukebox, the discs can be switched back and forth onto the drive mechanism without being handled by the user. The function is like the old jukeboxes that used to play 45rpm records.

Another type of multiple-disc CD-ROM drive is called a tower. A tower has multiple drives where the discs are stored. No switching mechanism is required since each disc in the tower is actually in a separate drive. Any of the discs can be activated very quickly. On a network, all the discs in a tower can be used simultaneously.

The number of networkable discs on the market today is increasing rapidly. Publishers are recognizing schools' need to be able to network their computer facility and offer the same information in multiple locations. User manuals for discs give instructions for network installation, and some companies provide customer service support for network installation and maintenance questions. Some companies, however, recognizing the extreme variance possible in school networks, reluctantly refuse to offer technical assistance for networking situations or problems. In this case, you must get acquainted with your local support people and make sure that at least one person on your staff has some technical expertise and training.

The price of single-user discs and networked discs varies with the producer. Usually it is more expensive to network the disc, but not as expensive as it might be if you had to buy multiple copies of the disc for several locations. Ask, ask, and ask again for networking information and prices.

CONCLUSION

Hardware is definitely not the easiest subject to understand. Most of us learn about computers and software and these things the hard way—when something breaks or stops working, we get into it with our bare hands and figure out. Cables and connections, memory upgrades and acquisitions all make it necessary for us to learn at least a little about how all of these devices work together. Ask questions of sales people, company representatives and colleagues at conferences or on LM_NET. Read current library and computer literature, product descriptions and reviews, and online files in an effort to get the latest and best information.

Some day, maybe having a computer will be as simple and easy as having a television set or a telephone, and we won't have to ask questions about how to use it. Until then, don't let the technical terminology scare you off. There's a lot of very good computer equipment and CD-ROMs available now. Learn and grow with the new developments, and have fun—all at the same time.

SELECTED RESOURCES FOR FURTHER READING

Benford, Tom. *Welcome to...CD-ROM*. New York: MIS Press, 1993. Chapters 1, 3-7, Appendices B and C.

Bosak, Steve and Jeffrey Sloman. *The CD-ROM Book*. Indianapolis, IN: Que Corporation, 1993, Chapters 1-5.

Derfler Jr., Frank J. and Les Freed. *How Networks Work*. Emeryville, CA: Ziff Davis Press, 1993.

Glass, Brett. "Buyers' Guide: 31 Multispeed CD-ROM Drives." *Multimedia World* 1, No. 4 (March 1994): pp. 74-79.

Glass, Brett. "CD-ROM Drive Acceleration Programs: Modest Speedups, No Miracles." *Multimedia World* 1, No. 4 (March 1994): pp. 81-85.

Holsinger, Erik. "Make Your Own CD-ROMs." *MacUser* (June 1994): pp. 100-107.

Jacsó, Péter. *CD-ROM Software, Dataware, and Hardware: Evaluation, Selection, and Installation*. Englewood, CO: Libraries Unlimited, Inc., 1992.

Jordahl, Gregory. "Networking CD-ROM." *Technology and Learning* 14, No. 3 (November/December 1993): pp. 48-55.

Kinnell, Susan K. "What You Really Need To Know About Buying a CD-ROM Drive." *Information Searcher*, Vol. 5, No. 1, (1992): pp. 17-19.

Martin, James A. "Double-Speed CD-ROM Drives." *Macworld* (July 1993): pp. 99-103.

Nicholls, Paul T. *CD-ROM Buyer's Guide and Handbook*. Wilton, CT: Eight Bit Books 1993, Chapters 3 and 4.

Parker, Dana and Bob Starrett. *Technology Edge: Guide to CD-ROM*. Carmel, IN: New Riders Publishing, 1992, Chapters 1-6.

Pope, David. "Driving in the Fast Lane: Lower Prices and Multi-Speed Capabilities Accelerate Adoption of CD-ROM Technology." *Digital Imaging* (March/April 1994): pp. 26-31.

Quain, John R. "Going Mainstream: CD-ROM Drives." *PC Magazine* 13, No. 4 (February 22, 1994): pp. 110-154.

Rizzo, John. "Passport to the Future: CD-ROM Drives." *MacUser* (March 1993): pp. 124-144.

Samis, Mark. "Sound Advice: Walking through the Confusing World of MS-DOS Sound Cards." *Electronic Learning*, (January 1993): pp. 30-33.

Scheib, Charlene M. "Planning for Networking in School Libraries." *Computers in Libraries* 13, No. 4 (April 1993): pp. 22-26.

White, Ron. *How Computers Work*. Emeryville, CA: Ziff-Davis Press, 1993.

CHAPTER 3

PLANNING AND MANAGING CD-ROM IN THE SCHOOL LIBRARY MEDIA CENTER

C D-ROM burst upon the library media center with a bang! In 1989, there were only a handful of CD-ROM titles; now in 1994, there are over 4,000. The number is still growing. The *New York Times* predicts that CD-ROM sales will skyrocket to over $9 billion in 1995. Despite the rapid growth of CD-ROM, or perhaps because of it, few library media specialists stop to consider the influences this technology may have on the library media center and its programs. Having a management strategy in place that includes CD-ROM will ensure that the instruction goals of the library media center will remain a priority and that student learning will continue to be the heart of the program.

NEEDS ASSESSMENT PLANNING

Introducing CD-ROM technology into the school library media center will cause major changes in management, student instruction and staff training, but it is impossible to predict exactly what these changes will be. However, unless the process is given considerable forethought, this new research tool can have a disastrous impact on your program and staff. Failure to plan not only jeopardizes the success of CD-ROM integration into the library media program, but could also adversely affect the rest of the library's services to the school. You need to consider those issues that influence the library's goals and objectives, which in turn affect other services as well as students, teachers and administrators.

School districts need a long-range, curriculum-based technology plan with specific goals that can be implemented in phases. Reassessment, incorporating new developments, should be made at each phase. The plan needs to be curriculum-based, not technology-driven. The goals of the district plan should be based on student learning outcomes. New technologies must help students reach these goals. CD-ROM is one of these technologies and must be viewed as part of the school library media center plan, which also encompasses online databases, local area networks (LANs), electronic mail, bulletin boards, the Internet and facsimile.

Planning involves organizing related activities to achieve specific results consistent with the school library media center's mission and the school's overall instructional plan. A planning document helps evaluate the benefits of a CD-ROM program, determine the costs, and outline a course of action. The document should include:

- **Library Goals and Objectives.** Goals for the CD-ROM program must be identified and objectives developed to focus action. The objectives should cover instructional, service and management requirements.
- **Personnel Requirements.** Staff will need time to monitor the physical needs of the workstation, help students conduct and revise searches, change CD-ROMs, train faculty, etc.
- **Hardware.** The number of workstations needed is based on student population. Consider the advantages and disadvantages of a local area network. Be aware that hardware must be constantly upgraded by adding more memory, replacing old printers, etc.
- **Software.** The cost of a CD-ROM varies greatly, depending on whether it is a single-copy version or networked; a one-time cost or a subscription. Some programs are produced for only one platform, either DOS/MPC-based or Macintosh.
- **Facilities.** The location of CD-ROM workstations are crucial to student access, instruction and security. Computer tables, comfortable chairs, electrical extensions and good lighting are necessary.
- **Other Services.** Consider how online searching, interlibrary loan, document delivery, staff training and other library services will be affected by the introduction of CD-ROM.
- **Evaluation.** The CD-ROM program must be evaluated continuously regarding its impact on student learning outcomes. Consider how to monitor the program and its impact. Involve faculty and students in the process.

It is also helpful to have a vision of what "school" and "school library media center" will mean in the future. How will students, teachers, administrators and the community use information? Will the school library media center be the hub for locating, retrieving and using information? Will it be a specific location or will its resources be networked into every classroom and home, providing needed information at that "teachable moment" and on demand? How will network access affect collection development or student instruction? If you can visualize your goal, you have a better chance of achieving it.

ESTABLISHING POLICIES AND PROCEDURES

Written policy should serve as the basis for establishing understanding and cooperation in managing information services. How the information service is to be delivered and to whom it is directed must be clearly communicated. You may wish to include CD-ROM in an electronic resources policy, or address it individually. Some issues may also be addressed in a collection development policy. Often a policy statement can be developed only after CD-ROM technology has been in place for a while, and after its effect on the curriculum and library media center is clearly understood.

Questions to consider when writing a CD-ROM program policy are:

Selection Criteria
- Are faculty and students involved in selecting CD-ROM products? If so, what is the process?
- What are the reviewing sources? Preview policy? Maintenance procedures?
- How do you plan to keep up with new and emerging CD technologies?
- Which platform or platforms will be used?
- How will equipment be selected?
- Do you have a selection/evaluation tool?

Budget
- Who prepares the budget?
- Under which line items is CD-ROM placed?
- Is CD-ROM included only in the media center budget?
- What items will be included? (Hardware, software, documentation, furniture, supplies?)

Bibliographic Control
- Will CD-ROMs be classified and cataloged?
- How will they be stored: in closed stacks or available for browsing?
- Will CD-ROMs circulate? For how long? To all patrons?
- How will copyright and licensing restrictions be handled?
- Will support materials be cataloged?

Physical Set-Up
- Where will the workstations be located?
- Is the location easily accessible for students?
- Is staff available to provide help?
- Is there adequate security?
- Is there ample work space?
- Is there sufficient electrical power?
- Is lighting adequate?
- Can the area be expanded?
- What supplies and materials will be kept at the workstation? (Printer ribbons, disc cleaner, paper, system diskettes, blank diskettes?)

Conditions for Use
- How will terminal time be allocated? Will classes have priority over individual students? Can students reserve time? Are there time limits?
- How will search results be saved?
- Are there restrictions on printing or downloading to a disk?

Student Instruction
- Who will receive instruction in using CD-ROMs?
- What form will instruction take? One-on-one? Classes?

- What will students be taught?
- Will it be integrated into the curriculum?
- Who will teach the students?

Staff Training
- Will you offer staff training?
- Who needs special training?
- Who will do the training?
- What will the staff be taught?
- What initial and ongoing training will be needed?

Documentation
- Who is responsible for maintaining the manuals and other documentation?
- How will they be accessible?
- How will they be updated?

Maintenance
- Who is responsible for maintaining equipment and discs?
- Who is responsible for turning the workstations on and off?
- Who is responsible for ordering supplies?

Contracts and Vendor Support
- Who keeps track of contracts and service agreements?
- Who negotiates service agreements?

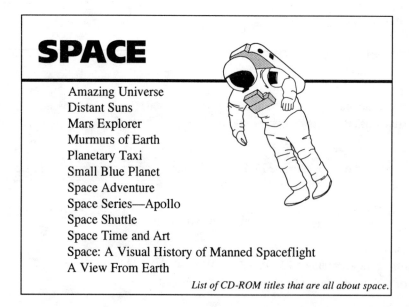

SPACE

Amazing Universe
Distant Suns
Mars Explorer
Murmurs of Earth
Planetary Taxi
Small Blue Planet
Space Adventure
Space Series—Apollo
Space Shuttle
Space Time and Art
Space: A Visual History of Manned Spaceflight
A View From Earth

List of CD-ROM titles that are all about space.

- Who maintains contact with vendors?
- What support do you need?
- What support will you pay for?

Evaluation
- How will the service be monitored and evaluated?
- Who will conduct the evaluations?
- Will students and faculty be involved?

ADMINISTRATION

Understanding the additional responsibilities a CD-ROM program incurs will help the program reach full potential and provide a smooth transition during its adoption and integration. Staff size and configuration will determine who will be primarily responsible for implementing and managing the CD-ROM program. For the benefit of library staff, faculty, students and vendors, it is important to make clear from the beginning who will administer and maintain the various components of the program.

Additional staff responsibilities include:

Overall Coordination of CD-ROM Functions. This includes long-range planning as well as daily maintenance.

Vendor Contact and Contracts. This includes keeping current with new products and services.

Maintenance of Equipment and Supplies. It is necessary to be aware of new and updated versions of software and emerging CD technologies, and to troubleshoot hardware problems and maintain computer supplies so that the CD-ROM installation runs smoothly.

Increased Student/Staff Assistance. There is an ongoing demand for assistance from the library staff to develop search strategies, identify keywords, help with printing or downloading, etc.

Training. Training staff and students requires time often taken from other responsibilities.

Evaluation. The CD-ROM program must be evaluated continuously regarding its impact on student learning outcomes. Involve library staff, faculty and students in such evaluation efforts.

Bibliographic Control. All public access materials, including CD-ROMs, must be classified and catalogued.

CD-ROM Budget. New budget line items for incorporating CD-ROM must be established and maintained. Consider how CD-ROM impacts other budget areas.

Copyright Concerns. Ongoing education for students and staff regarding copyright issues for electronic resources is required.

As reported in the literature, various school library media centers have delegated responsibilities differently. Library media specialists are usually responsible for overall coordination, vendor contracts, student/staff assistance, training, and bibliographic control. Computer directors or coordinators usually maintain equipment, particularly when networks are involved. Budgeting, evaluation and training may be shared.

STAFFING ISSUES

Researchers Carol Tenopir and Ralf Neufang surveyed research libraries in the United States and Canada and found widespread use of electronic products. They learned that CD-ROM products increased activity at the reference desk. Librarians said that patrons needed more help using CD-ROMs, and librarians needed extra time themselves to learn how to use the programs. Many said they found it difficult to keep up with CD-ROM software and hardware and commented they learn the product as they teach it to patrons. Some librarians felt they were giving more instruction to students and spent increased time understanding the patron's information needs (*ONLINE* May 1992, pp. 54-60).

These findings are consistent with our experience in the school media centers and must be included in staffing considerations. Remember additional time will be spent:

- Changing CD-ROMs for students
- Monitoring the physical needs of the workstation (making sure the CD-ROM drive and computer are working, correcting paper jams, providing general security for equipment and disks)
- Overseeing patron computer time
- Completing interlibrary loan slips
- Handling increases in document delivery services
- Helping students conduct and revise searches
- Helping students find sources from their searches

One staffing solution is to recruit teachers to play more active roles in the media center, or train student aides and volunteers. Otherwise, you must rely on computer-assisted tutorials and printed guides for assistance and schedule small group instruction to supplement regularly scheduled classes.

Common Problems In Teaching CD-ROM
• Shortage of staff
• Shortage of equipment for group instruction
• Lack of standard search software
• Convincing students they need to practice their searching skills
• Time to develop instruction for students

LOCATION AND ACCESS

Location of the CD-ROM workstation is key in providing help to students using the CD-ROM products. Although many CD-ROM producers want us to believe that CD-ROM products require no instruction, professional journals indicate otherwise. It is, therefore, critical that the library staff have easy access to students using the CD-ROM workstation.

School library media centers often lack extra space, however, so workstation accommodations must be carefully considered. Most university and public libraries place CD-ROM stations, alone or in clusters, near the reference desk so the reference librarian can see if a patron is having trouble. In a school library media center, CD-ROM workstations are best placed in an open, central location. This placement is inviting and helps the library staff quickly recognize assistance needs and gives the opportunity to teach one-on-one.

Many teaching situations involve entire classes visiting the library media center, so CD-ROM workstations need to be clustered for group instruction. In that case, try to place them in a configuration where staff and students can view all the screens to encourage cooperative learning and information sharing. Student learning must be the primary consideration—don't position workstations based on the location of electrical cords and wiring.

If you have only one workstation and a large class, other methods must be developed to give all students a chance to experience the technology. Perhaps use the CD-ROM workstation as one of many curriculum or information skills stations where students work in groups or use an LCD panel to display computer output on a large screen.

Teaching Tip!

If you have a standalone station, load a popular CD-ROM title, such as Guinness Disc of Records during lunch periods. As students gravitate toward it naturally in groups, use the opportunity to demonstrate how to do a keyword search, or download text. Encourage them to share these searching techniques with other students.

SECURITY

Security requirements complicate the physical location of CD-ROM workstations. Careful consideration needs to be given to protecting against theft because of the expensive, and easily portable, hardware and software. Students must also be prevented from tampering with the drives and removing the discs. Lockable covers or cabinets to encase the microcomputer are available, as well as cables to secure the equipment to the table.

If there is only one CD-ROM workstation and switching of CD-ROMs occurs daily, establish an efficient and secure routine to prevent theft or damage. Small, thin CD-ROMs can be lost or misplaced easily. Producers will not replace lost or stolen discs free of charge. Invest in caddies and have one for each CD-ROM or purchase a mini-changer that can hold up to six discs out of sight.

Computer virus programs are an important security problem. Computers with a floppy disk drive for downloading search results to a disk are susceptible to receiving and transmitting a virus. Information on a CD-ROM cannot be damaged or changed in any way, but files on a computer hard drive may be. Also, unsuspecting students can contaminate floppy disks with a virus when downloading citations from the CD-ROM workstation, which will then spread the virus to their home computer.

WORKSPACE

Ample workspace for a microcomputer, keyboard, printer and CD-ROM drive requires at least 40 square feet and a minimum surface area two feet deep and four feet wide. Also consider additional electrical outlets for the computer, monitor, printer and CD-ROM drive, plus a telephone line for online searching, and air ventilation for the heat the equipment generates. Evaluate how to protect the area from glare, dust and dirt. Consider the need for antistatic mats and carpets, surge protection and an available power supply. Review traffic patterns and the need for noise control.

If possible, stock a nearby cabinet with microcomputer supplies such as computer paper, printer ribbons, extra disks, screen wipes, a disk drive cleaner kit, keyboard cleaner, spray for static, and a mild cleaner for machines and tables.

PRINTING OR DOWNLOADING PROBLEMS

With a CD-ROM system, users may save (download) search results to a disk, print them, or manually copy the results from the screen. One appealing aspect of CD-ROM is the ability to print results instead of manually writing or photocopying them. However, this sometimes fosters indiscriminate printing, and some libraries have decided not to offer the print option to their users. Others have limited the number of pages or citations that can be printed. Still others charge for printer paper. Teaching students to download search results to a disk for later, unhurried evaluation in a word processor encourages thoughtful research and avoids this problem.

The ability to download complete sections of full-text information to a disk tempts students' propensity to plagiarize. For example, it is simple to quickly download a complete section on Japan from an electronic encyclopedia. Next, the file can be transferred to a word processor. A student could then rewrite the first few sentences of each paragraph, paraphrase a few statements, print the section and submit it as a research paper. Usually, schools cannot set an enforceable policy to prohibit this practice. Even if downloading were prohibited, online search services via home computers and modems provide access to other electronic encyclopedias and full-text resources.

The solution lies with the assignment, not the technology. Carefully scrutinize requirements for research assignments. If students can fulfill an assignment by merely copying facts, reconsider the assignment. Consider Bloom's taxonomy which identifies different levels of thinking. "Identification" is the lowest level, i.e., identify the geography, climate, government of Japan. Using computers and electronic resources, identifying factual information is no longer difficult. Therefore, assignments should reflect changes in research capabilities due to advances in technology and demand a higher level of thinking, such as "Comparing and Contrasting." A more appropriate assignment would be to compare the economic conditions in pre- and post-war Japan.

Another potential problem is the sound level of the multimedia discs. Students get very excited when they first hear the fastest backwards talker in Guinness Disc of Records, or the sound of a violin in Microsoft Musical Instruments, and often want to share it with other students. Headphones placed near the computer or signed out by students can minimize the noise level.

Control and access to computers is an ongoing debate in libraries and is the focus of location considerations. Try to foster the least restrictive environment because well-coordinated physical and intellectual access to information is a high priority for all school library media centers. Most school library media center specialists find that fears about uncontrolled access, excessive printing and lack of security are unfounded in a school library media center where issues are openly discussed and handled in a respectful manner.

DOCUMENTING USE

With tight budgets, it is important to document statistically the use of the CD-ROM program. These statistics can be used to:

- Demonstrate accountability for continuing the program.
- Improve CD-ROM scheduling decisions.
- Improve budgeting resources.
- Provide insights for collection development.
- Indicate where resource sharing between libraries and other school
  library media centers can occur.
- Provide evidence useful for assessing students' performance.

(From Aversa and Mancall, *Management of Online Search Services in Schools,* 1989.)

PRODUCT ISSUES: OWNERSHIP, DISC RETURN AND PRICING

Most single-title or single-subject CD-ROMs are purchased and owned by the library. In some situations, particularly for bibliographic databases such as magazine indexes that are updated regularly, an issue of ownership arises. The principal question is whether the library owns the disc and its data or only has a license to use it.

If you own the disc and the data, you are not required to return the disc if you cancel your subscription to the product. It is the library's permanent property. If you license a CD-ROM product from a vendor, the license is a detailed contract that gives the library certain rights and contains a few or many restrictions. Some vendors require the library to return all discs when the contract expires or when an updated disc is delivered. If you cancel the contract, you must return all discs and data.

Read the purchase or license agreement carefully before you sign. Question the vendor if some clauses are not clear. Know what you are or are not buying. Also be aware of the contract's boundaries. Many vendors charge an additional fee or site license to distribute the CD-ROM on a network.

When evaluating the price of a product, include the support cost and the impact the product may have on other information services and supplies, such as print subscriptions, document delivery, interlibrary loan, and supplies such as paper, printer ribbons, etc.

PROMOTION AND PUBLIC RELATIONS

After searching the latest CD-ROM for information, a sophomore social studies student once remarked, "This library is just like a real library!"

A CD-ROM program offers a wonderful opportunity for the school library media center to shine. Students and faculty quickly understand the significance of the resource. They have heard about the new information technology in the media and appreciate the chance to try it out. The media center becomes known as the place where the latest information can be found.

Since the cost is fixed, it is cost-efficient to promote use of a new CD-ROM program. The program gives the library increased visibility and the opportunity to reach out to new users and encourages students' excitement in the research process.

Suggestions for marketing the CD-ROM program include:

- Demonstrate a CD-ROM search during a faculty or department meeting.
- Offer a presentation at a PTA meeting.
- Write an article for the school paper, parent newsletter, etc.
- Designate one computer for demonstrations and trial use of new CD-ROMs; encourage feedback.
- Plan half-hour, mini-demonstrations of CD-ROM programs several times a week.
- Encourage students to design a brochure about the CD-ROM program.
- Plan a "Grand Opening" of the CD-ROM workstation with balloons and flyers.

Other promotion methods fall into the following categories:

- Personal communications, both formal and informal
  Staff communications
  Special programs and events
  Orientations
  Meetings
  Quality of service and word of mouth

- Published materials
  Brochures and leaflets
  Newsletters
  Handbooks
  Annual Reports
  Information Packets

- Atmospherics (physical and psychological)
  Displays
  Physical Space
  Ease of Use
  Attitude of Service

(From Mancall and Aversa, *Management of Online Search Services in Schools,* pp. 77-78.)

Remember to involve the total education community including superintendents, assistant superintendents, principals, assistant principals, department heads, curriculum leaders, teachers, parent leaders, student leaders, newspaper and yearbook editors.

BUDGETING

Adding CD-ROMs to your library resources will not save you money. Beware of common cost-saving myths attributed to CD-ROM, such as: CD-ROM eliminates online searching costs; replaces or decreases print costs; decreases staff time; and minimizes the need to upgrade equipment. Unfortunately, none of these are true, so careful budgeting is a necessity.

When planning the budget, consider the following:

CD-ROM Program Objectives. Review what hardware, software, and personnel is necessary to accomplish the program objectives. If the objective is to integrate CD-ROM into the entire curriculum using a wide area network, the program will operate differently than if the approach is interdisciplinary, i.e., with one grade using three standalone computer workstations in the library. Factors such as training requirements and hardware needs will differ greatly.

Present Resources. Evaluate the present resources such as the number of computers and CD-ROM drives, the number of computer-literate teachers, in-house opportunities for training, etc.

Develop an initial start-up budget based on these needs:
Computer
CD-ROM drive
Printer
Software
Sound board
Speakers
Modem
Cables
CD-ROM subscriptions

CD-ROM single title discs
Electrical extensions cord
Power supply unit
Installation
Supplies: paper, printer ribbons, etc.
Furniture: desks, tables, chairs.
LCD panel for large group instruction
Overhead projector
Initial staff training
then
Calculate your total startup costs.

Develop an ongoing budget to support your CD-ROMs including the following items:
Newsletters/journals/directories
Staff development
User aids
CD-ROM subscriptions
CD-ROM single title discs
Public relations efforts
Product upgrades
Maintenance
then
Calculate your total ongoing costs.

CD-ROM is growing in popularity, due to decreasing production costs and the ease of searching CD-ROMs. It will soon be a basic electronic resource in all libraries. By consciously incorporating CD-ROM technology into the school library media center program school through careful planning, library media specialists can ensure that students' information needs are met.

SELECTED RESOURCES FOR FURTHER READING
Bankhead, Betty. "Through the Technology Maze: Putting CD-ROM to Work for You." *School Library Journal* (October 1991): pp. 44-49.

Dede, Christopher. "Planning Guidelines for Emerging Instructional Technologies." *Educational Technology* (April 1989): pp. 7-12.

Farrell, Rod and Stephen Gring. "5 Steps Toward Planning Strategically." *Media & Methods* (January/February 1993): pp. 14-17.

Foulds, M.S. and L.R. Foulds. "CD-ROM Planning and Managerial Issues." *CLJ* (April 1991): pp. 111-114.

LaGuardia, Cheryl and Stella Bentley. "Electronic Databases: Will Old Collection Development Policies Still Work?" *ONLINE* (July 1992): pp. 60-63.

Malinconico, S. Michael. "What Librarians Need to Know to Survive in an Age of Technology." *Journal of Education for Library & Information Service* (Summer 1992): pp. 226-241.

Reese, Jean. "CD-ROM Technology in Libraries: Implications and Considerations." *The Electronic Library* (February 1990): pp. 26-35.

Teger, Nancy. "MultiPlatter Goes to School." *CD-ROM Librarian* (June 1991): pp. 21-28.

Zink, Steven D. "Planning for the Perils of CD-ROM." *Library Journal* (February 1, 1990): pp. 51-55.

CHAPTER 4
EVALUATION AND SELECTION OF CD-ROMS FOR SCHOOLS

....

valuating CD-ROMs is an ongoing part of collection development. It is not, unfortunately, a quick, one-step process.

A comprehensive, systematic method for evaluating potential products has benefits including:

- Offering an opportunity to involve and educate faculty and students in CD-ROM technology.
- Developing ownership of the library media center and information skills instruction.
- Helping to determine the need and extent of student and staff training.
- Raising the level of student/staff acceptance of a product.
- Helping to determine the potential impact of CD-ROM on other services.

STEPS IN THE EVALUATION PROCESS

IDENTIFY PRODUCTS

CD-ROM products can be identified informally through advertisements, catalogs, promotional material and conferences, as well as word of mouth. A more systematic approach is to consult the Core Collection and Additional Title Listings in this book or to use some of the standard directories listed in this chapter.

At this preliminary stage, check to make sure you have the correct hardware requirements. Don't waste your time considering a product if your computer doesn't meet the minimum requirements. Equally important, don't make the mistake of purchasing a product and then discovering your computer doesn't have sufficient memory to handle the program or that the full-motion video does not function because the monitor is CGA instead of SVGA.

Write down the hardware configuration of your computer and carefully compare it to the program's requirements. (Read Chapter 2 for a basic understanding of the necessary components.) When checking for compatibility, consider these questions:

- How fast does the CPU need to be—25MHz/33MHz or beyond?
- How much RAM is needed to run the most advanced features?
- How fast a CD-ROM drive is required? Access time? Transfer time?
- Is a double/triple speed CD-ROM drive necessary to access the multimedia?
- What video display is necessary—SVGA? VGA?
- Do you need a sound board and speakers or earphones?
- Is the disc networkable?
- Is the disc on the correct platform? IBM? Macintosh?
- How much free hard drive space is needed to run the program?

FOOD

Food/Analyst PLUS
John Schumacher's New Prague Hotel Cookbook
New Basics Electronic Cookbook
Santé
The Herbalist

List of CD-ROM titles about food and nutrition.

LOCATE REVIEWS

CD-ROMs are starting to be reviewed in library and educational journals and newsletters. *Booklist, School Library Journal, Information Searcher, Wilson Library Bulletin, MULTI-MEDIA SCHOOLS, Technology Connections* and *Technology and Learning* are all publications that include reviews for schools. A full listing and comparison of the types and number of reviews per issue are included later in this chapter.

All reviews are not equal. As you read the reviews in computer magazines, keep in mind that K-12 educators are not the target audience. The reviews are not written with students in mind, nor is any attention given to curriculum integration—which is *our* primary concern. *PC World, BYTE, Macworld* and *MacUser* are good sources to help determine the content authority, the ease of use, screen design, etc. But remember, they are evaluating for a different audience. It is very likely that the "Top Ten Titles" for the home market will not be the top ten considered for purchase in a school library.

A CD-ROM must be more than entertaining. It must be unique. It must also meet the school's curriculum needs and attract students intellectually. For example, some highly-rated titles directed at the home market do not have printing capability, a major drawback for a school library.

IDENTIFY CURRICULUM NEEDS

CD-ROMs need to match the curriculum, as does any other information source. After potential products are identified, group them according to curriculum area and consider how they support the curriculum. Ask questions such as:

- What content is covered?

- How do similar print or other resources compare?

- Do these products contain information that teachers and students often request?

- Can this information enhance/highlight a particular curriculum?

- Will the CD-ROM support a frequently studied topic, such as animals, on the elementary level, or countries, on the secondary level?

- Can you identify specific instructional uses for the CD-ROM?

- Are there cross-curricular applications?

- Will it offer access to information unavailable in the school library?

- Does it present the information in a unique way?

Consider how these programs are going to be used. Similar to print resources, CD-ROMs fall into categories, such as reference works, circulating titles and classroom collections. Titles such as Contemporary Authors, Magill's Survey of Science, and Granger's World of Poetry are used as reference resources, while single-subject-specific titles, such as The Family Doctor, Microsoft Musical Instruments, or Clinton: Portrait of Victory circulate to the classrooms and are borrowed for students' personal use.

TALK TO TEACHERS

It is crucial for teachers to be involved in the evaluation and selection process—not only for their input as content and curriculum specialists, but to acquaint them with what is available. Approach them individually and also request time at department and faculty meetings to share information on products you have identified. Take advantage of their help in rating the products and identifying curriculum tie-ins. Explain how you selected these titles and solicit their help in targeting more titles.

Invite teachers and administrators to a short workshop on CD-ROM and its evaluation. It might be helpful to demonstrate how to assess a CD-ROM, using a computer with a large display. Most teachers have little or no experience with CD-ROM and need a brief explanation of what it is, its advantages, disadvantages. They need to understand the various types and see examples of curriculum applications.

DECIDE ON REQUIREMENTS AND FORMULATE QUESTIONS

The most important consideration is your requirements—exactly what you are looking for. Suppose, working with the social studies teachers, you have decided to purchase a CD-ROM with current facts on countries, *and* you want to be able to put it on 100 networked computers in the school. This, then, demands that the product be networkable.

If you don't have a sound board and speakers, you can't consider a multimedia title. If you need a magazine index on CD-ROM but do not have an adequate print collection to support it, nor access to interlibrary loan, you need to look at products with full text. Compile questions based on your needs and particular situation. If you have specific hardware configuration limitations, software needs, network configuration, etc., prepare detailed questions to address these issues. As you test the product, you can systematically address them.

NETWORK WITH COLLEAGUES

Talk with other school librarians who have used the product. Ask how they are using it in their curriculum. What are the teachers' and students' reactions? Very enthusiastic? Passive…just another resource? Would they buy it again? Why or why not?

LISTSERVs, such as LM_NET on the Internet, allow easy and timely sharing of personal experience with using CD-ROM products. Both positive and negative comments are helpful. More than once we have read a message on LM_NET warning that a producer is stating that a product is networkable, but it is not—yet! Sharing information and experiences can save hours of time and aggravation, as well as provide valuable tips on exciting new products.

ORDER DISCS FOR REVIEW

The ideal arrangement is to be able to test the product for a reasonable period of time. When you are considering purchasing a magazine index, this is possible. All of the companies offer trial subscriptions, and some will even lend you the hardware to run the product.

Unfortunately, many of the lower-priced, single-subject CD-ROMs cannot be borrowed for review. The next best approach is to try getting them on a 30-day return policy. Make sure it is stated in writing that you can return the product in 30 days if it doesn't suit your needs. This will give you time to test it with faculty and students.

The Search Off: Testing Demo Discs

Request a 60-day trial of the top three CD-ROM magazine indexes you are considering subscribing to. Plan ahead with your faculty for students to use these resources in completing research assignments. Publicize "The Search Off," inviting administrators, faculty and students to participate.

When the products arrive, place all three near each other in a central location in the library media center. Ask students to conduct their research on at least two of the products, using the same search terms and keywords. Then have them rate the products on ease of use, contents, screen design, results. Encourage other library patrons to test the products and compare them. Leave short evaluation sheets next to the products for patrons to fill out. Summarize the results and discuss them with faculty and students.

ENCOURAGE OPEN TESTING

It is not enough for school library media specialists to judge a CD-ROM or, for that matter, only faculty. Students should be encouraged to become knowledgeable consumers of electronic information. What better way than to be involved in evaluating and selecting CD-ROMs? It is very helpful to hear the different perspectives offered by faculty and students. To insure success, reach out to all the people who will actually use the product—health teachers, freshmen, etc.—and try to include all types of users—computer-literate, beginner, technophobic, etc.

Plan to have one workstation available. Announce the evaluation period ahead of time with flyers, memos and signs. Describe which CD-ROM is being evaluated, the curriculum

---

Student Evaluation

Sometimes children can be good judges. Here is an evaluation form designed by Nancy Larkin for her second-grade class at the Malcolm S. Mackey School in Tenafly, New Jersey. Some of their comments appear verbatim below.

Evaluation Form

Name

Name of CD-ROM

Circle YES or NO

1. This program was easy to understand.		YES	NO
2. It is easy to read.		YES	NO
3. The sound is good.		YES	NO
4. The pictures are clear.		YES	NO
5. It's fun.		YES	NO
6. It's challenging.		YES	NO
7. The CD taught me things.		YES	NO
8. It is easy to quit this program.		YES	NO
9. I can use this CD without the teacher's help.		YES	NO
10. I would use it again.		YES	NO
11. I would recommend that other children use this CD.		YES	NO

The BEST thing about this CD is

The WORST thing about this CD is

Children's Comments

I like Mammals because I like the people in the program. I also liked the movies especially the chipmunks. I didn't know what to do in Mammals at first but I wold like the Mammals to have some more movies for me to like. This CD helped us learn how animals talk and move. That's important because I don't know about all those animals. —Shira Tukl, Age 8

I liked Countdown better then all the other C.D. roms because it helps you learn about addition. And also because it's fun. I liked it better then all the others because it helps you learn to add. Mammals doesn't and all the other don't THE END. —Omri Boiko

You need to make an instruction book for the children so they can find out how to use the CD. The book should have a tape so if the kids can not read it will tell them what to do. If you need help it should tell you how to use it and not what to do. It should tell you how to solve your problem. —David Rivera

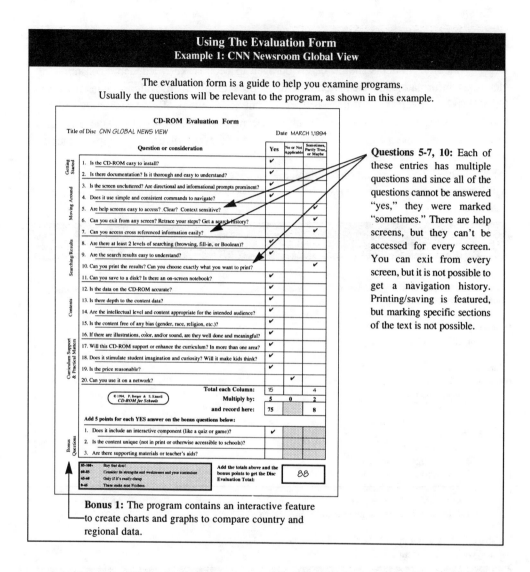

Using The Evaluation Form
Example 1: CNN Newsroom Global View

The evaluation form is a guide to help you examine programs.
Usually the questions will be relevant to the program, as shown in this example.

CD-ROM Evaluation Form

Title of Disc *CNN GLOBAL NEWS VIEW*   Date MARCH 1,1994

	Question or consideration	Yes	No or Not Applicable	Sometimes, Partly True, or Maybe
Getting Started	1. Is the CD-ROM easy to install?	✓		
	2. Is there documentation? Is it thorough and easy to understand?	✓		
Moving Around	3. Is the screen uncluttered? Are directional and informational prompts prominent?	✓		
	4. Does it use simple and consistent commands to navigate?	✓		
	5. Are help screens easy to access? Clear? Context sensitive?			✓
	6. Can you exit from any screen? Retrace your steps? Get a search history?			✓
	7. Can you access cross referenced information easily?			✓
Searching/Results	8. Are there at least 2 levels of searching (browsing, fill-in, or Boolean)?	✓		
	9. Are the search results easy to understand?	✓		
	10. Can you print the results? Can you choose exactly what you want to print?			✓
	11. Can you save to a disk? Is there an on-screen notebook?	✓		
Contents	12. Is the data on the CD-ROM accurate?	✓		
	13. Is there depth to the content data?	✓		
	14. Are the intellectual level and content appropriate for the intended audience?	✓		
	15. Is the content free of any bias (gender, race, religion, etc.)?	✓		
	16. If there are illustrations, color, and/or sound, are they well done and meaningful?	✓		
Curriculum Support & Practical Matters	17. Will this CD-ROM support or enhance the curriculum? In more than one area?	✓		
	18. Does it stimulate student imagination and curiosity? Will it make kids think?	✓		
	19. Is the price reasonable?	✓		
	20. Can you use it on a network?		✓	
	Total each Column:	15		4
	Multiply by:	5	0	2
	and record here:	75		8

© 1994, P. Berger & S. Kimell
CD-ROM for Schools

Add 5 points for each YES answer on the bonus questions below:

Bonus Questions	1. Does it include an interactive component (like a quiz or game)?	✓		
	2. Is the content unique (not in print or otherwise accessible to schools)?			
	3. Are there supporting materials or teacher's aids?			

85-100: Buy that disc!	
60-85: Consider its strengths and weaknesses and your curriculum	Add the totals above and the bonus points to get the Disc Evaluation Total: **88**
45-60: Only if it's really cheap	
0-45: These make nice Frisbees	

Questions 5-7, 10: Each of these entries has multiple questions and since all of the questions cannot be answered "yes," they were marked "sometimes." There are help screens, but they can't be accessed for every screen. You can exit from every screen, but it is not possible to get a navigation history. Printing/saving is featured, but marking specific sections of the text is not possible.

Bonus 1: The program contains an interactive feature to create charts and graphs to compare country and regional data.

area, and include a short description of the product. Be specific about the location of the workstation, the time frame of the evaluation process (one week, two weeks) and who is invited to participate. Develop a one-page sheet to record opinions. Make it short.

Students are never too young to learn how to appraise technology. Second-grade students in Tenafly, New Jersey are judging CD-ROMs for the *Information Searcher* newsletter. Their teacher, Nancy Larkin, introduced them to the technology, discussed the responsibilities and duties of a critic, set up a schedule for computer use and turned them loose. (See student evaluation form on page 45.)

Using The Evaluation Form
Example 2: CountDown

Filling out an evaluation form for a CD-ROM title like CountDown illustrates some of the problems in trying to use a standard form for a wide range of products. The explanation below will show how this particular disc scored only 72 on the form; but it is, in fact, an excellent product and one that we recommend. When you follow these explanations, you will begin to understand the discrepancies in the different types and levels of CD-ROMs.

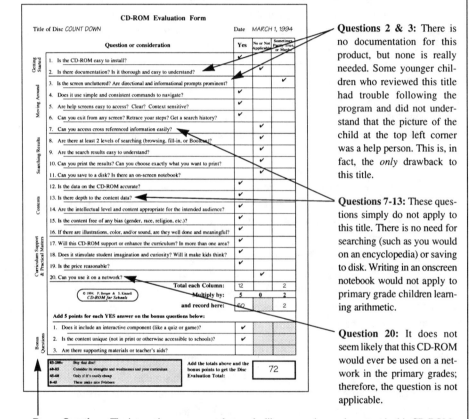

Questions 2 & 3: There is no documentation for this product, but none is really needed. Some younger children who reviewed this title had trouble following the program and did not understand that the picture of the child at the top left corner was a help person. This is, in fact, the *only* drawback to this title.

Questions 7-13: These questions simply do not apply to this title. There is no need for searching (such as you would on an encyclopedia) or saving to disk. Writing in an onscreen notebook would not apply to primary grade children learning arithmetic.

Question 20: It does not seem likely that this CD-ROM would ever be used on a network in the primary grades; therefore, the question is not applicable.

Bonus Questions: The interactive component that works like a game is very important in this CD-ROM, as is its uniqueness. It would be an excellent supplement to other print materials for teaching arithmetic in the primary grades. The lack of teacher's materials also didn't seem important for a disc like CountDown.

USE AN EVALUATION FORM

There are many evaluation forms and checklists available in library literature. Unfortunately, most are either too lengthy for practical application or they don't apply to school libraries. The evaluation form in this book was developed specifically for evaluating titles for student use in K-12. It has been tested by school librarians and teachers around the country. (See blank form on page 49.)

Block out some time to sit down at the computer with a disc and move step by step through the evaluation form. Jot down any interesting side trips, information or unique aspects of the disc. As you begin the rating process, maintain a file on the product by recording any questions, comments or problems you or the faculty or students encounter. This is very helpful when you later speak to salespeople or customer-support staff.

The form reproduced in this chapter is a guide to help you structure the examination process. The questions are organized in a logical, sequential order to help you survey the positive features and shortcomings of a product efficiently. It is designed to help analyze the true educational value of the CD-ROM, rather than the bells and whistles.

This form was designed by compiling as many checklist questions as possible to scrutinize every CD-ROM component. Initially, it totalled ten pages, single-spaced. Using it to evaluate a new resource would have taken about five days! Because our goal was to develop a one-page assessment tool, we went back to work to categorize, classify and reorganize the relevant topics. Other school librarians tested the result and gave us the feedback that helped us to synthesize and streamline the tool into a manageable size.

There are many CD-ROMs and simply no easy way to judge all of them. The purpose of this form is to guide you through the evaluation process, to teach you to ask appropriate questions. We hope that after using the form several times you will develop an intuitive feeling about what CD-ROM programs will be successful in your school.

Any evaluation process is subjective. The CD-ROM product is assessed within the general categories outlined in the form, but also according to specific requirements of your school. You need to look at the product with the curriculum, teachers and students in mind. The CD-ROM needs to be developmentally appropriate for its audience. Thus "user-friendliness" depends on who the users are—second graders, eighth graders, resource-room students, ESL students or teachers.

There will be tradeoffs between content and user interface. For example, the content might be right on target, but the search screens confusing and difficult to use. Often it is a balancing act, but the important thing to remember is the student. What will the student learn by using this resource? Many discs will fall into the 70-85 bracket on the form, and the decision to purchase will depend on the school's curriculum needs.

Unfortunately, as hard as we tried, we must admit it is impossible to develop a standardized list of questions that can be applied to all CD-ROM products. Multimedia is so new and diverse and uses powerful search techniques that do not conform to standard database evaluation criteria. Highly effective multimedia storybooks do not use Boolean searching, while magazine indexes cannot function without this search feature. Text-based CD-ROMs allow flexible printing and downloading to disk, while the need to save multimedia segments has only recently been identified due to increased student use of hypermedia authoring programs.

Not every question on this form will be relevant for every CD-ROM title. It is not important for a children's storybook to have an onscreen notebook or for a CD-ROM dictionary to have Boolean searching. As you read the questions, consider the type and purpose of the CD-ROM and whether a question is appropriate.

CD-ROM Evaluation Form

Title of Disc   Date

	Question or consideration	Yes	No or Not Applicable	Sometimes, Partly True, or Maybe
Getting Started	1. Is the CD-ROM easy to install?			
	2. Is there documentation? Is it thorough and easy to understand?			
Moving Around	3. Is the screen uncluttered? Are directional and informational prompts prominent?			
	4. Does it use simple and consistent commands to navigate?			
	5. Are help screens easy to access? Clear? Context sensitive?			
	6. Can you exit from any screen? Retrace your steps? Get a search history?			
	7. Can you access cross referenced information easily?			
Searching/Results	8. Are there at least 2 levels of searching (browsing, fill-in, or Boolean)?			
	9. Are the search results easy to understand?			
	10. Can you print the results? Can you choose exactly what you want to print?			
	11. Can you save to a disk? Is there an on-screen notebook?			
Contents	12. Is the data on the CD-ROM accurate?			
	13. Is there depth to the content data?			
	14. Are the intellectual level and content appropriate for the intended audience?			
	15. Is the content free of any bias (gender, race, religion, etc.)?			
	16. If there are illustrations, color, and/or sound, are they well done and meaningful?			
Curriculum Support & Practical Matters	17. Will this CD-ROM support or enhance the curriculum? In more than one area?			
	18. Does it stimulate student imagination and curiosity? Will it make kids think?			
	19. Is the price reasonable?			
	20. Can you use it on a network?			

Total each Column:

© 1994, P. Berger & S. Kinnell
CD-ROM for Schools

Multiply by:	5	0	2
and record here:			

Add 5 points for each YES answer on the bonus questions below:

		Yes		
Bonus Questions	1. Does it include an interactive component (like a quiz or game)?			
	2. Is the content unique (not in print or otherwise accessible to schools)?			
	3. Are there supporting materials or teacher's aids?			

85-100+	Buy that disc!
60-85	Consider its strengths and weaknesses and your curriculum
45-60	Only if it's *really* cheap
0-45	These make nice Frisbees

Add the totals above and the bonus points to get the Disc Evaluation Total:

The overall score the CD-ROM title receives will be subjective. And the final decision to purchase a CD-ROM will also be subjective—it depends on your school's curriculum needs.

This approach allows for the unique features of CD-ROM products. It is only a beginning. As CD-ROM technology matures, new program types and genres will be developed, and the evaluation form will have to be updated and refined to reflect this growth. Periodic updates will be published in the *Information Searcher* newsletter. Please photocopy it, use it, share it and give us your feedback.

PUTTING THE EVALUATION FORM TO USE

The form has six sections:

- Getting Started
- Moving Around
- Searching/Results
- Contents
- Curriculum Support and Practical Matters
- Bonus Questions

1. Getting Started. The best-designed products install easily and coexist with other computer software. Using the instructions supplied, installation is straightforward. The installation program is interactive and tells you what is going on while the program is installing, aborts easily at the user's command and gives you choices for video and sound boards, if needed.

Installation programs should not change the AUTOEXEC.BAT or CONFIG.SYS files without the user's permission—or at very least, without a warning. It is still a good idea to have a copy (disk or print) of each of these files, in case they are altered.

Basic documentation should include a table of contents, an index, an installation section, searching instructions, and a set of sample searches and trouble-shooting suggestions—plus a phone number for help. Extras, like quick reference cards, promotional displays, templates, etc., are welcome but not necessary.

2. Moving Around. A good CD-ROM program allows users to perform desired tasks without frustration. The interface is intuitive, uses standard conventions and has an uncluttered, organized screen that provides a range of features to help the user access the content. It is easy to move between screens and within screens. Ask how quickly does it become unnecessary to think about the mechanics of navigating the program? The sooner this happens, the more intuitive the interface. The commands are consistent and readily apparent. When the main menu appears, the user's options for navigating the program and accessing context-sensitive help menus are evident. Tutorials are easily accessed and exited. Search paths can be reviewed and repeated.

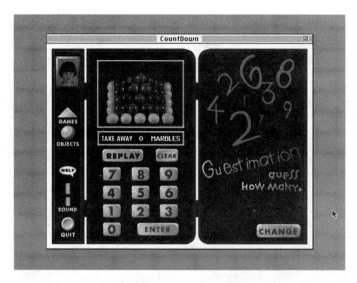

The program, CountDown, while an excellent product for primary arithmetic classes, has some problems with screen design. There is no clear way for users to know exactly what they are supposed to do, especially with the little picture at the top left corner. This is actually a QuickTime video, and if you click on it, it talks and gives an explanation of the various aspects of each game. Young children who tested the program said they needed a manual to understand what they had to do next.

Contrast the CountDown screen with this screen from Just Grandma and Me. Lil Critter asks users if they want to quit the program, and they have a choice of clicking on the No or the Yes box. Each child in those boxes is nodding or shaking his head—another visual clue about what to do next. There's no question about what actions are possible.

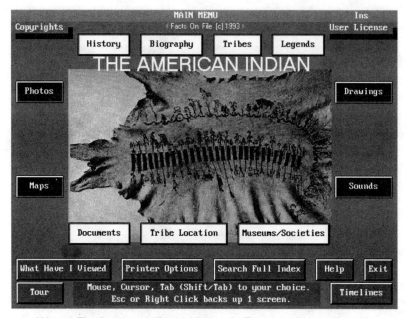

Although The American Indian: A Multimedia Encyclopedia is loaded with good information, the screens do not contain adequate visual clues to help the user begin the search process and easily navigate the program.

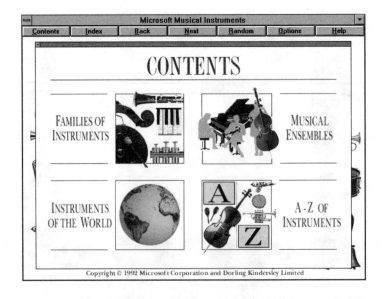

The screen design for Microsoft Musical Instruments is intuitive, and there is never confusion in navigating through the screens of information.

If the product is multimedia, test to see if there are separate or integrated pathways through text, sound, graphics and video. Are there hypermedia links from one part of the program to another? Are they cross-referenced? Are voice, animation and music synchronized? Can you end or exit a multimedia segment at any time?

3. Searching and Results. A good CD-ROM program offers at least two ways to look for information: browsing and searching. Search techniques allow a user to locate specific information quickly and efficiently. Browsing presents the opportunity to explore the program's information. The choice depends on whether you are interested in general or specific information. In either case, the user is guided through the process by a series of prompts or menus. The search software is transparent, so that a student can concentrate on the informational content, and is designed to encourage students to use higher-order thinking skills.

The capability of printing or downloading results to a disk is essential in a school media center. Most schools do not have enough computers to allow students to use a single computer for an extended period of time when major research papers are underway. Unfortunately, students must be on and off the computer quickly and still retrieve the desired information. To do this successfully, the student needs to be able to print the information or download it to a disk. Some products, such as the Multimedia Animals Encyclopedia and Newsweek Interactive do not have print functions. This non-print rationale is based, first, on the belief that the program's power is in its capacity to explore and navigate the multimedia information, not in the limited linear printout of text information. Second, the disc is intended to be used in the home, where students can spend hours on their computer uninterrupted.

Newer multimedia titles, such as National Geographic's Picture Atlas of the World, take the next step and allow downloading of the multimedia segments. Students can save the video clips, sound segments and graphics to a disk and incorporate them into a multimedia presentation of their own using Linkway Live! or HyperCard to put it all together.

Be sure to test-drive the program fully. Consider the content area and the intended grade level and develop a list of questions to put the program through its paces. If it is a full-text database, develop questions that search all appropriate fields, search multiword phrases, use Boolean and proximity operators, etc. If it is a multimedia title, then try to search multiple media simultaneously, display one media without the others, (such as only text, without graphics or sound) or search different media and display them side by side for comparison.

4. Content. Standard criteria applied to print and other resources are also used to determine the quality of CD-ROM content—scope, authority, uniqueness, comprehensiveness and depth, currency, freedom from culture or gender or racial bias, data quality and accuracy. In addition, content should be appropriate to student needs, curriculum area, purpose and grade level.

Taking Two Dictionary CD-ROMs For A Test Drive

Evaluating a dictionary CD-ROM should have the same flavor as looking at a brand-new print dictionary. You would open the book, find a word, check the cross-references and synonyms, and thumb through the different sections. Are you satisfied with the product? Is the print easy to read? Is the paper thick enough so the pages turn easily and the words don't show through? Are the definitions and pronunciation guides easy to understand? Is it so big you can't hold it, and you'll need a stand or a table? Is it so small that the really difficult words aren't in it? Is it up-to-date? Is it worth the price?

You can ask yourself similar questions about a CD-ROM dictionary, as far as the content of the dictionary is concerned. Is it up-to-date? How many words are in it? Is the print easy to read? The really nice thing about a CD-ROM dictionary is that it doesn't need a special table to hold it, but of course you still can't carry it around in your hip pocket and read it on the bus!

When a dictionary CD-ROM is first opened and is displayed on the computer screen, here are some questions to ask:

• Is it immediately obvious how to find a word?
• What tools do you have to move around? Is it easy to move around?
• Is the print big enough to read on your screen? Is the typeface OK?

After you have been browsing in the dictionary for a little while, ask these questions:

• Can you exit the dictionary at any point?
• Can you find other sections of the dictionary quickly?
• Can you print out the meaning of any word?
• Can you save a word and its meaning to your floppy disk?

The final questions that should be asked are probably the key ones in making a buy decision:

• What does this dictionary do for you that a print dictionary doesn't?
• Is it worth the price?

Most CD-ROMs have different features, so it is a good idea to do a comparison review to see which one you want to buy. We looked at two of the big dictionaries that are available on CD-ROM: Random House Unabridged Dictionary (over 300,000 words), and Webster's Ninth New Collegiate Dictionary.

These dictionaries are covered in-depth in the Reviews section of this book, but it is worth noting that there are indeed reasons to buy a CD-ROM dictionary, instead of a print dictionary.

Webster's has the unique feature of being able to pronounce any word that is selected. You can actually hear the word as it should be pronounced, so even if the phonetic spelling features are a mystery to you, you will now be able to repeat the word out loud.

The Random House Dictionary does not run on your computer as a separate program, but as a background tool. You can call it up at any point while you are working in another program (as long as the CD-ROM is in the drive). It is triple the size of most dictionaries that are included in the spell-check feature of word processing programs. And, of course, being able to print a lengthy definition or save it to disk is an added bonus. This feature is probably of most use to students doing reports, rather than to casual browsers who just want to know the meaning of a word.

If graphics and sound are included, they should be relevant to the content and student learning. In some programs, these features are added just to be able to label the title "multimedia." Monarch Notes, a CD-ROM containing the complete print version of the same title, is listed as "multimedia." When you click on the button, the first few lines of the book will be read to you, the graphic on the screen is of Patricia Richardson-Smith, the woman who is reciting. The same black-and-white photograph of the same woman appears for all audio clips. Hearing a few sentences from a book does not add to the relevance of the content, nor does seeing the photograph of Patricia Richardson-Smith.

5. Curriculum Support and Practical Matters. Curriculum support is a crucial step in the evaluation process. The CD-ROM can be a strong candidate for purchase—fulfilling all other criteria—but if it does not have a significant relationship with or connection to the curriculum, it is worthless. It must support the instructional concepts and themes of the school's curricula.

Look for titles that support interdisciplinary curriculum connections, in which a central focus or topic/question might be explored through many subject areas. TIME Almanac, a multimedia program, is used successfully in this manner with social studies, science and language arts. When examining discs, make sure the content/curriculum and the developmental level match. If you are looking for a multimedia CD-ROM on animals for students in the lower elementary grades, check to be sure that the reading level, type of information and presentation are appropriate for students of that age.

Does this CD-ROM stimulate student imagination and curiosity? Will it make students think? These issues are important considerations when rating CD-ROMs, even though they are placed in the bonus category. Good screen design and searching interfaces can be developed to encourage student interaction. The more students are involved, the more they are engaged, the more they are going to learn. We are hopeful that in the future this will be a basic requirement for all educational technology.

Price is a major consideration. How often will the product be used and by how many students? Is the price reasonable compared to its print counterpart? Are there ongoing subscription costs? How often does the program need to be updated, and what is the cost of program updates?

There is sometimes confusion about networking a CD-ROM. If you plan to network the program, be certain it can be accessed simultaneously by multiple users. Some producers state their CD-ROMs are networkable, but what they really mean is that it can run across a network with one user at a time accessing the program. Be sure to check the required hardware and software specifications, including the file server and workstations.

There are added network charges—sometimes a flat rate and other times incremental, based on the number of users accessing the system. Check to see what the network license includes, and whether it covers one building, multiple school buildings on a campus, dial-in at-home access, etc.

6. Bonus Questions. In some situations, CD-ROM products are accompanied by supporting curriculum materials or teacher's aids. This is a great benefit to educators and gives the product a major advantage. In California, school librarians feel strongly that all CD-ROM products should come with supporting material. In "Guidelines for CD-ROM in California Schools," the top rating is reserved for those titles that have curriculum-supporting materials. Watch for titles that make a unique contribution, such as Ethnic NewsWatch, a full-text collection of over 95 ethnic publications. Or, look at Street Atlas USA, a seamless atlas of every street, highway, river, etc., in the country—great for elementary students studying their community, as well as high school students planning a cross-country trip in American History.

COMPOSERS

Bach and Before: Vol. 1
Beethoven Symphony #9
Composer Quest
Jazz
Multimedia Beethoven
Multimedia Mozart
Multimedia Music Book: Mozart
Multimedia Stravinsky
Orchestra
Vivaldi: The Four Seasons

List of CD-ROM titles about musical composers.

SELECTION AND EVALUATION TOOLS

DIRECTORIES

Good directories will help you identify discs, compare titles and producers, and know where to call for questions. Most of the following directories are updated annually.

CD-ROM Directory 1995 (annual) Thirteenth Edition
George Bischiniotis, (ed.)
Print Version
TFPL, Washington DC, 1994
Distributed in the U.S. and Canada by Pemberton Press Inc.
462 Danbury Road
Wilton, CT 06897-2126
$139 (ISBN 1-870889-30-4)

CD-ROM Directory 1995 *On Disc*
TFPL, Washington DC, 1994
Hardware: IBM, 640K RAM recommended, DOS 3.0; MSCDEX, hard drive with 2.6MB free.
Distributed in the U.S. and Canada by Pemberton Press Inc. (see previous entry for address)
$155, 2-disc set (semiannual updates, January and July)

CD-ROMs in Print 1995: An International Guide to CD-ROM, CD-I, CDTV, Multimedia &
Electronic Book Products (print version)
Meckler Corporation
11 Ferry Lane West, Westport, CT 06880
$99.95

CD-ROMs in Print 1994: An International Guide to CD-ROM, CD-I, CDTV, Multimedia &
Electronic Book Products (CD-ROM version, DOS/Mac)
Meckler Corporation
11 Ferry Lane West, Westport, CT 06880
$49.95 (for annual, January)
$99.95 (for annual & semiannual, January & July)

CD-ROM Finder, Fifth Edition 1993
Print Version
James Shelton, (ed.)
Learned Information, Inc.
143 Old Marlton Pike
Medford, NJ 08055-8750
$69.50

MAGAZINES AND JOURNALS

Many periodical sources are available to help you keep current with CD-ROM. News-letters, journals and magazines concerning school librarians, educational technology, the CD-ROM and computer industries and mass media all address the burgeoning field of CD-ROM. (See the list of key titles on page 58.) The resources vary in depth and breadth of coverage, depending on their target audience.

The newsletter, *Information Searcher*, is specifically targeted for the use of CD-ROM in the school library and classroom. It was started six years ago by a school librarian (a co-author of this book) and remains a grassroots publication, written by and for school librarians. It covers major trends, reviews, integration of CD-ROM technology into the curriculum, conferences, etc., and offers practical advice and librarian-tested curriculum units.

MultiMedia Schools, is a new, highly acclaimed journal from Online Inc., pub-lishers of *CD-ROM Professional, DATABASE* and *ONLINE* magazines. The first

Magazines And Journals That Cover CD-ROM

Booklist
ISSN 0006-7385
American Library Association
50 E. Huron Street
Chicago, IL 60611
Twice monthly, $60
Look for the "Audiovisual Media
Section—CD-ROM."

CD-ROM Professional
ISSN 1049-0833
Pemberton Press
462 Danbury Road
Wilton, CT 06897-2126
Monthly (beginning January
1995), $98 year
$55 personal rate

CD-ROM Today
ISSN 1069-4099
GP Publications
23-00 Route 208
Fair Lawn, NJ 07410
Bimonthly, $20.95

CD-ROM World
ISSN 1066-274X
Meckler Corporation
11 Ferry Lane West
Westport, CT 06880
Monthly, combined issues
Feb./March, Nov./Dec., $87
$33 personal rate

Computers in Libraries
ISSN 1041-7915
Meckler Corporation
11 Ferry Lane West
Westport, CT 06880
Ten times per year, $80
Look for the column, "School
Time," by Catherine Murphy.

Electronic Learning
ISSN 0278-3258

Scholastic, Inc.
555 Broadway
New York, NY 10012
Eight times per year, $23.95

Information Searcher
ISSN 1055-3916
DataSearch Group, Inc.
14 Hadden Road
Scarsdale, NY 10583
Quarterly during the school
year, $34
Look for two columns:
"CD-ROM News," "CD-ROM
Reviews for Schools" by Pam
Berger and Susan Kinnell.

Library Journal
ISSN 0363-0277
Cahners Publishing Company
249 W. 17th Street
New York, NY 10011
Monthly, $79
Look for the column,
"CD-ROM Review," by
Cheryl LaGuardia.

MultiMedia Schools
ISSN 1075-0479
Online Inc.
462 Danbury Road
Wilton, CT 06897-2126
Bimonthly during the school
year, $38; 800/248-8466
Concentrates on practical, how-to
articles on CD-ROMs and the
Internet written by school profes-
sionals in the field.

NewMedia
ISSN 1060-7188
HyperMedia Communica-
   tions, Inc.
901 Mariner's Island Boulevard
San Mateo, CA 94404

Free to school library media
specialists.
Look for the column,
"Big Screen."

School Library Journal
ISSN 0362-8930
Cahners Publishing Company
249 W. 17th Street
New York, NY 10011
Monthly, $67
Look for the column
"Reviews Computer Software
and CD-ROM."

Technology Connections
Linworth Publishing, Inc.
480 East Wilson Bridge Road,
Suite L
Worthington, OH 43085-9490
10 issues, $29, newsletter

Technology & Learning
ISSN 105-67280
Peter Li, Inc
330 Progress Road
Dayton, OH 45449
Monthly, except June, July,
Aug, $24

Wilson Library Bulletin
ISSN 0043-5651
H.W. Wilson & Co.
950 University Avenue
Bronx, NY 10452
Monthly, $52
Look for these columns:
"Electronically Speaking"
by Merry Mattson, Bonnie
Morris and Renee Troselius;
"CD-ROM/Online Update"
by Martin Kesselman;
and "Reference on Disc,"
by Charles Anderson.

issue of *MULTIMEDIA SCHOOLS* appeared in May 1994. *MULTIMEDIA SCHOOLS* is directed to K-12 school librarians and teachers who are using CD-ROM and multimedia and online resources. It covers the trends and technology from a practical angle, includes how-to articles on CD-ROM, online and the Internet, all written by working teachers and school librarians. A significant component of the magazine will be critical, concise reviews of CD-ROM and multimedia titles, written for teachers, librarians and curriculum specialists.

Two other CD-ROM-specific magazines are directed at the emerging home market; *CD-ROM World* and *CD-ROM Today* are available on newsstands. While they do not include reviews with curriculum and students in mind: they, nevertheless contain many reviews and are good sources for current developments. Another magazine, *NewMedia*, concentrates on multimedia including CD-ROM and contains a review section entitled "Big Screen" and feature articles on CD-ROM.

Educational/library technology journals, such as *Technology and Learning*, *Computers in Libraries* and *Electronic Learning*, include articles and reviews on CD-ROM. *Computers in Libraries* has a section called "CD-ROM Librarian" that occasionally includes "School Time," a column by Catherine Murphy from the University of Texas at Denton.

Traditional library reviewing journals are now including CD-ROM reviews. These journals are *Booklist*, *School Library Journal*, *Library Journal* and *Wilson Library Bulletin*. Sporadically, these journals feature articles on CD-ROM.

ELECTRONIC SOURCES

Bulletin boards on commercial online services and LISTSERVs on the Internet are also good sources of CD-ROM information. The following are some key sources.

CompuServe
500 Arlington Centre Boulevard
P.O. Box 20212
Columbus, OH 43220
800/848-8199

CompuServe's CD-ROM Forum attracts all kinds of CD-ROM enthusiasts from home, industry and business. It is a clearinghouse for news, tips, discussions and related shareware programs. To access the forum at the CIS prompt, type GO CDROM.

CD-ROM Vendor's Forum is CompuServe's forum sponsored by software and hardware manufacturers. A few of the vendors represented are Bureau of Electronic Publishing, Bowker Electronic Publishing and Nimbus Information Systems. The forum includes demos, driver updates, press releases and other information, plus access to company representatives. To access the forum at the CIS prompt, type GO CDVEN.

The Multimedia Forum hosts both users and producers of multimedia software and equipment. It contains demos, and vendor representatives are accessible for questions. To access the forum at the CIS prompt, type GO MULTIMEDIA.

Subscribing To LM_NET

    To sign on LM_NET, send an e-mail message to: **LISTSERV@SUVM.SYR.EDU.** Leave the subject line blank. In the body of the message type: **SUBSCRIBE LM_NET firstname lastname**

    LM_NET is good place to share information on CD-ROMs. Jan Hosey posted a message asking LM_NETters to send her a listing of their top CD-ROMs. She offered to post the results to the list. The following message is the result of her informal survey.

Date: Fri, 11 Feb 1994 21:04:47 -0600
Reply-To: Jan Z Hosey <hoseyjz@MAIL.AUBURN.EDU>
Sender: School Library Media & Network Communications <LM_NET@SUVM.SYR.EDU>
From: Jan Z Hosey <hoseyjz@MAIL.AUBURN.EDU>
Subject: HIT> Top 10 CD-ROMs
To: Multiple recipients of list LM_NET <LM_NET@SUVM.SYR.EDU>

Thanks to all who responded to my request for your Top 10 CD-ROM products, and please forgive my delay in forwarding a summary of your responses.

The results were difficult to formulate into a top ten list. I received recommendations for 46 CD-ROMs, but there was very little overlap among titles. Also, most of the suggested titles were reference-rather than curriculum-related.

Still, the results were interesting and I appreciate your help.
Most of you are using indexes and encyclopedias, perhaps (as Catherine Murphy suggested to me) because these products were first on the market and appeal to a broad range of grade levels and curriculum areas.

    The following titles received four votes each:
        - Discovering Authors (Gale)
        - Time Magazine Almanac
        - SIRS full text
These titles received three votes each:
        - Groliers Encyclopedia
        - Tom Jr. Magazine Index
These titles received two votes each:
        - Granger's Poetry
        - Great Literature
        - World Fact Book
        - World Book's Information Finder
        - National Geographic's Mammals
        - Infotrac
        - CD Newsbank
        - Facts on File
        - Elite Magazine Article Summaries (EBSCO)
        - Software Toolworks World Atlas

    Although I couldn't lay my hands on Catherine Murphy's article in the Nov./Dec. '93 issue of CD-ROM World [both copies of that issue available from Auburn University libraries disappeared—that must be a TERRIFIC article, Catherine, since someone felt inclined to steal it :)], it has the results of a survey she conducted of top 10 CD-ROMs.

To the many of you who shared my interest in the topic, you might also check out two articles published in the Nov. '93 issue of CD-ROM Professional. The first lists "29 essential titles" for high school libraries, and the second lists MS-DOS CD-ROMs for grades K-9. The authors promise similar lists of Macintosh products in future issues of the magazine.

If any of you would like the complete list of titles you suggested to me, you can e-mail me directly at the address below.
Thanks again!

Jan Hosey
Auburn University
hoseyjz@mail.auburn.edu

America Online
8619 Westwood Center Drive
Vienna, VA 22182-2285
800/827-6364

This is an online service which has a special educator's section run by Scholastic, Inc.

The Internet
The Internet is a network of networks, linking millions of users worldwide. Once on the Internet, you can join a mailing list. A mailing list or LISTSERV is an organized system in which individuals receive messages on a particular topic. When one member sends a message to the list, all members receive the message in their personal mailboxes. They have the option to reply directly to the person posting the message or reply to the LISTSERV for group interaction. Participants also have the option to read only the messages posted to the list and not interact by sending messages. This is called "lurking" and is an excellent way to learn about a new topic like CD-ROM.

LM_NET is a LISTSERV for school library media specialists. Discussions, questions and answers, files, reports, jokes, etc., are shared by over 1,200 school librarians worldwide. Mike Eisenberg, Syracuse University, Syracuse, NY and Peter Milbury, Pleasant Valley High School, Chico, CA are the list owners. This is a good place to ask questions about CD-ROM products, networking, training, etc., as well as share your experiences as you learn. To subscribe to the list, send an e-mail message to: LISTSERV@SUVM. Leave the subject line blank and in the body of the message type: Subscribe LM_NET firstname lastname.

MultiMedia Schools' Gopher, is sponsored by Online Inc., and will be operational in late 1994. It will contain the full text of selected feature articles and columns from the magazine, plus reviews of CD-ROM titles for schools. Other items in the gopher will include the text of articles, columns and reviews about CD-ROM, multimedia, online and Internet topics of interest to school library media specialists, selected from the company's other publications. For information about the gopher address and availability, call Online Inc., 800/248-8466.

CDROM-L, started by Richard Hintz, University of California, is focused on technical content and discussion of CD-ROMs. To subscribe, send a message to LISTSERV@UCCVMA. UCOP.EDU. In the body of the message type: Subscribe CDROM-L firstname lastname.

CDROMLAN is a useful list to discuss technical aspects of CD-ROM products on local or wide area networks. It was started by Dan Lester at Boise State, Iowa. To subscribe, send a message to: LISTSERV@IDBSU.EDU. In the body of the message type: Subscribe CDROMLAN firstname lastname.

FAQs are a useful source of information on the Internet that contain answers to frequently asked questions (FAQ). You can access the following FAQ files on CD-ROM by using anonymous FTP and retrieve them from ftp.cdrom.com: FAQ (Questions and answers from CDROM-L); FAQ_MM (Multimedia CD questions and answers); CDROMLAN. FAQ (CD-ROMs on local/wide area networks).

Top Ten Highly Recommended Titles

CNN Newsroom Global View
Discovering French Interactive
Living Books
Macmillan Dictionary for Children Multimedia Edition
Microsoft Bookshelf 1994 Multimedia Edition
Microsoft Musical Instruments
Picture Atlas of the World
Prehistoria
The San Diego Zoo Presents...The Animals!
Time Almanac 1993

Look for the star marking these top ten titles in the Core List

---

CONFERENCES

The MULTIMEDIA SCHOOLS Conference (formerly DATABASES IN SCHOOLS) is the only conference devoted to the teaching and use of CD-ROM, online searching and the Internet in schools. Organized by Online Inc. and chaired by Pam Berger, the conference is held in one of three cities, San Francisco ('94), Chicago ('95), Washington ('96) in the fall. The conference is held in conjunction with the ONLINE/CD-ROM Conference and Exposition and shares a common exhibit hall.

MULTIMEDIA SCHOOLS concentrates on the most important issues facing library media specialists, teachers and administrators in their attempt to integrate technology meaningfully into the curriculum. It focuses on practical how-to aspects of teaching database searching, and features experienced practitioners in the field.

American Association of School Librarians (AASL) is a division of the American Library Association. AASL holds a national biannual conference every other fall. For information about the next conference, contact AASL/ALA, 50 East Huron Street, Chicago, IL 60611-2795.

Association for Supervision and Curriculum Development (ASCD) is an annual conference sponsored by the educational association of the same name. For more information, contact ASCD, 1250 N. Pitt Street, Alexandria, VA 22314-1453.

Florida Educational Technology Conference (FETC) is an annual conference held each spring that attracts a broad and diverse group of educators who use educational technologies. For more information contact FETC, 325 West Gaines Street, Florida Educational Center, B1-54 Tallahassee, FL 32399-0400.

National Educational Computing Conference (NECC '95) is an annual conference held in June. There are many CD-ROM exhibitors at this conference. For information about the 1995 conference scheduled in Baltimore, MD, contact Doris Lidtke, NECC '95, 1705 East West Highway, #611, Silver Spring, MD 20910.

The Technology+Learning Conference, sponsored by the National School Boards Association, is held in the fall at the Dallas Infomart. It is a large, general conference and expo with some CD-ROM topics. For information contact the NSBA at 1680 Duke St., Alexandria, VA 22314. Phone: 1-800/950-6722.

THE BOTTOM LINE

The final step of the evaluation process is to decide what is necessary to make a disc worthwhile. Ask:

- What will it take to ensure that this resource will be used by students?
- How can we guarantee that this technology will be integrated into the curriculum in a meaningful way?
- Is it staff development that's needed? Curriculum development? Presentations at faculty meetings? More hardware?

You have been evaluating information products in print and audiovisual media for years. Use those same skills to evaluate CD-ROM products and don't be intimidated by the technology. Look at lots of discs and *enjoy* the process. Remember that the bottom line is student learning. If you think a disc will enhance and support the learning process, go for it!

SELECTED RESOURCES FOR FURTHER READING

Berger, Pam. "Students Evaluate CD-ROM." *Information Searcher* 6, No. 1 (1993): pp. 29-32.

Jacsó, Péter. *CD-ROM Software, Dataware, and Hardware: Evaluation, Selection and Installation.* Englewood, Colorado: Libraries Unlimited, 1992.

King, Alan. "Kicking the Tires: The Fine Art of CD-ROM Product Evaluation." *ONLINE* (May 1992): pp. 58-60.

LaGuardia, Cheryl. "Virtuous Disc Selection: Or, How I Learned to Stop Worrying and Love To Buy CD-ROMs." *CD-ROM Professional* (January 1992): pp. 58-60.

Nicholls, Paul, Isaac Han, Karen Stafford, and Katherine Whitridge. "A Framework for Evaluating CD-ROM Retrieval Software." *Laserdisk Professional* (March 1990): pp. 41-46.

Nordgren, Layne. "Evaluating Multimedia CD-ROM Discware: Of Bells, Whistles and Value." *CD-ROM Professional* (January 1993): pp. 99-105.

CHAPTER 5
CD-ROM INSTRUCTION AND CURRICULUM INTEGRATION

....

- Is it necessary to teach students to use CD-ROM?
- Isn't CD-ROM user-friendly?
- Don't students already know about computers?
- How do you include CD-ROM in your instructional program?
- What type of instruction is most effective?
- What instruction do faculty need?

CD-ROM poses as many questions as it answers when it comes to instruction. There is a growing debate among librarians about the necessity of teaching students how to use CD-ROM. There are arguments for and against; however, the pros are more compelling than the cons.

REASONS TO TEACH CD-ROM USE

Unique Features of CD-ROM: CD-ROM has its own structure, design and features. Students need to learn the advantages and disadvantages unique to CD-ROM and be able to compare it to online and print formats when locating specific data to fulfill their information needs. In addition, students should be aware of the different kinds of CD-ROMs, such as reference, bibliographic, numeric, full text, multimedia, etc. Instruction about using traditional print sources should include teaching the basics of electronic resources. Students need to learn about using computers and CD-ROM to access information.

Prevalence and Accessibility of CD-ROM: Students will encounter CD-ROM technology in all kinds of libraries. CD-ROM is now available in many public, college and academic libraries. The acceptance and widespread use of CD-ROM is documented in surveys, professional literature and conference presentations. A survey conducted for UMI in 1993 indicates that in the next few years these percentages of libraries will have CD-ROM:

- 85 percent of high school libraries
- 99 percent of large research libraries
- 97 percent of most college libraries
- 89 percent of public libraries

Inescapably, students encounter CD-ROM.

CD-ROM use is increasing faster than online searching, due to its predictable costs and ease of accessibility. Unlike online, CD-ROM does not have the clock ticking away, adding charges by the minute. Students have the luxury of time to explore the system. Once the basic concepts are learned, students can search unassisted and are in control of their own searching, a benefit they all enjoy.

Instruction Increases the Comfort Level: Instruction decreases students' computer anxiety. School library media specialists need to be prepared to cope with the well-documented fear of computers that handicaps many people. Most students are comfortable with computers, enjoy exploring programs and are not intimidated by experimenting, but some who have never used computers are hesitant and sometimes fearful.

Faculty and staff are often the most computer-phobic, afraid of appearing foolish in front of students or colleagues. It's important to offer formal and informal instruction for these groups so they reach a critical level of comfort. Faculty require personal experience with CD-ROM before they can consider integrating it in their curricula. Don't underestimate the power of faculty who model computer use—and the impact on both students and other faculty members.

ARGUMENTS AGAINST TEACHING CD-ROM

Some of the most common excuses for not teaching CD-ROM are similar to the arguments for developing an instructional program.

User-Friendliness: CD-ROM producers argue that instruction is not required for their products, citing "user-friendly" software interfaces. Sometimes we are fooled by user-friendly menus that give quick access to the first level of searching. However, repeatedly in the literature librarians say they are concerned about patrons' low skill levels and gaps in the conceptual understanding necessary to search a database effectively.

On the college and academic level there is an ongoing debate about whether it is an academic librarian's responsibility to interfere when a patron appears satisfied with an ineffective or inappropriate search. Many students consistently under-use the search software because CD-ROM databases appear so simple. They search a bibliographic database and retrieve 135 citations or none at all. In either case, they are unaware of the techniques and strategies to narrow or broaden the search. Often they waste their time going through all 135 citations or believe that nothing is written on a topic. (Carol Tenopir summarizes the argument in an editorial, "Is It Any Of Our Business?" in *Library Journal*, April 1, 1992, p. 96.)

These experiences in college and public libraries further strengthen the argument for instruction about CD-ROM search strategies and techniques. On the K-12 level, it is our responsibility to teach students how to locate information effectively, CD-ROM included. Don't be fooled by user-friendliness—database concepts and search techniques are not intuitive; they must be learned.

Student Resistance: Students and faculty are sometimes resistant to CD-ROM instruction. Unlike online searches, which are conducted with the assistance of or by the school library media specialist, CD-ROM workstations are often freestanding in the center of the library.

ANIMALS

about COWS
Creepy Crawlies
Dictionary of the Living World
Kid's Zoo
LIFEmap Series, Vols. 1, 2, & 3
Mammals: A Multimedia Encyclopedia
Multimedia Animals Encyclopedia Library, Vol. 1
Multimedia Encyclopedia of Mammalian Biology
San Diego Zoo Presents…The Animals!
World Alive
World of Animals
Zoo Guide Series: Butterflies
Zoo Guide Series: Mammals of Africa

List of CD-ROM titles about all kinds of animals.

Since students and faculty are thus invited to use them without immediate assistance, the implication is that no instruction is needed.

Several recent studies of how people learn to use microcomputers indicated that they prefer to solve problems on their own, turning to outside help as a last resort. This might explain why some students express impatience and resentment at having to learn how to use the programs.

Some computer-literate students who are experienced with word processing, spreadsheets or electronic bulletin boards have a more difficult time accepting instruction and help from the library staff. They don't understand that searching a database or multimedia CD-ROM program requires a unique set of skills.

There is a false sense of competency about searching CD-ROMs. Students using an electronic retrieval system at its most superficial level unconsciously think they have employed its full capability. They need to be taught how to search a text-based database with its power and complexity including Boolean logic, truncation, field qualification, word proximity operators, keyword searching, multiple display and print format options. Knowing how to navigate user-friendly titles is not sufficient.

Lack of Time: Lack of time and fixed costs are frequent arguments for not teaching the use of CD-ROM. CD-ROMs are purchased on a subscription or one-time basis. There is no cost-per-minute for students' use of the system, unlike database searching online. Why not let the students learn to search by practicing and exploring on their own? This thinking is especially attractive considering the time it takes to design and produce teaching materials, develop curriculum units using CD-ROM, conduct workshops for faculty or provide individual assistance. Unfortunately, research shows that the skills needed to search CD-ROM properly are not learned by exploration alone. Despite CD-ROM's deceptive user-friendliness and everyone's—students' and faculty's—lack of time, students still need CD-ROM instruction.

CURRICULUM-BASED/LEARNER-CENTERED CD-ROM INSTRUCTION

Information skills (how to locate, retrieve, evaluate, present and use information) should be taught within curriculum areas. A skill is meaningless if taught out of context. Students will question, explore, analyze, compare, contrast and generally make sense of the information if they have a *need* to understand. Using CD-ROM is exactly the same.

Technology supports the inquiry process by allowing a student to be an active participant. Students can perform research with multimedia tools, information resources and human experts, locally or online. CD-ROM technology assists research by supplying large amounts of information and structuring it in ways that encourage exploration.

Steps In The Planning Process To Integrate Research Strategies With Curriculum

Responsibility	Planning Steps
Teacher	1. Decide on the instructional goal(s) of the research paper or project.
Shared	2. Assess students' expertise in using library resources and decide which additional skills will be required by the assignment.
Shared	3. Agree on teaching strategies to introduce the new search skills and specific resources.
Librarian	4. Identify specific reference sources, books, and current information to meet the depth of the assignment and the developmental level of the students.
Shared	5. Develop a lesson plan/calendar to: a. introduce assignment b. review sources students know c. teach search strategy and sample sources d. read for background information e. search for and evaluate materials f. make frequent progress checks for grades g. provide time for individual guidance h. teach required form of paper i. present project to class or other group
Shared	6. Evaluate papers or class presentations with librarian and note improvement in lesson plan for future classes.

Presented at DATABASES IN SCHOOLS '93, Washington, DC, Nov. 3, 1993, by Betty Bankhead.

In addition to being curriculum-based, successful and appropriate instruction must take a "learner-centered" approach. The user's needs should determine teaching objectives. Students' expertise in using electronic resources should be assessed to discover what additional skills are needed.

Remember too, that the learners may be students, faculty, administrators or library staff, and their needs may vary. Consider varying assignments such as learning how to use the Readers' Guide Abstracts, locating three articles on women's role in the Gulf War Crisis, developing a unit using NewsBank to support an elective course on practical law, or identifying current educational trends in ERIC. Assess the learner's level of expertise and base new instruction on those findings.

FACULTY AS PARTNERS

Both the library media specialist and the teacher should be involved in the instruction planning process. Each brings valuable expertise to the learning experience. The teacher is a content specialist who knows the students' abilities and the desired outcomes, while the librarian knows appropriate search methods, available resources and how to teach information skills and strategies.

Faculty need to know how to use CD-ROM and how the contents can support and enable the curriculum. Like print resources, they need to learn this new technology to integrate this information successfully into their curriculum. Roxanne Mendrinos (*School Library Journal*, October 1992, pp. 29-31) found there is a definite connection between training and curriculum use. Teachers who have been trained are more comfortable with the technology, opening windows of opportunities between library media specialists and classroom teachers. Librarians become more active in curriculum planning and classroom teachers understand the importance of developing information-literate students who can access a wide variety of discipline-specific information using high-tech tools.

Local area networks are connecting school library media centers to classrooms making electronic resources available through the school. Teachers, now more than ever before, must know how to use the tools skillfully and how to instruct and guide students in their use. This is a wonderful opportunity to really integrate information skills into the curriculum in every classroom.

WHAT TO TEACH?

What do students and faculty need to know?

Computer Technology: CD-ROM searching requires basic computer-literacy. For instance, a brief explanation of keyboard basics is required to minimize frustration

Presearch Questions
Before doing a search, students should ask themselves:
• Is the topic covered in this CD-ROM?
• Is the topic within the date range covered by the CD-ROM?
• Is the search narrow enough to produce good results?

when students begin using the software products. Vocabulary words—such as local area network, workstation, main menu and front end software—need to be defined. Students also need to know the basics of the hardware—about the CD-ROM drive, floppy drive and printer. Include a discussion on basics of the CD-ROM—how to hold it and how to load it. They need to understand how to handle problems such as adjusting screen contrast and dealing with printer malfunctions.

Elements Of An Instruction Program For Novice Users

What is a database?
How does a database compare to a printed index?
What constitutes a search strategy?
Why should you devise a search strategy?
How is a search strategy devised?
How to summarize your topic
How to identify main concepts
How to choose search terms
What is truncation and when do you use it?
How a thesaurus can help
What are connectors?
Boolean logic
How to use connectors with search terms
How to fine-tune a search
How to get help

Source: John Maxymuk, CD-ROM Professional, *May 1991, p. 47.*

Database Content: The user must know what information is on the disc and what is not. This might seem silly, but often students see a computer and assume all the information in the universe is in the machine! They are not aware that different CD-ROMs have specific subject content and types of information. Compare a CD-ROM to the print version if there is one. Seeing familiar indexes helps. Discuss the date ranges on the disc and the content, emphasizing how much CD-ROM databases vary. Discuss the differences between multimedia discs and text-only bibliographic discs.

Database Structure: Knowing how the records are stored on the disc can help students understand how to retrieve information. Show an example of a record, identifying each field. Explain how to retrieve these citations by searching for terms either in the entire record or the specific field. Explain how a multimedia program has text, graphics, sound and full-motion video, and is linked together.

Search Strategy: Students need to know how to summarize a topic, identify concepts, select terms and combine them using Boolean logic. Use a Venn diagram to explain AND/OR/NOT concepts and a strategy worksheet to help them organize the topic. Alternate spellings, truncation and the use of synonyms also need to be addressed.

Search strategies originally developed for searching online databases are still applicable for CD-ROM bibliographic databases such as magazine indexes. Introduce these concepts to encourage students to be creative and experiment during their searching:

- Building blocks: break the search down into smaller, manageable parts
- Citation pearl-growing: find one citation and use its descriptors to find other sources.
- Most specific facet first: start with the most specific terms and see if you can find the right citation.

Keyword and Subject Descriptors: Stress the use of descriptors and alternate search terms to broaden students' vocabulary and search topics. They need to understand the concept of keyword searching as opposed to using descriptors.

Evaluation of Results and Modification of Search Strategy: Students need to know how to analyze the results of their search. Is the information retrieved relevant to their needs? Does the search need to be narrowed or broadened? Use onscreen subject headings to find alternate choices. Consider publication year, type of periodical, scholarly or popular, other document types, book reviews, conference papers, reports, article length and subject. Evaluating search results is one of the most important steps in the searching process and the one most often overlooked by students.

HOW TO TEACH?

There are many different learning styles, so plan to provide instruction in several ways.

One-On-One, Point-of-Use Instruction

Personal assistance from library staff or student monitors is the best form of CD-ROM instruction for individual users. It is interactive, context-sensitive and flexible. The instructor recognizes the students' comprehension, puzzlement or anxiety and adjusts his response accordingly. When students in an academic library were asked their preference for instruction, they said they preferred one-on-one assistance and help available in CD-ROM labs and demonstrations, rather than group instruction.

They especially wanted training in developing search strategy, search procedures, Boolean logic and how to use the equipment (Gillian Allen, *RQ*, Fall 1990, p. 88). You will need to train your staff to conduct one-on-one assistance. They should be able to operate, demonstrate and troubleshoot the hardware, explain the system software, teach basic search strategy development, and recognize when CD-ROM is not appropriate and refer the student to the correct source.

The preferred learning style for faculty, in particular, seems to be point-of-use,

---

Basic Student Search Skills

At the very least students should be able to:

- Begin and end a CD-ROM search
- Retrieve information using search terms
- Combine terms
- Display references on the screen
- Print or download references selected
- Save a search

MOVIES/VIDEOS

Canadian Catalog of Media Resources
Cinemania
Complete Guide to Special Interest Videos
Movie Select
Roger Ebert's Movie Home Companion
Software Toolworks 20th Century Video Almanac

List of CD-ROM titles about video and film.

one-on-one instruction. They prefer this method because they don't feel "dumb" in front of their students. Time is another factor—faculty want to spend a minimal amount of time learning a CD-ROM product.

Lecture/Demonstration

Lectures are not the best way to teach. Frequently, however, we have no choice. Teachers still bring students into the media center in full classes, and they try to cover the important points as briefly as possible, with lots of examples. Most learning will occur when students are actively engaged in the research process. Involve students by asking them to compare what they know about print indexes and other resources. What problems did they encounter? How do they think searching on an electronic database will be different? What do they expect to find? Simple handouts showing a sample record from the database and basic commands can be helpful.

Always use a demonstration of the search process when lecturing. It is an excellent way to involve learners in the searching. Proceed from the lecture where you and the class develop sample search strategies to executing the strategies onscreen. Use topics relevant to the information they are seeking.

Point-of-Use Materials

These are important because they often provide the new user's first information about CD-ROM. They are nonintrusive until the user himself seeks guidance. Include handouts, posters, charts and similar materials that you keep or display at the workstations. Make certain they are easy to use and clearly accessible. They should be clear and concise as well as be colorful and attractive to draw attention. Design them using word processing or desktop publishing so they will be easy to alter when software changes.

This is a good way to involve students in developing ownership in the library. Ask a few students, maybe the computer applications class that is learning desktop publishing, to design handouts and charts for the CD-ROM products. This has an added benefit because the students will need to learn the products to be able to design the teaching aids.

A FEW TIPS FOR INSTRUCTION

Don't talk too much. Teach the basics and let students experiment. Identify the most relevant information the students need and emphasize it. Point out whatever is most essential about the skill or concept you are teaching, then let students experiment by searching the database.

Allow time for assimilating new information. Learners need time to rehearse and reflect on what they have learned. The instruction can be broken into multiple sessions on different days or perhaps different sections of the same class.

Solicit help with the instruction. Request help from knowledgeable students or faculty. Student "experts" who know the system will be happy to share their skills with the class. Encourage other members of the school community to take an active role in teaching information searching.

Use nontechnical language. It is easy for frequent users to lapse into computer-ese, which may overwhelm or alienate students and faculty. Use lay language instead and explain terms as you go along. Hand out a glossary or develop a crossword puzzle or other learning game using computer jargon for students to become familiar with the new terminology.

Involve the learner in the presentation. Information elaborated on is more easily remembered. Pose questions, invite comparisons, solicit responses and conduct live demonstrations of searches to keep learners mentally involved in the presentation.

Emphasize a conceptual approach to obtaining information. Define the information need, choose the best source to find it and decide on the best terms or subject headings. The primary goal is to teach skills that can be applied to any system. By teaching the basic concepts of database structure, Boolean logic, the function keys, etc., the student should gain the confidence and know-how to sit down at any CD-ROM product and figure it out.

Make use of the "teachable moment." Use situations or circumstances to teach whenever the opportunity presents itself. A skill is best remembered when it is relevant to the user in his attempt to understand or gather information. The ideal time to learn is when you are ready.

Conduct live demonstrations. These are extremely helpful but must be pre-planned to get the maximum effect from the instruction. Decide which search techniques to emphasize and which databases to cover, so as to best impress the audience. Bostian and Robbins, at Plymouth State College, found in a study on effective instruction for searching CD-ROM databases that, "The only level of instruction that resulted in a significant difference was a live demonstration of a few searches....Our gut feeling is that you can talk about computer searching from now until the cows come home, and the students won't know much more than when they started" (Bostian, Robbins, *Laserdisk Professional*, January 1990, p. 14).

Use audiovisual aids. If live demonstrations or hands-on experimentation are not practical, then use other audiovisual aids. Overhead transparencies, slides or handouts are helpful. Ask students to prepare a brief, one-page search guide to each system highlighting the pertinent points a new user needs to know. Hand these out, making sure to give the students credit.

Tips For Live Demonstrations

- Check the lighting in the room. Make sure it is low enough for all students to see the screen but light enough to see the keyboard.
- Display one screen at a time and go slowly. Allow extra time for students to stop and ask questions.
- Have a student type at the keyboard as you explain the steps in the search process. Plan ahead with the student so he feels comfortable.
- Don't worry about making mistakes. Ask the students to troubleshoot and learn from making mistakes.

Structure cooperation. Design the instruction so students work in groups. Place computers in configurations that encourage cooperation. Also design assignments and tutorials to encourage collaboration.

Don't touch the keyboard. Always have the student sit at the keyboard. You can point to the screen, but resist the temptation to do it for the student. When conducting a demonstration, pre-arrange to have a student do the keyboarding while you explain the process.

Use signs as an instructional format. Don't overlook a teaching opportunity. Clearly mark the CD-ROM workstations with large, bold-lettered signs stating the title of the CD-ROM database/program *and* the contents, for example, "Readers' Guide Abstracts— Index and Abstracts of Popular Magazines from 1983 to Present."

Distribute tailored handouts. Give students handouts tailored to specific assignments. Students tend to dismiss general instruction sheets presuming, "We've done that before." Use desktop publishing or word processing programs to customize handouts, including information such as the teacher's name and class, topic assignment and due dates, different graphics, etc. Clearly highlight the learning outcomes.

EVALUATE THE INSTRUCTION PROGRAM

Evaluation of the CD-ROM instruction program needs to be done continuously. Each year, as computers are more available in classrooms and at home, students come to the library more computer-competent. The instruction program needs to be flexible and reflect these changes. Constant monitoring of the program will ensure that students are getting the instruction they need.

Involve teachers and students in the process, asking for criticisms and suggestions for improvement. Develop a short questionnaire with a few pertinent questions for faculty and students to fill out at the completion of a research assignment. Base your evaluation of your instruction's effectiveness on answers to these questions:

- Do the students understand the search process?
- Can students perform an effective search?
- Can students locate and retrieve materials cited in the search?
- Do the students use citations in their papers?
- Do students synthesize the data found in the citations?
- In what ways has CD-ROM changed students' search behaviors?
- Is there evidence of increased subject area knowledge?

(John Maxymuk, *CD-ROM Professional*, May 1991)

In summary, students encounter CD-ROM in all kinds of libraries. To be information-literate, they need to understand its unique features and capabilities and learn to search it with ease and dexterity. Since research shows such skills are not learned by practice alone, and because some students have no experience using the personal computers integral to CD-ROM systems, instruction is critical.

SELECTED RESOURCES FOR FURTHER READING

Allen, Gillian. "CD-ROM Training: What Do the Patrons Want?" *RQ* (Fall 1990): pp. 88-93.

Barron, Ann and Donna Baumbach. "A CD-ROM Tutorial: Training for a New Technology." *Educational Technology.* (June 1990): pp. 20-23.

Bostian, Rebecca and Anne Robbins. "Effective Instruction For Searching CD-ROM Indexes." *Laserdisk Professional* (January 1990): pp. 14-17.

Broughton, Nancy, Patricia Herrling and Nancy McClements. "CD-ROM Instruction: A Generic Approach." *CD-ROM Librarian* (November 1991): pp. 16-19.

Johnson, Mary E. and Barbara S. Rosen. "CD-ROM End-User Instruction: A Planning Model." *Laserdisk Professional* (March 1990): pp. 35-40.

Maxymuk, John. "Considerations For CD-ROM Instruction." *CD-ROM Professional* (May 1991): pp. 47-49.

Mendrinos, Roxanne Baxter. "CD-ROM and At-Risk Students: A Path to Excellence." *School Library Journal* (October 1992): pp. 29-31.

Mendrinos, Roxanne Baxter. "Successful Experiences Integrating Technology and Information Literacy." *Information Searcher* 6, No. 1 (1993): pp. 11-14.

Nash, Stan and Myoung Chung Wilson. "Value-Added Bibliographic Instruction: Teaching Students to Find the Right Citations." *Reference Service Review* (Spring 1991): pp. 87-92.

Tenopir, Carol. "Is It Any of Our Business?" *Library Journal* (April 1, 1992): pp. 96-98.

CHAPTER 6
CORE COLLECTION OF CD-ROMS FOR SCHOOLS

This chapter contains evaluative reviews of 100 CD-ROM titles, including several series that have multiple titles. It was difficult to select discs for this Core Collection. The process involved looking at, reviewing, reading and talking about hundreds of CD-ROM titles. We chose only discs that are suitable for the educational market or that will enhance a library collection. As new discs appeared, titles we once considered very good no longer made the grade. The CD-ROM field is growing fast and the level of expectations is quickly rising.

We applied several general criteria to our selections: 1) the content had to be relevant to school use; 2) the price had to be reasonable; and 3) the discs had to be readily available. Next we looked at other broad, but more specific areas: 1) the quality of the content had to be high, with no questionable areas; 2) the interface had to be good-looking and well-designed; and 3) the search capabilities had to be fast and seamless.

We always asked, would kids use this disc? Would they learn from it? Would it be useful in a classroom? A library media center? If the answers to any of these questions were no, then the disc was set aside in favor of others in the pile.

Finally, we evaluated each disc according to the standards that evolved as we looked at more titles. We began with the evaluation form which appears in Chapter 4. The exercise of developing that form gave us some good insight into the process of evaluation. It also showed that there is still room for improvement in the art of evaluation! Several discs that we both liked very much did not score highly on the form, so we had to re-evaluate some of our own criteria.

Many of our decisions came from comparisons—this disc is good, but it doesn't do what that disc does; this disc is better. Would this disc work better in a history class than that disc? Why?

Questions that we asked during the evaluation process for each disc always centered around students. Would it be easy for kids to use? Would it be confusing? Is this a disc that contributes something different and unique to the learning process, or is it simply an electronic form of material already available in print?

Ten discs in this Core Collection carry our highest recommendation. These discs set the standards for excellence in content, interface design, and usefulness. They are the ones by which we judged all others, and to which we will compare new titles. These top ten discs are clearly marked with a big star.

The other 90 titles in the Core Collection reflect the current balance in the marketplace, both as to platform and to curriculum area. There are almost twice as many IBM/compatible discs as Mac ones—more companies are putting out DOS, Windows, or MPC titles than Mac titles, but the gap is narrowing. There are many more titles in curriculum areas such as social studies and science, and far fewer in math and language arts. There are also many more middle and high school-level titles than titles for the elementary level. Producers are not developing as many titles for lower grade levels, and primary and elementary schools don't yet have an established CD-ROM hardware base.

Each review includes information about the price, producer, hardware platform, technical support, and documentation. The producer data includes the name, address, voice telephone number, and fax and 800 telephone numbers if available. The minimum requirements for running the disc on a DOS machine, a DOS machine with Windows, an MPC machine, or a Macintosh machine are given in the minimum hardware requirements information. We listed all of the platforms for each disc as we know them, but we did not, in all cases, have the minimum hardware requirements for each platform. In addition, there is some confusion over the labeling of some discs by the manufacturers. Discs that are not certified MPC discs may be labeled Windows (but have exactly the same hardware requirements), and may or may not run on a DOS-only platform as well. Please check the listing on each package to make sure that the disc will run on your equipment. Call the technical support number listed for each product if you have specific questions about your equipment's capabilities. Remember to check the MPC Level 1 and Level 2 box on page 15 for a detailed explanation of those hardware requirements. Recommended grade level (Primary, Elementary, Middle, and Senior High) and curriculum area are also given. For most titles, a screen shot is included to convey the "look and feel" of the product.

The text of each review contains descriptive and evaluative comments about the disc. All the titles are recommended, but not all are perfect. Some may not be as strong as we would have liked in certain areas, but their strengths definitely outweighed any weaknesses.

As you use these discs in your library media centers, your classrooms, or at home, please let us know your reactions to them, favorable or not. We have shared our reviews and our evaluation form with teachers, students, and media specialists, and their feedback was invaluable in our decisions about the composition of this Core Collection.

Adventures of Pinocchio
(*See* Talking Storybook Series)

Aesop's Fables
(*See* Discis Books)

American Vista:
The Multimedia U.S. Atlas
Applied Optical Media Corporation, 1450 Boot Road, Building 400A, West Chester, PA 19380; 800/321-7259, 610/429-3701, 610/429-3810 (fax).
Price: $59.95.
Minimum Hardware Requirements:
MPC Level 1: 386 25MHz/compatible, DOS 5.0, Windows 3.1, MSCDEX 2.21, 4MB RAM, CD-ROM drive, SVGA monitor, audio board and speakers, mouse.
Platform: *MPC.*
Documentation: *Eight-page user guide in disc case.*
Technical Support: *800/321-7259.*
Curriculum: *Reference & Interdisciplinary, Social Studies*
Grade Level: *Middle, Senior High.*

....

American Vista contains maps, symbols, images and facts for all the states in the U.S. After installing American Vista in the Windows environment, click on its icon to launch the program. The opening screen offers four main areas to explore—States, Topics, Bookshelf, Maps—and a standard Windows-type Help function. Selecting States leads to a list of all the states, while Topics takes you to Maps, Symbols, Images, and Facts. The

Bookshelf includes Thematic, History, Travel, Cities, Culture, Facts, Documents, and Areas. Then, for example, History leads to a choice of Timeline, Maps, Presidents, Flags, and Songs. Presidents includes a picture and brief biography of all the presidents plus a cutaway view of the White House with its various rooms and parts labeled.

While the maps aren't as finely detailed as one might wish, they are taken from the Hammond cartographic database. Interestingly, under Symbols, you can see the state flag and seal, and also an example of each state's driver's license and car license plate.

Other sections include major historical documents, a timeline of historical events, 38 city maps and data sheets, and a collection of photographs from various locations. The Travel section lets you calculate the mileage from any point on the map. Click to find distances to other points. Another section points out differences in regional speech patterns, with an audio section that includes a verbal demonstration.

This is an atlas that is easily accessible and quite complete. It will be an asset to most library media centers.

Animals
(*See* LIFEmap Series)

Animals and How They Grow
(*See* Wonders of Learning CD-ROM Library)

Animals with Backbones
(*See* LIFEmap Series)

Following the kitten out of the warm sand and into the cool grass, Annabel stopped for a moment at the river's edge, stretching out over the water to pluck a white lotus blossom.

Annabelle's Dream of Ancient Egypt

Texas Caviar Inc., 3933 Steck Avenue, Suite B115, Austin, TX 78759; 800/648-1719, 512/346-1393 (fax).
Price: *$89.95; $39.95, home.*
Minimum Hardware Requirements:
Macintosh: *LC/II or Performa, System 6.0, 1MB RAM, CD-ROM drive;* **Windows:** *IBM 286/compatible, DOS 3.1, Windows 3.0, 640K, CD-ROM drive, mouse.*
Platform: *Macintosh, Windows.*
Documentation: *Six-page user guide in disc case.*
Technical Support: *512/346-7887.*
Curriculum: *Language Arts.*
Grade Level: *Primary, Elementary, Middle.*

....

Annabelle's Dream of Ancient Egypt is intended for ages six to ten. It is a unique multimedia program featuring Annabelle the cat who, entranced by the music of Aida, dreams of herself in ancient Egypt, "far across the rippling sands, just this side of the reeds and rushes that border the quiet blue river." This delightful children's program combines text, graphics and sound, along with a variety of auxiliary materials and projects for "developing reading skills, music appreciation, learning about far away places, coping with life's problems and just having fun."

Annabelle's Dream of Ancient Egypt is an original children's story that tells the narrated tale of a young cat that falls asleep after her mother tells her the story of Aida. As she journeys through ancient Egypt, visits the pyramids and Sphinx and meets the cat Goddess Bastel, Annabelle learns how to handle some of life's problems, such as anger and sibling rivalry. The program also has interactive features. You can have the text of the story appear on the screen and pause the story at any time with a mouse click. You can also select words or sections of the story and have them repeated, insert an electronic bookmark, or double-click on any word and find its meaning and pronunciation.

With just a mouse click, a student can access any of the activities designed to enhance general knowledge, music appreciation, vocabulary or reading comprehension. What's Happening Now is a series of drawings from the story intended to increase recall, while Scrambled Letters is a fun vocabulary builder.

The program also provides a series of illustrated information articles on Egyptian history. "Art galleries" contains outline drawings from the story, which can be colored onscreen or printed on paper for an entire class. "Facts About Cats" is a rock music presentation. There is also a complete audio recitation of Rudyard Kipling's poem "If," plus projects for paper-making with students, a hieroglyphics translator, backyard archaeology, the complete audio of Celeste Aida and more.

Installation is simple, as is navigating the program. Creative icons are used to move from place to place, such as a cat's paw to pause, a cat head for the main menu, right-facing cat head to move forward, etc.

This program is unique. Annabelle is endearing, and the combination of materials and activities engage and motivate children to experience literature and music in many ways.

Arthur's Teacher Trouble
(*See* Living Books)

Atlas of U.S. Presidents
Applied Optical Media Corporation, 1450 Boot Road, Building 400A, West Chester, PA 19380; 800/321-7259, 610/429-3701, 610/429-3810 (fax).
Price: $39.95.
Minimum Hardware Requirements:
Macintosh: System 7.0, 4MB RAM, 12-inch monitor with 512KB VRAM, CD-ROM drive; MPC: IBM 386/ compatible DOS 3.1, Windows 3.1, 2MB RAM, VGA monitor, CD-ROM drive, audio board, speakers, mouse.
Platform: Macintosh, MPC.
Documentation: Four-page user guide in disc case.
Technical Support: 800/321-7259.
Curriculum: Social Studies.
Grade Level: Middle, Senior High.

Atlas of U.S. Presidents is a multimedia history program containing brief biographies, audio speeches, historical maps, election statistics, histories of the 41 presidents, biographies and portraits of the first ladies, symbols of the Presidency and searchable facts about each administration.

Installing Atlas of U.S. Presidents is, like all AOMC products, fast and easy. The installation program places an icon on the Windows menu for easy loading and, within minutes of placing the disc in the drive, the main menu appears. The choices are Presidents, First Ladies, Maps, Facts, Symbols, and Help. Click on Presidents, choose a time period or a specific president and a screen containing his portrait appears, along with buttons to access details of his presidency.

Although the maps are interesting, Roosevelt's request to Congress for a declaration of war is chilling and Kennedy's inaugural speech inspiring, the program's strength is its Facts section. Clicking on any president in the alphabetical list displays a screen containing facts about the man and his administration including political party, state, term of office, vice president(s), prior occupation, age at inauguration, birth date, birthplace, parents, religion, ancestry, date of death, and place of burial. Nine of these fields can produce a President Fact Table listing specific information for every president in a table.

Did you know that besides having 21 lawyers, the U.S. has had one teacher, a clerk, an historian, a newspaper publisher and a tailor serve as president? Not to mention the professor and the actor! The possibility for students to explore the information and compare facts about the

presidents is a valuable learning experience, as well as a fun activity.

Another intriguing feature of this program
is a complete full-color drawing and a
detailed floor plan of the White House. A
graphic, larger than the computer screen,
exposes all the rooms with furniture and
decorations and is accessible by using the
up, down and sideways arrow keys.

Searching is simple and intuitive. Every
screen contains buttons to go the main menu
and to get help. Access to the First Ladies'
portraits and biographies and maps is available both through the individual presidents'
screens and in a separate section. However,
the ability to hyperlink to the presidents'
fact tables from the individual presidents'
screens and pop-up windows to provide a
brief background about the historical map
items would increase access and enhance
the program.

An updated version that will include
Clinton should be available by the time this
book is published. It will include digitized
video, the ability to print and copy standard-
information, and portraits of each president.

Bach and Before

The Voyager Company, 578 Broadway,

*New York, NY 10012; 212/431-5199,
212/431-5799 (fax). Also: One Bridge
Street, Irvington, NY 10533; 800/446-
2001, 914/591-6481 (fax).*
Price: *$24.95.*
Minimum Hardware Requirements:
Macintosh: *Macintosh Plus, System 6.0.5,
HyperCard 2.1, 1MB RAM, CD-ROM
drive, external speakers or headphones.*
Platform: *Macintosh.*
Documentation: *Four-page getting-started
card in jewel case.*
Technical Support: *914/591-5500.*
Curriculum: *Arts & Music.*
Grade Level: *Senior High.*

....

This disc is Volume 1 in the So I've
Heard Series. Others in the series are The
Classical Craft, Beethoven and Beyond,
Romantic Heights, plus Here and Now. It is
positioned between the home user and the
educational market, with good applications
for each area.

As always with a Voyager disc, it is easy
to load and install, quick and intuitive to
run with a HyperCard interface and a
delight to browse. This series of discs
looks at recorded music throughout the
history of music to help collectors build a
personal collection of fine digitally-
recorded music.

Each selection on the disc has a description of its history, musical importance and
recording information. It also has a preview
of the selection so you can listen to it and
judge whether or not to add it to your collection. If you have attached good speakers
to your CD-ROM, you can hear the excellent quality of these digital selections.

Each selection can be marked for inclusion in a personal catalog, and there is also a pop-up notepad for writing down thoughts as you go through the catalog. You can also create new catalog cards for your own musical selections, so that a truly personal catalog of music can be created. The essays that accompany the musical selections were written by Alan Rich, who lectures in music at UCLA. A glossary of musical terms relevant to the period in each disc is also included.

These discs could qualify as a starting place for students of music history.

Beauty and the Beast
(*See* Talking Storybook Series)

The Big Green Disc
Media Design Interactive, The Old Hop Kiln, 1 Long Garden Walk, Farnham, Surrey, GU9 7HP, England; International 011/44/252-737630, 011/44/252-710948 (fax).
Price: $69.
Minimum Hardware Requirements:
Macintosh: System 6.0.7, 4MB RAM, CD-ROM drive, color monitor; MPC: 486 PC/compatible, DOS 5.0, Windows 3.1, MSCDEX 2.1, 4MB RAM, audio board and speakers, CD-ROM drive, mouse.

Platform: Macintosh, MPC.
Documentation: Four-page booklet in jewel case.
Technical Support: 800/654-8802.
Curriculum: Science.
Grade Level: Senior High.

The Big Green Disc is an interactive look at the environmental issues facing our planet. Although created with a British/European point of view, it is very relevant to studies here in the United States.

The disc is divided into six sections, with specific environmental issues covered in Problems, Solutions, Ask the Experts, and Resources. Issues such as pollution, global warming, fossil fuels, population growth, alternative energy, and waste disposal are dealt with in pictures, text and video. A section at the end of the disc is a Slideshow covering the Good, the Bad and the Ugly in our environment. The photographs are superb and the story they tell is extremely powerful.

Another excellent section on this disc is a series of graphs relating to issues of the environment. Population growth in developed and developing countries and the rate of extinction and number of species becoming extinct are examples of the clear graphics shown.

While the issues and the solutions are not covered in great detail or depth, this disc remains a valuable tool for depicting the number and variety of problems facing our global planners. The quality of the images makes this disc a very good buy.

Bodyworks 3.0:
An Adventure in Anatomy
Software Marketing Corporation, 9830 S.

51st Street, Building A131, Phoenix, AZ 85044; 602/893-3377, 602/893-2042 (fax).
***Price:** $69.95.*
Minimum Hardware Requirements:
***Windows:** IBM/compatible, 4MB RAM, VGA monitor, CD-ROM drive, Windows 3.1, sound board, mouse.*
***Platform:** Windows.*
***Documentation:** 31-page booklet.*
***Technical Support:** 602/893-8481.*
***Curriculum:** Science.*
***Grade Level:** Senior High*

....

Body Works 3.0 is an interactive journey through the body, exploring its systems, structure and functions in detail. Using text, graphics, 3-D rotating views, animations and videos, users study the body from head to toe, focusing on different internal systems such as the skeletal, muscular, nervous, cardiovascular, respiratory, digestive, sensory organs, endocrine, lymphatic, and genito-urinary systems along with topics such as Health & Fitness and Living.

The screen is divided into four main areas including the picture view box, item list, text box and control buttons. A menu bar at the top of the screen provides access to functions that let you control your session and customize your program. If you want more in-depth information about a topic, click on its name in the item list to find the topic's text entry. Then draw a line to the item on the picture and hear the correct pronunciation. A small square appears before an entry to indicate that there is another picture associated with the item.

Bodyworks has three different types of animation. Some occurs in the current image, such as in the Circulatory System image in which the heart beats. Some is the use of animation cutaways such as those used in the muscular system where circles of muscles move off the main image to reveal what lies beneath. The last type is movie sequences. When a movie is available, a small projector icon appears in the upper right corner of the screen. Three-dimensional views are also available. They can be rotated, enlarged and decreased in size.

The program has nine lessons that let you explore the anatomic systems in a step-by-step fashion. When you finish, take a quiz. The quizzes are a combination of multiple choice and identification questions, with ten questions for each group. If you don't know the answer, you can press the Surrender button to have the program display the correct answer. The number of correct answers and how fast you answer the questions is recorded. Names of high scorers are kept.

Exporting pictures and program text to use in your own documents can be done through Windows Clipboard. Direct printing of both text and graphics is also available. Hypertext links, bookmarks, a full-topic index, glossary and online help are all available to help exploration and navigation. This well-designed program encourages students to explore the world of anatomy.

Broadcast News
Research Publications International, 12

Lunar Drive, Woodbridge, CT 06525-9957; 800/774-7741, 203/397-3893 (fax).
Price: *Price varies. Call for information.*
Minimum Hardware Requirements:
DOS: *IBM 286/compatible, MSCDEX 2.0, 640K RAM, 5MB minimum hard drive space, VGA monitor, CD-ROM drive, mouse.*
Platform: *DOS.*
Documentation: *22-page user guide.*
Technical Support: *800/RPI-RPI-1.*
Curriculum: *Reference & Interdisciplinary.*
Grade Level: *Middle, Senior High.*

....

Broadcast News is a monthly, full-text, reference database of the news and current affairs programs of ABC, CNN, PBS and NPR (National Public Radio). It supports keyword and full-text searching. You can purchase all the transcripts or only ones from selected networks.

The main menu offers four choices including Current Issues, Networks and Shows, Simple Search Mode, and Advanced Search Mode. Current Issues is a selection of recent transcripts about significant recurring issues and topics frequently found in today's headlines. Networks and Shows accesses transcripts in specific networks and shows. Simple Search Mode provides powerful direct access to the basic search fields for transcript retrieval. Advanced Search Mode accesses all search fields in the database using Boolean logic.

Selecting Current Issues brings up a list of 21 significant issues and topics in today's news, such as abortion, civil rights, drug abuse, endangered species, gun control, right to die, rape, religious cults, homelessness, terrorism, and women's rights. Selecting an issue obtains a partial list of

headlines related to that issue. For example, click on "drug abuse" and headlines of 26 news stories from all four networks appear. To further explore the topic and navigate the database, access the full-text of the transcripts or choose the control panel on the right side of the screen that contains buttons.

The Overview button gives an eleven-screen essay of background and context for studying drug abuse. Key Events presents a chronological list of events in the history of drug abuse from 1971 to 1993. Research This Issue suggests keywords relevant to the issue "drug abuse," such as AIDS, cocaine, education, heroin, marijuana, needle, testing, etc., all of which help narrow the issue. Combining drug abuse and marijuana retrieves 27 transcripts ranging in length from one to 12 pages, most around six pages or so.

Navigating the database is easy. Menu bars on the bottom of the screen offer options to print or export, go to main menu, get help or see other relevant screens of information. Broadcast News on CD-ROM has radio and TV news programs, talk shows, interviews, documentaries and specials—a medium students feel comfortable with and will use readily for research.

Capitol Hill
The Software Toolworks Inc., 60 Leveroni

Court, Novato, CA 94949; 415/883-3000, 800/231-3088, 415/883-3303 (fax).
Price: $49.95.
Minimum Hardware Requirements: Macintosh: System 6.0.7, 4MB RAM, 13-inch 256-color monitor, CD-ROM drive; MPC: IBM 386/compatible, DOS 3.1, Windows 3.1, 4MB RAM, 5MB minimum hard drive space, SVGA monitor, CD-ROM drive audio board, speakers, mouse.
Platform: Macintosh, DOS, MPC.
Documentation: Two double-sided cards.
Technical Support: 415/883-3000.
Curriculum: Social Studies.
Grade Level: Middle, Senior High.

....

"Congratulations! Your aggressive campaigning and well-rounded experience have paid off. In a landslide victory, you have just been elected to a seat in the House of Representatives to represent your state..." Capitol Hill takes you on an exciting tour of Congress as an active participant. It contains more than 45 minutes of video clips and 500 photographs, plus narration and original music.

When you arrive in Washington, DC, you receive your Personal Digital Assistant (PDA) to guide you through the ins and outs of Congress. Instructions explaining the buttons on your PDA are provided in a narrated tour. These buttons include First Day, Orientation, Your Office, Capitol Hill, Power Play, Terms, and Help, Exit and Put Away. In addition, you are told that during your exploration you might be asked to vote on a bill—yea or nay—and accept mail or phone calls.

Click on the First Day button to be sworn in, meet colleagues and find your office. The Orientation button gives details about the history and structure of Congress. It describes how Congress is set up, its powers, and requirements to become a member. It also contains a state-by-state list of the Representatives, information about committee power and structure, how the different arms of Congress interact and how a bill becomes law.

Click on Your Office button to choose staff, learn about your budget, schedule, and support staff on the Hill. It's here where you'll first meet Lynn Woolsey, a Representative from California who gives you advice about how to be successful. You'll meet other House and Senate historians along your route to help you. The Capitol Tour button is a tour of the Capitol building starting in the Grand Rotunda with a video clip of Mike Michaelson, Vice President of C-Span. Explore different parts of the building by clicking on sections of the floor plan.

When you have learned about your new position, click on the Power Play button. Answer questions about the structure and history of Congress to move up through the ranks to become Speaker of the House. Be prepared to be quick or someone will beat you to it! The final buttons on the PDA include an explanation of terms and phrases used in Congress such as Pro Tempore, mark-up and hopper.

From choosing your office, checking your $197,800 budget and voting on bills, to touring Capitol Hill and playing the power game, the experience teaches about government in an interesting, interactive and entertaining manner.

CD NewsBank

NewsBank, Inc. 58 Pine Street, New Canaan, CT 06840-5426; 800/762-8182, 203/966-1100, 203/966-6254 (fax).
***Price:** Price varies; call for information.*
Minimum Hardware Requirements:
***DOS:** IBM 286/ compatible, 500K RAM, DOS 3.0, 5MB on hard drive for installation, MSCDEX, CD-ROM drive, monochrome monitor;* ***Macintosh:** Mac II, System Software 7, 4MB RAM, 2MB minimum hard drive space, CD-ROM drive, monochrome or color monitor.*
***Platform:** DOS, Macintosh.*
***Documentation:** User's guide, hot topics sheets (issued monthly), teaching units, pathfinders and a point-of-use poster.*
***Technical Support:** 800/762-8182.*
***Curriculum:** Reference & Interdisciplinary.*
***Grade Level:** Middle, Senior High.*

CD NewsBank provides the full text of 40,000 articles annually from more than 100 newspapers and eight newswire services from the U.S. and around the world. Monthly updates are provided to keep the service as current as possible.

The first of two search levels is menu-driven and provides quick and easy access for the beginner or person in a hurry. The second level has keyword and proximity searching, as well as Boolean capability for in-depth and precise searching. A search can be customized by defining a date range. Any article can be marked for future reference, printed or downloaded to a disk. Printing itself has two options, full text or the bibliographic citation only.

There are no images in the database, which means fewer problems and faster searching, not to mention lower costs and memory requirements.

A Spanish-language module is available separately. This module features articles from *Efe* and the Reuter Spanish language news service. The accompanying Spanish software and interface makes it doubly nice for Spanish-speaking students to access needed information.

There is no extra cost for a site license to run multiple copies of CD NewsBank on a LAN. WAN situations are negotiated individually.

The depth and breadth of information in national newspapers makes CD NewsBank an extremely valuable tool for the study of current events, the environment, politics and government, social history, economic issues, or arts and literature.

CD Sourcebook of American History

Candlelight Publishing, P.O. Box 5213, Mesa, AZ 85211-5213; 800/677-3045,

801/373-2499 (fax).
Price: $69.95.
Minimum Hardware Requirements:
DOS: IBM 286/compatible, DOS 3.1, 512KB
RAM, VGA monitor, CD-ROM drive.
Platform: DOS.
Documentation: *28-page user guide in*
disc case.
Technical Support: *800/677-3045.*
Curriculum: *Social Studies.*
Grade Level: *Senior High.*

....

The CD Sourcebook of American History, Volume 1, contains nearly 1,000 primary source documents, plus 28 volumes of interpretive history, including first-hand accounts, official documents and contemporary histories of the people and events that shaped the nation.

The opening screen organizes the information into seven main categories including Preface, Founding Documents, First-Hand Accounts, Interpretive Histories, Search by Author, List of Illustrations, Bibliography, and Citations Index. Clicking on Interpretive Histories provides ten choices, one of which is Inaugural Addresses of the Presidents. Every inaugural address is listed, from George Washington's on April 30, 1789 to George Bush's address on January 20, 1989. Presidents who were not inaugurated are noted, such as Chester A. Arthur and Gerald R. Ford. Click to read the full text of the speech, save it to a file or print it out.

You can search the contents for any given word, subject or phrase. Once located, selected passages of famous historical documents can be compared in multiple windows, printed or copied to a file. In exploring World War II documents, you can read General Gallieni's passionate and courageous

speech to the French people telling them that President Poincare and his ministers had left Paris to establish the French seat of government at Bordeaux. Next you can read "How the 'Taxicab Army' Saved Paris," "Burning of Louvain," and more. History comes alive in these first-hand accounts.

This is an excellent resource to help students learn to work with primary sources.

Cinderella: The Original Fairy Tale (*See* Discis Books)

Cinemania

Microsoft Corporation, One Microsoft Way, Redmond, WA 98052; 800/426-9400, 206/936-7329 (fax).
Price: $79.95.
Minimum Hardware Requirements:
IBM 386/compatible: DOS 3.1, Windows 3.1, 2MB RAM, 30MB minimum hard drive space, SVGA monitor, CD-ROM drive, audio board, speakers, mouse.
Platform: Macintosh, MPC.
Documentation: *22-page user guide in disc case.*
Technical Support: *206/635-7172.*
Curriculum: *Arts and Music.*
Grade Level: *Middle, Senior High.*

....

Cinemania is a multimedia movie guide containing capsule reviews of 19,000 movies and detailed reviews of 245 current and 500 selected film classics spanning the early days of movies to the present (1914 to 1993). Reviews are culled from the text of *Leonard Maltin's Movie and Video Guide, 1992,* with additional information from *The Motion Picture Guide, The Encyclopedia of Film,* and *The Film Glossary,* and are enhanced by movie stills, portraits and dialog.

The Table of Contents screen introduces you to the Controller, a look-alike remote control device that allows you to access desired sections of the program. The top three sections on the Controller are filled with articles offering information, photographs and dialog clips. These three sections are Movie Listings, Biographies, and Topics, which make up the heart of Cinemania.

The Movie Listings section contains reviews and other information about the movies. The Biographies section offers biographical articles on nearly 3,000 film personalities, with a filmography for each personality. The Topics section has topical articles on film-related subjects, such as directing, special effects and the history of major studios.

Additional sections on the Controller include the Award List, MultiMedia Gallery, Glossary, and List Maker. The Award List offers a complete list of Academy Awards in every category from 1927 to 1991. The MultiMedia Gallery lets you browse all Cinemania's photographs and dialog clips. The Glossary presents definitions of film terms, and the List Maker lets you create lists of movies to save, modify and print.

Since Cinemania works under Windows, there is a menu bar at the top of the screen for additional navigation. The Index button leads to indexes of movies, biographies and topical articles. Using the Controller you can narrow down the list to one index. Through the menu bar you can return to the Contents screen, go to a previous screen, see a listing of the last 40 screens you visited, or go to Awards List, MultiMedia Gallery, Glossary, or Listmaker.

"Toto, I have a feeling we're not in Kansas anymore." You can quickly find the Movie Listings Screen for the Wizard of Oz, 1939. It is 101 minutes long, in color and black and white, available on videocassette and won the Academy Awards' Best Song.

There is a narrated, animated introductory tutorial offered, along with a 20-page user's guide and "Quick Help" on the Controller for the timid few, but most will find this program easy to use and very addictive. Did you know Judy Garland was second choice for Dorothy's part and the lion's costume weighed 100 lbs...?

With a firm lead over both of his rivals on the day Perot rejoined the race, Clinton enjoys a Wisconsin afternoon with his adoring public. 1 October 1992

Clinton: Portrait of a Victory

Time Warner Interactive Group, 2210 West Olive Avenue, Burbank, CA 91506-2626; 800/593-6334, 818/955-9999, 818/955-6499 (fax).
Price: $39.99.
Minimum Hardware Requirements:

Macintosh: Macintosh, 4MB RAM, CD-ROM drive; DOS: IBM 386/ compatible, DOS 3.1, 640K RAM, VGA monitor, CD-ROM drive, audio board, speakers.
Platform: Macintosh, DOS.
Documentation: Six-page user guide in disc case.
Technical Support: 800/565-TWIG.
Curriculum: Social Studies.
Grade Level: Middle, Senior High.

....

Clinton: Portrait of Victory is a multimedia, photojournalistic CD-ROM that chronicles Bill Clinton's run for the White House, through the primaries, the scandals and ultimately to victory on Election Day 1992. It contains over 300 black-and-white photographs shot by award-winning *TIME* magazine photojournalist, P.F. Bentley.

With Clinton's full cooperation, Bentley traveled with the Clinton entourage during the campaign. He snapped candid photographs of Bill Clinton, Hillary and Chelsea, Al Gore, and Clinton aides, strategists and long-time friends as they made their way down the campaign trail. The program is divided into three major themes, The Assignment, The Candidate, and The Campaign. Enhancing the photographs is an audio and text prologue by *Vanity Fair* and *The New Republic* contributing editor Roger Rosenblatt. There are captions by Rebecca B. Taylor, executive director for Epicenter, and an epilogue by Michael Krammer, chief political correspondent for *TIME*.

Each theme is composed of several categories. The Campaign is divided into five sections including The Primaries, The Convention, On the Road, The Debates, and The

Bold Finale. Each section contains 40 to 80 captioned prints telling a little story and includes Milestones, which records and rates each significant event that happens during the campaign. The Primaries goes behind the scenes to view Clinton as a father helping Chelsea with algebra and as a regular guy playing pool.

Through the photo tour users learn about Bill Clinton, the political candidate and the person, as well as the events that shaped his campaign. Krammer's epilogue, "On Being Tough," uses 14 screens of text to study Clinton's tenacity, which kept him going when everyone thought he was finished. He also writes about Clinton's famous pursed lip, which could mean he was in deep thought, or experiencing extreme satisfaction, or consuming anger. In From His Speeches, users can hear actual excerpts from Clinton's speeches while watching related photo selections. The Man from Hope is a three-page biography of the native son from Arkansas.

Clinton: Portrait of a Victory provides a photodocumentary of a candidate's highs and lows as he campaigns for the presidency and offers students a rare glimpse of the political arena.

★ CNN Newsroom Global View

Compact Publishing Inc., 5141 MacArthur Boulevard NW, Washington, DC 20016; 800/964-1518, 202/244-6363, 202/244-6363 (fax).
Price: $49.95.
Minimum Hardware Requirements:
IBM 386/compatible: DOS 3.3, MSCDEX 2.0, 640K RAM, 1MB minimum hard drive space, VGA monitor, CD-ROM drive.
Platform: DOS, MPC.
Documentation: 32-page user guide; 84-page activity guide.
Technical Support: 800/964-1518.
Curriculum: Social Studies.
Grade Level: Middle, Senior High.

....

CNN Newsroom Global View lets a student enter the CNN newsroom and view world events through video essays on simulated video monitors. The disc contains more than one hour of narrated video, plus hundreds of commentaries by leading authorities and transcripts of speeches by world leaders. Pros and cons and analyses from international newspapers and magazines cover important global trends, such as the collapse of communism, cultures in conflicts, famine in Africa, third world, earth matters, and waging peace.

The CNN Newsroom's main menu emulates a "studio," with six video monitors plus a calendar to keep your daily schedule and reminders. Click on the Cultures in Conflict's photo image to view video coverage or click on the title bar to read text articles. After choosing the text, a second screen appears presenting specific subjects, such as Israeli-Arab, Northern Ireland, Casual Factors, Battles Brewing, Drug Wars, and Balkans. A note explains Battles Brewing, which focuses on nationalism, while leaders discuss separatism, ethnic problems, tribalism and ethnic divisions. South Africa, Canada, India and Pakistan are a few of the countries discussed.

Select the Globe and zoom in on detailed maps of every country and region. Select the Chart program for a powerful educational tool enabling students to select and display statistical data on countries all over the world. Complete descriptions and data for all nations and regions are included. Click on the chart icon from the Newsroom to select a chart from any text article in Main Menu. Choose the Topic, Region, Type of Graph, and Year Range to build color charts or graphs. Up to 12 countries can be compared at once.

Select Worldclock and, in addition to current time or time of sunrises and international time zones, the distance between any two points on the globe is measured with the location's latitude and longitude. When you first load the program, you are asked for your zip code and location. Your hometown appears on the world map to help measure distance.

CNN Newsroom Global View is a "must" for school libraries. It's right on target for curriculum use, encouraging critical thinking skills through comparing countries and examining current issues.

This generation of students is being raised on television. In fact, most Americans get their news from TV. What could be more appropriate than to have a current issues CD-ROM based on CNN coverage? The coverage is not editorialized—it explores different points of view, allowing students to analyze the facts and come to their own conclusions.

Columbia Granger's World of Poetry

Columbia University Press, 562 West 113th Street, New York, NY 10025; 800/944-8648 (orders), 212/666-1000, 212/316-3100 (fax).
Price: *$699; Networking, no charge in single building LAN, multibuilding network option available.*
Minimum Hardware Requirements: DOS: *IBM 386/compatible, DOS 3.1, MSCDEX 1.0, 640K RAM, CD-ROM drive.*
Platform: *DOS.*
Documentation: *One-page insert in disc case.*
Technical Support: *800/767-7843.*
Curriculum: *Language Arts.*
Grade Level: *Senior High.*

....

The Columbia Granger's World of Poetry contains the complete text of 8,500 classic poems, 3,000 quotations from 1,500 more recent poems, anthology locations for an additional 80,000 poems, indexing for 550 anthologies with full descriptions, and evaluations of the nearly 400 most important anthologies. In total, the program contains anthology citations for 70,000 poems written by 12,000 poets on 4,000 subjects.

The Columbia Granger's World of Poetry on CD-ROM offers significant additional benefits over the printed edition. These benefits include keyword searching for titles or for the first line of the poem, and keyword or keyword phrase searching in the body of 8,500 poems. It can also identify quickly classic and contemporary poems on a specific topic relating to curriculum, such as Christopher Columbus, civil rights, etc., and it has access to the full text of 8,500 of the most sought-after poems.

Installation is easy. The opening screen provides access to poems by Author, Title, First Line, Subject, Title/First Line/Subject, Word(s) Within Poems, Combined Searching, Anthology Information, Introduction, and Help. Searching for an author with the author search mode produces an alphabetical list of authors with the number of their poems that are on the disc. Highlight the author, press <Enter> and the title of each poem and the first line appears.

A "P" or a "Q" to the left of the entry indicates that the database includes the full text or a quotation from that poem. Function keys at the bottom of the screen flash to alert you to the full text or quotation entry. You may print the screen, print the poem or quotation, or save the information to a disk. Help is available on every screen and is context-sensitive.

The poems in full text or in quotation are the poems most often anthologized, according to the *Columbia's Granger World of Poetry*, ninth edition. The CD-ROM combines the indexing capabilities of the *Granger's Index to Poetry*, eighth edition (1986), *Granger's Index to Poetry*, ninth edition (1990), *Columbia Granger's Dictionary of Poetry Quotations* (1992) and *Columbia Granger's Guide to Poetry Anthologies* (1990).

Schools that have copies of the print Granger's and use it frequently or schools that have a heavy poetry concentration in the curriculum will find this program helpful, especially with keyword searching and full-text access.

Compton's Multimedia Encyclopedia

Compton's NewMedia Inc., 2320 Camino Vida Roble, Carlsbad, CA 92009; 619/929-2500, 800/862-2206, 800/216-6116 (catalog sales), 619/929-2555 (fax).
Price: $395.
Minimum Hardware Requirements:
Macintosh: System 7, 4MB RAM, 5MB minimum hard drive space, 8-bit 256 color monitor, CD-ROM drive; IBM 386/ compatible: 4MB RAM, 3MB minimum hard drive space, DOS 3.1, Windows 3.1, VGA monitor, CD-ROM drive.
Platform: Macintosh, Windows.
Documentation: 51-page manual.
Technical Support: 619/929-2626.
Curriculum: Reference & Interdisciplinary.
Grade Level: Elementary, Middle.

....

Compton's Multimedia Encyclopedia for Windows contains the full text of Compton's 26-volume encyclopedia, 13,000 images, maps and graphs, 50 minutes of sound music and speech, 90 multimedia sequences (videos, slide shows and animations), 5,000 charts and diagrams plus the complete Merriam-Webster's OnLine Dictionary, which contains definitions of 60,000 words.

The encyclopedia offers the user a pathbar and buttons used to locate information including Idea Search, Articles, Multimedia, Infopilot, Atlas, Topic Tree, Picture Tour, Timeline, Dictionary, and Backtrack. The pathbar is always on the screen. Most of the buttons are self-explanatory except Idea Search, Topic Tree, and Infopilot.

Idea Search allows users to type words or phrases that prompt the program to search text, picture captions and fact boxes using the Boolean operator AND. Results include articles, photographs, sound clips, graphics or video clips, all of which can be selected, played or heard.

The Topic Tree helps students narrow searches. It takes the user from a broad list of 19 topics—such as the arts, the earth, geography, government, literature, sports and leisure, or religion—along a list of sub-topics until he gets to a topic represented by an article. All articles consist of a text window with icons providing easy access to related photographs, audio and video clips, charts and tables, cross-references and maps.

Infopilot presents a selection of active article windows and groups of article titles that relate to a topic or question. When the user enters a request, the program searches for articles related to the subject and displays them in an array of active windows. The user can browse through each window and "link" to additional information.

Text from any article can be printed or saved in a notebook. Graphics can be exported via the Windows clipboard into a graphics applications program. Three lesson guides—Lesson Guide to Math Excursions, Lesson Guide to Science Excursions, Lesson Guide to Social Studies Excursions—and an activity guide are included with the program.

What makes this version of the encyclopedia unique is the concept of "virtual workspace," which enables a user to navigate among multiple open windows. Click on Go To Expert Mode (Virtual Workspace) from the View Menu, and a Workspace Map opens up in the lower left of the screen. It displays a representation of every open window on the screen. The user can move these representations as if they were pieces of paper on a desktop. Windows provides the ability to have multiple windows open on the screen; however, the number is limited to those that can fit on the monitor's screen. Virtual Workspace has no limit. Any open window can exist beyond the borders of the screen.

Students can work with and manipulate many media objects in Virtual workspace, including pictures, animation and text. They can create a new workspace for each topic and save the information with each use, much like being able to save the layout of books, paper and photographs on a desktop. This capability adds a new dimension to electronic research.

CountDown

The Voyager Company, 578 Broadway, New York, NY 10012; 212/431-5199, 212/431-5799 (fax). Also: One Bridge Street, Irvington, NY 10533. 800/446-2001, 914/591-6481 (fax).
Price: $29.95.
Hardware Minimum Requirements:
***Macintosh:** Macintosh II, System 7.0, 2.2MB RAM, hard drive, color monitor.*
***Platform:** Macintosh.*
***Documentation:** 12-page user's guide.*
***Technical Support:** 914/591-5500.*
***Curriculum**: Mathematics.*
***Grade Level**: Primary, Elementary.*

First in a series of products based on Apple Computer's *Visual Almanac*, Count-Down consists of three games designed to teach young children basic mathematical concepts. Introduced in a QuickTime video by a young child named Chris, the games can be played with different sets of objects. Bright, colorful and based on sound educational practices, the games will intrigue and delight young users.

CountDown is, on the surface, a simple product. There are three games with nine sets of objects to use as playing pieces in the games. These objects range from eggs and marbles to noodles and pennies. The first game is Guestimation, in which a single player, or two players (two teams), try to guess the exact number of objects pictured. When the correct answer is typed on the keyboard (or number pad), there is a "surprise ending" so that the player knows when the answer is right.

The second game is Nimbles, and the goal is to be the player that removes the last object from the picture. Again, there is a choice of objects; and each player can remove one, two or three objects by clicking that number and then <Enter>. Once a player understands the game, the quantities can be changed.

The third game is Leftovers, and here the object is to guess how many groups it will take to remove all the objects you started with. The size of the group or number of objects can be changed to make it come out even so there won't be any leftovers.

The little user's guide is written in the first person by "Chris" and provides hints and clues about how to win the games. It also has ideas and challenges that enhance the learning experience for the players.

This CD-ROM would be suitable for all the younger grades, for both group activities and individual tutorials. Older children will be able to work out more complex puzzles by increasing the number of objects and working with different variables. The color QuickTime video inserts of Chris, the sounds, and the solid educational principles comprising this disc make it a very good buy.

Desert Storm: The War in the Persian Gulf

Time Warner Interactive Group, 2210 West Olive Avenue, Burbank, CA 91506-2626; 800/593-6334, 818/955-9999, 818/955-6499 (fax).
Price: *$49.99 (DOS, MPC); $39.99 (Mac).*
Minimum Hardware Requirements:
Macintosh: *Macintosh Plus, System 6.0.5, 1MB RAM (color machines require 2MB RAM), CD-ROM drive;* ***DOS:*** *386/compatible, DOS 3.1, MSCDEX 2.2, Windows 3.1, 4MB RAM, VGA monitor, CD-ROM drive.*
Platform: *Macintosh, MPC, DOS.*
Documentation: *Ten-page booklet in jewel case.*
Technical Support: *800/565-TWIG.*
Curriculum: *Social Studies.*
Grade Level: *Senior High.*

....

Just weeks after the war in the Persian Gulf ended, Warner New Media and *TIME* magazine collaborated to produce an in-depth look at the events of the war as they had unfolded. The disc, one of the first to be produced so quickly after a major global event, has been called a new form of journalism. The events of the war are still so recent that the disc does not use it as a history lesson, but instead as a look at current events and their on-going implications.

The disc is easy to install and use, and its various sections are readily accessible. The sections include a week-by-week description of the war's events, including correspondents' recorded and/or filed reports, recorded speeches and interviews, and short video clips of major events. Supporting material on the disc includes maps of the Gulf area, charts, more than 400 archival photographs, biographies of key political and military figures like Saddam Hussein, and a glossary of the weapons used.

The Gulf War is the first event in modern history covered so extensively by print and television journalists. The opportunity this coverage gives the teacher and student of current events or modern world history is priceless. Desert Storm is a significant tool for examining and understanding the events that took place and their implication for the future.

Dictionary of the Living World

Applied Optical Media Corporation, 1450 Boot Road, Building 400A, West Chester, PA 19380; 800/321-7259, 610/429-3701, 610/429-3810 (fax).
Price: $149.95.
Minimum Hardware Requirements:
Macintosh: Macintosh II, Performa (68020); System 6.0.7; 4MB RAM; CD-ROM drive; MPC Level 1: 386 25MHz/compatible, DOS 5.0, Windows 3.1, MSCDEX 2.21, 4MB RAM, CD-ROM drive, SVGA monitor, audio board and speakers, mouse.
Platform: Macintosh, MPC.
Documentation: 16-page user's guide.

Technical Support: 800/321-7259
Curriculum: Science.
Grade Level: Middle, Senior High.

The Dictionary of the Living World is a multimedia product based on an alphabetic listing of over 2,600 files about different animals, species, biological definitions and terms. The disc includes illustrations (either photographs or drawings), sounds, video clips and distribution maps for species that greatly enhance the text files.

Installing and launching the disc is relatively easy on either a Macintosh or MPC platform. The Macintosh version requires copying the HyperCard stack and the MacroMind Player file from the disc to the hard drive. This enables the program to run faster and smoother. The HyperCard stack is especially big and requires at least 2MB of RAM to run the larger animations and video clips. The MPC version requires installing Multimedia Movie Player to run the larger video sequences. This driver is located in Drivers section of the Control Panel in the Main Windows screen.

Starting the program is quick and easy. Clicking on the Index icon takes you right to the beginning of the entries—"abaxial" (upper leaf surface). You can then explore through the alphabet, request a specific term, look at related pictures, listen to sounds, or run a video or animation. If you are searching for a specific topic, you can bring up the search window and type in the desired terms. In the Mac version, you can request that those words be actual terms in the index or just found in other parts of term definitions. In the MPC version, you can use Boolean operators to combine or exclude certain terms from your request.

In the Mac version after you find several entries that contain your search terms, you can create a "Collection" by using the Compass button to gather the terms together. In the MPC version, Search brings up a list of "hits" that can be manipulated in much the same way.

The Dictionary of the Living World is a good resource, with content depth and good multimedia features. It is the first commercially available CD-ROM that has full-motion video on it. It will enhance any natural sciences collection.

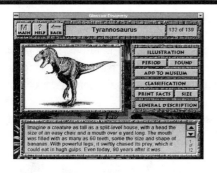

Dinosaur Discovery

Applied Optical Media Corporation, 1450 Boot Road, Building 400A, West Chester, PA 19380; 800/321-7259, 610/429-3701, 610/429-3810 (fax).
Price: $39.95.
Minimum Hardware Requirements:
MPC: IBM 386SX/compatible, 2MB RAM, SVGA monitor, CD-ROM drive, sound board, mouse, Windows 3.1;
Macintosh: System 7, 4MB RAM, 512K VRAM, 13-inch color monitor.
Platform: *Macintosh, MPC.*
Documentation: *Four-page user guide in disc case.*
Technical Support: *800/321-7259.*

Curriculum: Science.
Grade Level: Middle, Senior High.

Dinosaur Discovery is a multimedia program about approximately 140 dinosaurs and associated prehistoric animals representing life that existed throughout the Triassic, Jurassic and Cretaceous periods of earth's evolution. Students can search for dinosaurs by name, classification, period, size, location, profile or any combination of these categories. They can view illustrations, listen to pronunciations and read detailed descriptions and other pertinent facts.

The opening screen lets students select a specific dinosaur, displays a color illustration and provides information about the dinosaur's classification, period of existence, area found, name pronunciation and general description.

Choosing Bookshelf on the main menu, enables the user to find dinosaurs with certain characteristics or to browse any of the items presented in the dinosaur description screen. A student chooses the characteristics and then selects from a list of dinosaurs that share those traits. For example, clicking on size and choosing 71+ feet narrows the list to seven dinosaurs.

Topics from the main menu allow exploration of several topics related to dinosaurs. Museum reviews dinosaurs tagged for placement in a personal museum. Chronicles enables learning about the theories and behaviors that surround these creatures through 24 adventurous and informative presentations. Associate is a listing of other species of reptiles and flying animals that were closely associated with the dinosaur. Glossary defines the terminology used in the program.

The Activities button on the main menu challenges the user's knowledge of dinosaurs in three games. Anyone can build his own dinosaur with Dinobuild, complete a dinosaur crossword puzzle in Puzzle or test his knowledge with Dinokraze, a dinosaur trivia game. A librarian can print the Puzzle and leave it near the computer or on display to entice students to learn about dinosaurs. The printout consists of three pages including the puzzle, answers and questions.

Peter Dodson of the University of Pennsylvania and George Olshevsky, editor of *Mesozoic Meanderings*, served as consultants for the program. The interface and menus are well-designed and easy to navigate. Facts about the dinosaurs can be printed or saved to the clipboard and help is available from all screens. Junior and senior high school students will enjoy exploring this program, and teachers will appreciate the design features that encourage higher-order thinking skills—comparing, contrasting and categorizing.

Dinosaurs! The Multimedia Encyclopedia

Media Design Interactive, The Old Hop Kiln, 1 Long Garden Walk, Farnham, Surrey, GU9 7HP, England; 011/44/252-737630, 011/44/252-710948 (fax).
Price: *$99.*
Minimum Hardware Requirements:
Macintosh: *System 6.0.7, 4MB RAM, CD-ROM drive, color monitor;* **MPC:** *486 PC/compatible, DOS 5.0, Windows 3.1, MSCDEX 2.1, 4MB RAM, audio board and speakers, CD-ROM drive, mouse.*

Platform: *Macintosh, MPC.*
Documentation: *Two-page booklet in jewel case.*
Technical Support: *800/654-8802.*
Curriculum: *Science.*
Grade Level: *Middle, Senior High.*

Dinosaurs! is another disc in the MDI family of discs created in England. It is thorough, carefully created, easy to use, and has a substantial amount of material in many different formats.

Installing the disc is straightforward and requires only making sure that QuickTime is installed in the system folder. Using the disc is also easy and intuitive. The opening screen is a contents page with six sections including an Introduction, Age of the Dinosaurs, Dinosaur Directory, Story of the Fossils, Ask the Experts, and Dinosaur Gallery. The largest and most informative section is the Dinosaur Directory which lists over 200 individual and dinosaur species in alphabetical order.

Each dinosaur has its name at the top with the meaning of the name underneath (for example, "Megalosaurus" means "great reptile.") with a small illustration at the right. This illustration, if clicked, expands to the whole screen, and can be exported as a large picture without accompanying text.

The family and order of the dinosaur is listed, along with a timeline showing the duration of its existence and a scale drawing showing its size relative to something familiar in today's world (man, giraffe, elephant, etc.). Along the bottom of the screen, a row of buttons leads to additional information, if there is any, about that particular dinosaur. A map shows the places the dinosaur lived and museums where fossils are located today. There are photographs of those fossils, a video of an animated sequence, and a text-searching field for specific word searches.

With the sole exception of a misspelling of Belgium, this disc seems to be put together with great care. The background of the contents pages and index pages looks like chiseled stone. When a name or item is clicked, it is surrounded by a bright red box; there is no question which one was selected. Since all the material is exportable to disk or paper, it should provide students with a wealth of research information on dinosaurs.

Discis Books

Discis Knowledge Research Inc., 45 Sheppard Avenue East, Suite 410, Toronto, Ontario M2N 5W9, Canada; 800/567-4321, 416/250-6537, 416/250-6540 (fax).
Price: *Individual Discis titles are $59.95. Classroom Edition Library is $450.00. Emergent Level titles are $49.95.*
Minimum Hardware Requirements:
Macintosh: *System 6.0.5 (including System 7), 1MB RAM for black and white, 2MB RAM for color, keyboard and hard disk not required;* **DOS:** *IBM 286/compatible, DOS 5.0, MSCDEX 2.0, 2MB RAM, VGA or SVGA (VESA compliant) monitor, audio board, speakers, mouse, optionally installed under Windows 3.1.*
Platform: *Macintosh, MPC, DOS.*
Documentation: *Includes laminated quick reference card with very clear instructions,*

user manual (28 pages for DOS and Windows users, 36 pages for Macintosh users), 91-page teacher's guide, assorted teacher notes and black line masters for activities.
Technical Support: *800/567-4321.*
Curriculum: *Storybook.*
Grade Level: *Primary, Elementary.*

(Series includes ten individual titles that together constitute the Classroom Edition Library. Each title is also available separately. Discis also produces the Emergent Level CD-ROM series, as well as other individual titles. The ten titles in the Discis Books series are the Paper Bag Princess, The Tale of Benjamin Bunny, Scary Poems for Rotten Kids, Mud Puddle, The Tale of Peter Rabbit, Cinderella: The Original Fairy Tale, Thomas' Snowsuit, Moving Gives Me A Stomach Ache, A Long Hard Day on the Ranch, and Heather Hits Her First Home Run. Other individual titles include Aesop's Fables and The Tell-Tale Heart (see separate review). There are currently two volumes in the Emergent Level series.)

....

Storybooks are a delightful new and growing field within the general field of CD-ROMs for schools. Because CD-ROM's large storage capacity lends itself so well to adding animation and sounds, storybooks have taken on a whole new dimension in this electronic format. The Discis series of storybooks is a very good example of this new format. Not only is the text read aloud to the user in the preferred language, but music is added and pop-up definitions or synonyms can be heard and read.

All Discis storybooks, either single titles or in a series, have the same format. The screen looks like the pages of a book, and the pages turn as the story is read. The reader can choose between having the entire story read aloud, or choose to turn the pages "manually" by clicking on the turned corner at the bottom right. A single click of the mouse on any word results in the pronunciation of the word. A double-click pronounces the word in syllables, and a press-and-hold gets the pronunciation and a synonym. The part of speech and explanation of the word in context is available in both English and Spanish, as are the help screens.

When a child clicks on a word for pronunciation or clarification, the word is added to the Recall List so the teacher can review the words that gave the child some difficulty. The teacher's guide contains relevant research and descriptions of the way children learn to read and write. Interesting and informative!

These discs are superb for the classroom, school library and home use. The stories have been chosen well, the narrator's voice is good and the illustrations are clear and appropriate.

DiscLit: American Authors

G.K. Hall & Co., 866 Third Avenue, 18th Floor, New York, NY 10022; 212/702-6789, 800/257-5755, 212/605-9350 (fax).
Price: $995.
Minimum Hardware Requirements: DOS: IBM 286/compatible, MSCDEX 2.0, 640K RAM, 20MB minimum hard drive space, CD-ROM drive.
Platform: DOS.

Documentation: 103-page manual; reference cards.
Technical Support: 617/232-0412.
Curriculum: Language Arts.
Grade Level: Senior High.

....

DiscLit on CD-ROM contains two databases, Twayne's United States Authors Series and OCLC American Authors Catalog. It is a joint venture between the publisher, G.K. Hall & Co. and OCLC. The program contains 143 volumes of Twayne's series, each about the life and works of a different American author, plus OCLC American Author Catalog containing bibliographic information for more than 100,000 books, serials, recordings, videos and other material by and about the 143 authors. The two units are searched separately, but their information is linked so users can move easily between them.

The databases can be searched in either the New or Casual User or the Experienced User mode. The interface allows complete Boolean and proximity searching. You can limit searches to twelve different fields in the Books database and twenty in the Catalog database. The New or Casual User mode provides pull-down menus to give access to field-specific and adjacency searches and a full system of help screens. The user may also go through a ten to 15-minute interactive tutorial at the beginning of the session.

Opening the book, the user is presented with the table of contents, with search word occurrences of the search terms. The user can select chapters or "Jump to search word" or look at the back-of-the-book index and select a page number for a particular topic. Every page of the book is contained in the database.

The Catalog unit can be searched by term or author's name as well as by type of material. This is helpful for students who are looking for a video about a particular author and his works. However, for the most part, this is not a useful resource for schools. There is a brief Search Tips card that can be set up next to the computer plus additional reference cards that summarize how to search, view, print and save to a disc and a detailed manual.

OCLC and G. K. Hall also publish DiscLit: British Authors, the full-text of 145 books from Twayne's English Author Series plus over 20,000 bibliographic citations from OCLC Online Union Catalog.

DISCovering Authors

Gale Research Inc., 835 Penobscot Building, Detroit, MI 48226-4094; 313/961-2242, 800/877-GALE, 313/961-6083 (fax).
Price: *$500.*
Minimum Hardware Requirements: *DOS: IBM 286/compatible, 500K RAM, 1MB minimum hard drive space, DOS 3.1, MSCDEX 2.0, CD-ROM drive.*
Platform: *Macintosh, DOS.*
Documentation: *70-page manual; reference cards.*
Technical Support: *800/877-4253, Ext. 6021.*
Curriculum: *Language Arts.*
Grade Level: *Senior High.*

....

DISCovering Authors features 300 of the most commonly studied authors in high schools and colleges—from Aristotle to Maya Angelou—and includes full-text biographical essays on the authors' lives and careers, critical essays on their writings, full bibliographies, a summary of media adaptations of their works and sources for further study. The program gathers information from *Contemporary Authors*, *Dictionary of Literary Biography* and *Gale's Literacy Criticism Series*, plus some material written specifically for the disc to make author entries complete.

The opening menu offers five choices to search the database including Author, Title, Subject Term/Character, Personal Data on Author, and Advanced Search Mode (Full Text.)

Type the letter "A" to choose Author and see a screen offering a dialog box to type the author's name and an alphabetical list of authors. The search is letter-specific so, as you type the first few letters of an author's name, the index automatically displays the closest match, letter by letter. Title and Subject Term/Character function the same way.

Personal information—an author's birth and death statistics, nationality, education, politics, religion, addresses, military, memberships, honors/awards, interests, media adaptations and genre—can be searched as a separate field or in combination. The advance search mode allows a search for any word or phrase in any part of an author's biography or criticism. By pressing the function key, <F4>, a word list appears. Begin typing and the scroll bar moves to the closest spelling. Boolean operators, AND, OR, and NOT can be used, plus the proximity operator, NEAR, to locate words within 30 characters of each other. The range can be changed.

Printing is accomplished in two ways. Print or copy entire sections or mark the desired text and print or save it to a disk. The author entries are quite long. If F. Scott Fitzgerald's entry were printed in its entirety, it would be nearly 50 pages. The menus are well-designed and the program is easy to navigate. Students will find this program intuitive and extremely useful due to the amount of critical and biographical information available in one place.

★ Discovering French Interactive

DC Heath and Company, 125 Spring Street, Lexington, MA 02173; 800/235-3565, 800/334-3284 (orders), 800/824-7390 (fax orders), 617/860-1927 (fax).
Price: *Level A: $199 for CD-ROM, $25 for Student Disc ($100 for five Student Discs). Special prices for additional copies or subsequent Level B and C packages; call for information.*
Minimum Hardware Requirements:
Macintosh: *Macintosh II or LC II, System 7.0, 4MB RAM, CD-ROM drive, color monitor, microphone.*
Platform: *Macintosh.*
Documentation: *44-page CD-ROM teacher's*

guide; six-page user's guide in the disc case.
Technical Support: *800/235-3565, Ext. 1767.*
Curriculum: *Foreign Language.*
Grade Level: *Middle, Senior High.*

Discovering French Interactive (DFI) is the first in a series of high school textbooks on CD-ROM developed by DC Heath. Based on the textbooks and pedagogical methods in *Discovering French,* a series of traditional textbooks and methodology by Rebecca and Jean-Paul Valette, these interactive CD-ROMs hold great promise for the future of language instruction.

Discovering French Interactive (DFI) comes in three levels, A, B, and C, and provides self-contained lessons with activities on each level, each based on specific but ordinary topics and events in day-to-day life in France. Each level contains three units, with accompanying lessons and information. Each lesson includes communication functions and activities (such as self-expression), communications topics (including vocabulary), and linguistic goals (i.e., accuracy of expression). Each unit is structured exactly the same way so that learning the interface is quick and easy and does not interfere in the student's learning process.

The interactive part of DFI comes to light with the Explorations section of each unit. Included in Explorations are a notebook for writing and recording, documents to supplement each topic (authentic looking menus, invitations, etc.), a review section for difficult words or concepts plus a truly unique section called Créa-dialogue. In this section, students can place characters into a scene, and then write and record dialog for each person in a conversation in that scene. The conversation can be placed on the scene in a cartoon-like bubble, and the bubbles can be sorted for audio dialog sequencing. The scene can then be played and replayed in sequence with the alternating dialog. Subsequent sessions can add to the dialog, and other groups of students can listen to the dialogs, try to predict the conversations, and create new comments or develop explanations.

Of particular interest to French teachers is the capability of the program to record the student's voice when pronouncing certain words or phrases. The student can listen to a native French speaker, record his or her own voice repeating the same thing, and then compare the two. Five seconds of recording time is available at each "Record" control box.

This CD-ROM adds a new dimension to the study of foreign languages. The ease of use, the intuitiveness and interactivity, the voice recording, the creation of dialog between characters, and the superb technical quality of the disc combine to give it our "gold star" recommendation.

Emergent Level CD-ROM Series
(*See* Discis Books)

Encarta Multimedia Encyclopedia

Microsoft Corporation, One Microsoft Way, Redmond, WA 98052; 800/426-9400, 206/936-7329.
Price: $395; $79, update price.
Minimum Hardware Requirements: MPC: IBM 386/compatible, DOS 3.1, Windows 3.1, 2MB RAM, VGA monitor, CD-ROM drive, audio board, speakers, mouse.
Platform: Macintosh, MPC.
Documentation: 21-page user guide; search aid cards.
Technical Support: 206/635-7172.
Curriculum: Reference & Interdisciplinary.
Grade Level: Elementary, Middle, Senior High.

....

Microsoft's Encarta Multimedia Encyclopedia contains the full text of *Funk & Wagnall's New Encyclopedia*, *Webster's Concise Electronic Dictionary* (83,000 words), and *Webster's College Thesaurus* (44,000 words, a total of nine million words in 26,000 articles). It also includes 15,000 multimedia elements including 106 full-motion video clips; 8,283 photos, illustrations and graphics; 3,598 audio clips of national anthems, foreign languages, historical audio, sound effects, popular/jazz music, literary audio, etc. resulting in over seven hours of sound.

Encarta's editorial staff has revised more than 25 percent of the topics, including complete rewrites and updates for the 1994 edition. The text is current through September 1993 including the historic handshake between Yasser Arafat and Yizhak Rabin after they signed the Middle East peace accord. New articles appear on figures such as Ruth Bader Ginsberg, Hillary Clinton, Charles Barkley, and Chuck Berry.

Encarta is organized around three distinct areas, the Article Frame, the Category Frame, and the Gallery Frame. The Article Frame shows the current article and the buttons for hot links to related information in the Gallery Frames, such as maps, illustrations, charts, tables and the like. Words marked in red are linked to other articles. The Category Frame indicates which of the 93 major subject areas the article belongs in and includes a visual illustration of the subject. Menu bars on the top and the bottom of the screen allow the user to easily navigate easily one category forward or backward, to change categories, to show an alphabetic listing of categories, to link to other articles, to view the outline window, and more.

The encyclopedia can be searched several ways, including content searching by article title, category or subject browsing, word searching with hints, Boolean operators and wildcard characters, gallery browsing for multimedia components, plus atlas or timeline searching.

The Category Browser is divided into major areas of interest including Physical Science and Technology, Life Science, Geography, History, Social Science, Religion and Philosophy, Art, Language and Literature, Performing Arts and Sports, Games, Hobbies and Pets. The search can be limited by any combination of keywords, areas of interest or media types (pictures, animations, sounds, or maps). Click on History and Animation to view the animated sequence of the Battle of Gettysburg. Type Jazz in the search box and choose Audio from the media types to view a list of 52 topics to hear about or research further.

Encarta is an excellent multimedia reference source. It encourages students to explore and browse information, while offering good search methods to target a topic.

Encyclopedia of Dinosaurs

Gazelle Technologies, Inc., 7434 Trade Street, San Diego, CA 92121; 619/693-4030, 800/843-9497 (orders), 619/536-2345 (fax).
Price: *$59.95.*
Minimum Hardware Requirements:
Macintosh: *Macintosh II, LC, System 6.0.7, 5MB RAM, CD-ROM drive, 8-bit color monitor.*
Platform: *Macintosh.*
Documentation: *None.*
Technical Support: *619/536-9999.* ·
Curriculum: *Science.*
Grade Level: *Middle, Senior High.*

....

The Encyclopedia of Dinosaurs is a good, large program that must be loaded onto the hard disk before you begin. The file is over two megabytes, so make sure you have enough space. It runs well, albeit slowly, and an excellent guided tour gets you started.

The Encyclopedia includes information about more than 400 dinosaurs and other creatures. The easiest way to access this information is to use the browse feature. You can flip through the "pages" of the encyclopedia and see up to seven different dinosaurs on each page. Click on the one to see a text information screen, a small picture of the dinosaur that can be enlarged to full-screen size, a map showing the location of its habitat, and buttons for additional video clips, more photographs (usually of fossil sites), and its family tree.

The small outline images of the dinosaurs on the maps are shaped so they can be identified by general family group. They are also green if they are herbivores, and red if carnivores. Text or terms from the encyclopedia can be saved on a Stored Terms list. This list can be kept or erased as the need arises and also saved to a disk or printed.

Other features of the program include a slide show of all of the dinosaur illustrations, a movie show showing all the video clips of dinosaur animations and fossil sites, and special animations of fossil formation and history of the earth.

Enduring Vision

DC Heath, 125 Spring Street, Lexington, MA 02173; 800/235-3565, 800/334-3284 (orders), 617/860-1927 (fax), 800/824-7390 (fax orders).
Price: *$44.95.*
Minimum Hardware Requirements:
Macintosh: *Macintosh II or LC, System 6.0.7, 4MB RAM, CD-ROM drive.*
Platform: *Macintosh.*
Documentation: *15-page user's guide.*
Technical Support: *800/235-3656, Ext. 1797.*
Curriculum: *Social Studies.*
Grade Level: *Senior High.*

This CD-ROM is the interactive edition of *The Enduring Vision: A History of the American People* by Paul Boyer, et al. It contains the entire text of the printed version plus audio and video files, maps, charts, and search tools.

The program must be copied to and run from the hard drive. You need at least 1.5MB of space on your hard drive to run it successfully and QuickTime 1.5 must also be installed.

The opening screen of the program is the table of contents, which has the look and feel of the printed version. Selecting a chapter (or the Prologue or Epilogue) by clicking once takes you directly to that chapter, where you can then select sections or subsections. As soon as any chapter or section is selected, a timeline at the bottom of the screen is activated.

You can read the text of the chapters, choose an audio or video selection if it is indicated, or access the buttons at the bottom of the screen above the timeline. These buttons let you quit, take notes in a notebook, cut a selection from the text and paste it in the notebook, access numerical data, look at the chapter chronology, look at primary documents relevant to the current chapter, take a self-test, or view the chapter bibliography or glossary.

Clearly, one of the best features about Enduring Vision is its ability to create dynamic charts and maps showing statistical data. For example, you can select a specific time period and ask for the map to show the population of African-Americans at that time. Or you can ask for the African-American population in all of the states over the whole history of the country. The map builds in increments, showing states with differing populations, adding states as they were added to the union, and changing the density of the population in each state over time. Visual data like this adds incredible weight to the learning process.

Another extraordinary feature of Enduring Vision is the video discussion by the historian-authors of the text about why they included or did not include certain information. It is beneficial for students to realize that every text, every book, and every learning tool has a perspective or point of view. Understanding that perspective will help them evaluate the material and arrive at their own reasoned and informed opinions.

Ethnic NewsWatch

Softline Information Inc., 65 Broad Street, Stamford, CT 06901; 203/975-8292, 800/524-7922, 203/975-8347 (fax).
Price: *Varies depending on frequency, $1195/$1495/$1895.*
Minimum Hardware Requirements: DOS: *IBM 286/compatible, DOS 3.1, MSCDEX 2.1, 512KB RAM, 20MB minimum hard drive space, CD-ROM drive.*
Platform: *DOS.*
Documentation: *40-page user guide.*
Technical Support: *203/975-8292.*
Curriculum: *Social Studies.*
Grade Level: *Middle, Senior High.*

....

Ethnic NewsWatch (ENW) is a bilingual, full-text collection of newspapers and periodicals published by the ethnic minority press from the Americas. It gives you the unique ethnic and minority per-

spective, "the other side of the stories," on issues of local, national and global importance. ENW contains over 50,000 articles from 1991 with 2,500 new articles added each month from African-American, Hispanic, Latino, Chicano, Native American, Asian, Arab, Jewish, and European and American publications.

Included are original news stories, editorials, obituaries, columns, reviews of books, theater, movies, arts, music and recordings. There are some limitations on the number of local news stories included in the database. Some publications included are *Asian Pages, New India, Call and Post, Irish Voice, New York Voice/Harlem Inc., Polish-American Journal, El Diario/La Prensa, Jewish Advocate, New Lebanese American, Sho-Ban News, Cherokee Advocate, Michigan Citizen, Miami Times* and *La Voz de Houston.*

The database can be searched by keyword, controlled subject access, or browse-and-search windows for all fields, and Boolean connectors. Within the fields, you can search or browse terms using an article keyword, article subject, author/byline, article type, publication date, named people, geographic location, ethnic group and publication name. By pressing the <F2> function key, users can browse an alphabetic list of terms found in a field. The database can be searched in English or Spanish. Switch from one language to another by choosing Options on the main search screen, then pressing two keys. Articles can be printed or saved to a disk.

Ethnic NewsWatch expands students' access to important and relevant multicultural information. It is an extremely important alternative to the mainstream press.

Exotic Japan: An Interactive Introduction to Japanese Culture and Language

The Voyager Company, 578 Broadway, New York, NY 10012; 212/431-5199, 212/431-5799 (fax). Also: One Bridge Street, Irvington, NY 10533; 800/446-2001, 914/591-6481 (fax).
List Price: $59.95.
Minimum Hardware Requirements:
Macintosh: *Macintosh Plus, System 6.0.7, 1.5MB RAM (3MB RAM if running System 7), amplified speakers or headphones if CD-ROM drive is external;* ***DOS:*** *IBM 386/compatible, DOS 3.3, Windows 3.1, MSCDEX, 4MB RAM, SVGA monitor, audio board, speakers.*
Platform: *Macintosh, DOS.*
Documentation: *Nine-page user's guide (booklet).*
Technical Support: *914/591-5500.*
Curriculum: *Foreign Language.*
Grade Level: *Senior High.*

....

Developed by Nikki Yokokura, teacher of Japanese at McMaster University in Canada, Exotic Japan is a unique attempt to help students of Japanese develop the perspective necessary to learning this language. Without a background understanding of Japanese culture

and way of life, the student cannot be expected to grasp the intricacies and slight differences in spoken and written Japanese. The product was developed to help anyone interested in the Japanese language and culture, not just students in a classroom situation. It contains everyday phrases and polite exchanges, and even things like important telephone numbers to know when traveling in Japan.

The product is easy to install and getting started is not difficult. If it is run on a black and white monitor, it will work satisfactorily since the original art work is not in color.

There are four basic sections in the program—Lessons, Games, Stations, and Quizzes. There are 150 different lessons, including language practice. To reproduce your own voice as you follow these lessons, you must have some kind of sound input software and hardware, including a microphone. There is a quiz for each lesson, and you can record your progress through the lessons because Exotic Japan keeps track of your quiz scores.

The Stations section includes 53 scanned images from a series of woodblock prints by Hiroshige Ando. Each is accompanied by a description and historical explanation, as well as appropriate Japanese music. The images are used as interludes as you move from one part of Exotic Japan to another and also as the squares in the game board section. The game is a variation of "snakes and ladders" and asks questions based on the lessons covered. You can play against the computer or with another person.

This is an excellent program for independent tutorial language work, to supplement course work in Japanese culture, or simply as a travel guide and introduction to the country.

Exploring Ancient Architecture

Medio Multimedia Inc., P.O. Box 2949,
Redmond, WA 98073-9964; 800/788-3866,
206/885-4142 (fax).
Price: *$49.95.*
Minimum Hardware Requirements: MPC:
IBM 386/compatible, 2MB RAM VGA with
256 colors, Windows 3.1, DOS 3.1, CD-ROM
drive, audio board with speakers, mouse.
Platform: *MPC.*
Documentation: *None.*
Technical Support: *206/867-5500.*
Curriculum: *Arts and Music.*
Grade Level: *Senior High.*

Exploring Ancient Architecture is an interactive multimedia program concentrating on four periods of architecture including Neolithic, Egyptian, Greek, and Roman. Through video and animation sequences the user is given an overview of the period and the opportunity to take a self-directed tour. The main menu presents the periods of architecture in colorful photos. Each architectural period includes an overview section and buildings to explore.

The Neolithic period explores the Dolman Tomb and Stonehenge. The Egyptian period presents the Mentuhotep and Temple of Khons. The Greek period explores the Parthenon and Ecclesiaterion. And the Roman period offers the Basilica of Maxentius to visit. After you have picked an area to explore, click on overview. Dr. Bruce Meyer takes you on a historical overview of that period. Each slide is accompanied by text and narration, although you can turn off the narration if you want.

Listening to the Egyptian overview, the user learns about the historical significance and development of Greek culture, the Palace of Minos, the Treasury of Atreus, the Mycenae Citadel, the Greek theater 350 B.C., Doric, Ionic, and Corinthian classical styles, Greek sculpture, the Temple of Zeus, the Acropolis, the Temple of Hepestis, Temple of Poseidon, the Erectheum, and the Theater of Epidaurus.

Buildings from each period were recreated using a 3D art animation system. Each was rendered from many different angles, so you can choose your own walking tour through each building. Key points through a building are narrated to explain what you are seeing. The experience is similar to sophisticated video games in which, for example, the player uses the arrow keys to direct a princess through a maze of castle rooms. A floor plan of the building is displayed on the right side of the screen with the user's exact location marked with a red dot.

Exploring Ancient Architecture is a higher-level CD-ROM program, placing the user in control of his movements and enabling him to stop, turn right or left to look more closely at the pillars, or to view the ceiling or even to retrace his steps.

Navigating the program is simple. The menu bar at the top of the screen is always there, providing a choice of views of periods, overviews, building tours or navigational choices. In addition, Options offers full-screen video or fast video playback for slower computers.

Students enjoy this program—the bonus of movement and narration increases their involvement in learning about architecture and ancient cultures.

Facts on File News Digest CD-ROM

Facts on File, Inc., 460 Park Avenue South, New York, NY 10016-7382; 800/322-8755, 212/683-2244, 212/683-3633 (fax).
Price: *$995 subscription with quarterly updates; $695 initial subscription, $195 each annual update.*
Minimum Hardware Requirements: DOS: *IBM XT/compatible, DOS 3.1; MSCDEX 2.1; 640K RAM; CD-ROM drive; monitor with graphics capability.*
Platform: *Macintosh, DOS.*
Documentation: *74-page user guide; template and reference guide*
Technical Support: *800/322-8755.*
Curriculum: *Reference & Interdisciplinary, Social Studies.*
Grade Level: *Middle, Senior High.*

Facts on File has been a library staple for the past 50 years. Now in its latest evolving electronic format, it is just as useful and just as solid as ever. Facts on File contains over twelve years of weekly news story digests, cumulative indexes, and maps of more than 300 countries and regions.

More than 75 leading U.S. and world news sources are surveyed to summarize and index significant current events around the world. All the articles from the last twelve years of *Facts on File News Digest* are contained in this single CD-ROM—more than 45,000 in all.

The CD-ROM is strictly a text file, with the added enhancement of a fast search engine. Now you can search through thousands of articles using Boolean operators or keywords. Cross-references make finding related stories a quick and easy process.

The depth and breadth of information contained in Facts on File makes this a good disc, and the added attraction of being able to search it to find what you're looking for makes it even more valuable.

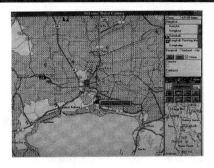

Global Explorer

DeLorme Mapping, Lower Main Street, P.O. Box 298, Freeport, ME 04032; 207/865-1234, 800/452-5931, 207/865-9291 (fax).
Price: *$125 (direct); $169 (retail).*
Minimum Hardware Requirements:
IBM 386/compatible: *DOS 4.1, Windows 3.1, 4MB RAM, 3MB minimum hard drive space, VGA monitor, CD-ROM drive, mouse.*
Platform: *Windows.*
Documentation: *16-page user guide in disc case.*
Technical Support: *207/865-7098.*
Curriculum: *Social Studies.*
Grade Level: *Senior High.*

Global Explorer contains seamless, full-color maps of the world featuring detailed topographic information, national and provincial boundaries, bodies of water, urban area and major highways, elevation data, and land overage patterns indicating wetlands, glaciers, oil fields, and other features. The disc includes an index with searchable references to more than 120,000 places and street maps of 100 cities through the world. It also includes country profiles with up-to-date information about the geography, government, economy and populations of countries around the world.

The screen shows a detailed map containing the geographic information, Gazetteer symbols, contour data and street maps. This map is linked to the overview map in the lower right-hand corner of the screen. The area of the detailed map is indicated on the overview map by a black box. Panning in the overview map allows you to move over vast geographic distances quickly. You can also type the name of a location, and Global Explorer displays the correct map.

The right side of the screen houses the interfaces and tools. The Gazetteer interface lets you locate places and points of interest with text description and also access the Profiles of Countries and Dependencies. The Street Find interface locates and highlights street names. The Airnet interface allows you to fly around the commercial air routes. The Legend provides a key to colors, patterns, lines and symbols used on the map.

The program features descriptions of 20,000 historical, cultural, geographical and social phenomena all over the world. In any country, users can select icons displayed on the maps to call up descriptions of notable features. These descriptions fall into more than 100 different categories, ranging from volcanoes to wildlife reserves, national monuments to ocean trenches, and battlefields to shrines. For instance, caves, canyons, mountains, mountain passes, cities, small towns, waterfalls, religious sites, glaciers, castles and more were highlighted in the Italian/Austrian Alps area around Innsbruck.

By clicking on Info in the Gazetteer interface, you can access information about a country's population, health, economy, military and law enforcement, communications, government, and wildlife.

Air routes are also included in the program. Users can request a route between any two cities and the program displays two options for likely commercial air routes between the two locations and the approximate travel distance.

Maps can be copied into the clipboard as a bitmap file for use in other applications or printed. The printout includes any air routes and Gazetteer item symbols displayed on the map, but not the text descriptions.

Goldilocks and the Three Bears in Spanish
Syracuse Language Systems, 719 East

Genesee Street, Syracuse, NY 13210;
315/478-6729, 315/478-6902 (fax).
Price: $29.95.
Minimum Hardware Requirements:
IBM 386/compatible: *DOS 3.1, Windows*
3.1, 2MB RAM, 3MB minimum hard drive
space, VGA monitor, CD-ROM drive,
audio board, speakers, mouse.
Platform: *MPC.*
Documentation: *Eight-page user guide*
in disc case.
Technical Support: *800/688-1937.*
Curriculum: *Foreign Language.*
Grade Level: *Elementary, Middle.*

....

Goldilocks and the Three Bears is a foreign language program designed to teach children basic Spanish words and phrases. Users click an icon that moves them through the pages of a story, similar to turning the pages of a book. Each page is a full-screen illustration with characters that, after clicking the mouse, explain their roles. Instead of a text, a narrator speaks a few sentences in Spanish. The characters each have a unique voice and are endearing as they strike different poses on the 20-screen story.

Icons at the bottom of the page allow the user to move through the program, either page by page or by jumping to one of five different sections in the story, choosing the games or having the narrator read the section.

Story-related games are accessed by clicking an icon. Most use multiple-choice questions to teach numbers, colors, hot or cold, hard or soft, large or small, etc. Each game opens with an introductory screen. After clicking on the objects or activity on the screen and hearing it in Spanish, the user clicks on the icon to start the game. One game

asks questions about the story and the user is given a series of choices. If an incorrect answer is chosen, the program handles it playfully, showing a graphic of the incorrect answer, such as the three bears eating flowers or chairs instead of their porridge or living in a bus rather than their house.

Beginning Spanish students will have fun learning new vocabulary while exploring this program.

Guinness Disc of Records

Grolier Electronic Publishing, Inc.,
Sherman Turnpike, Danbury, CT 06816;
203/797-3530 800/356-5590, 203/797-
3130 (fax).
Price: $99.
Minimum Hardware Requirements:
Macintosh: *Macintosh LC, System 6.0.7,*
1.5MB RAM, CD-ROM drive, 256 color
monitor; ***Windows:*** *IBM 286 10MHz/*
compatible, DOS 3.3, Windows 3.1,
MSCDEX 2.21, 4MB RAM, 4MB minimum
hard drive space, VGA monitor, CD-ROM
drive, audio board and speakers, mouse;
DOS: *286 16MHz/compatible, (386 highly*
recommended), DOS 3.3 (5.0 highly
recommended), MSCDEX 2.1, 2MB RAM,
4MB minimum hard drive space, VGA

monitor, CD-ROM drive, audio board and speakers, mouse.

Platform: *Macintosh, MPC, DOS.*

Documentation: *Two-page user guide in disc case.*

Technical Support: *800/356-5590, Monday through Friday, 8:30a.m. to 4:30p.m., Eastern Time.*

Curriculum: *Reference & Interdisciplinary.*

Grade Level: *Elementary, Middle, Senior High.*

....

The 1993 version of the Guinness Multimedia Disc of Records runs under Windows and on the Macintosh platform. It is a point-and-click interface and allows browsing through the incredible collection of facts that make up the various "records." Every feature and fact from the printed version is contained in the disc version, with the added benefits of sound ("the loudest animal") and video sequences.

To begin working with the Guinness Multimedia Disc of Records, first load the program or application onto the hard drive. Double-clicking on the Guinness icon brings up the main window with its various selections for searching. The choices are Record Titles (e.g., Aircraft: Largest Airliner), a screen for entering a word search using AND and NOT, a Topic Index, and the Random Record Explorer, which allows the user to sample various records without a direction or goal. Also included is a Superlative Index (e.g., Highest, Largest, Loudest, etc.), a Picture Index, and finally a Movie Index.

After a specific topic is selected, buttons appear across the bottom of the screen. If these buttons are not grayed out, they can be clicked to produce a picture or a movie clip

of the selected topic. An example is the Birds: Longest Bills. After the picture of the hummingbird is displayed, the user can then click on the Caption button to see the caption for that topic without closing the picture.

The variety of topics is intriguing and the addition of color, sound, and video increases the enjoyment and the "browseability" of these records. Add the power of word searching and electronic cross-referencing, and the 1993 Guinness Multimedia Disc of Records is a valuable and entertaining tool.

Heather Hits Her First Home Run (*See* Discis Books)

How Computers Work

Time Warner Interactive Group, 2210 West Olive Avenue, Burbank, CA 91506-2626; 800/593-6334, 818/955-9999, 818/955-6499 (fax).

Price: *$79.99.*

Minimum Hardware Requirements: Macintosh: *Macintosh II or LC, System 6.0.7, 4MB RAM with 2.2 available, CD-ROM drive.*

Platform: *Macintosh.*

Documentation: *Six-page booklet in jewel case.*

Technical Support: *800/565-TWIG.*

Curriculum: Science.
Grade Level: Middle, Senior High.

....

How Computers Work is an interactive guide to the complex workings of all kinds of computers. Based on the Time-Life books, *Understanding Computers*, and *How Things Work*, this disc is a complete history of computers as well as a look at their internal workings.

To run How Computers Work requires QuickTime installed on the hard drive and QuickDraw on machines older than the Mac IIci. The program runs faster if the application is transferred to the hard drive, but it is not essential.

To open the program, click on the HCW icon. The opening screen is a table of contents that includes Introduction and Activities, Input, Processing, Memory and Storage, Output, Programming, Applications, and Timeline. A row of buttons at the bottom of the screen gives access to audio sections, bookmarks, a guided tour, help, a notebook, index and glossary (where you can also type in a word search), credits, and the exit button.

A unique feature of this disc is the Applications section, which contains demo versions of several well-known (and expensive) software programs. These demos include QuarkXPress, Audioshop, FileMaker Pro, Excel, SuperPaint, Word, Machine, and Logo (a programming language used extensively in education).

Each of the seven main section buttons contains a mini-list of topics, so the user can scan the lists and go directly to the topic of choice. For example, the Timeline list contains seven different time periods, ranging from before the 1940s and extending to the 1990s and beyond. Each section contains text, illustrations, animations, and predictions or visions of future developments.

Understanding the workings of computers is difficult at best. For those who need to understand them, this disc is an enormous help and ranks with the dictionary and encyclopedia as a basic reference tool.

The Human Body (*See* Wonders of Learning CD-ROM Library)

Information Finder Encyclopedia

World Book Educational Products, 101 Northwest Point Boulevard, Elk Grove Village, IL 60007; 708/290-5300, 708/290-5370 (fax).
Price: $395.
Minimum Hardware Requirements: DOS: IBM 286/compatible, DOS 2.0, MSCDEX 2.0, 640K RAM, 3MB minimum hard drive space. Windows: IBM 386/compatible, 4MB RAM, 5MB hard disk space, DOS 3.1, Windows 3.1, VGA monitor, CD-ROM drive. Macintosh: Macintosh LC, System 6.0.5, 2MB RAM, 5MB minimum hard drive space, 14-inch color monitor, CD-ROM drive.
Platform: Macintosh, DOS, Windows.
Documentation: 96-page user manual with template.
Technical Support: 800/323-6366
Curriculum: Reference & Interdisciplinary.
Grade Level: Elementary, Middle, Senior High.

....

Information Finder is the electronic version of the *World Book Encyclopedia*. It contains 17,000 articles, 1,700 tables, and 139,000 entries from the *World Book* dictionary. There are 150,000 index entries,

60,000 cross-references and 1,600 reading lists. The new 1994 Windows and Macintosh versions have incorporated 3,000 pictures and 360 maps. Users can search for articles by topic or full-text keyword searching.

The opening screen places the user in the Topic Search Mode. Type in a search term and the program displays the article containing the most relevant information about the topic. Other articles that contain information about the topic can be called up in alphabetical order in Related Topics. The GOTO feature allows easy access to any cross-references in the article. Bookmark can be used to save text screens for further reference.

The Keyword Search Mode uses the full range of Boolean operators to search the entire encyclopedia. The user can adjust the proximity operators so that search terms can be next to one another in the same sentence, paragraph, article, or heading. The default searches for terms in the same sentence. Both right and left truncation is supported. The Search Log feature provides a numbered history of previous searches with the number of hits.

New search features have been added to the Windows and Macintosh versions. Gallery offers instant access to graphics using an illustrated display of categories. Atlas allows you to study maps and related text and also to navigate around the world by clicking from map to map. And InfoTree invites you to browse through topics and articles organized by subject area.

Articles are displayed on a split screen. The left one-third of the screen is an outline, the right two-thirds contains the full text. As the user moves through the outline on the left, the text on the right quickly moves to keep him in the correct place in the article. The split screen helps students understand the context of the full-text information they are viewing. Full articles or portions of the articles can be printed or saved to disk.

Jazz: A Multimedia History

Compton's NewMedia Inc., 2320 Camino Vida Roble, Carlsbad, CA 92009; 619/929-2500, 800/862-2206, 800/216-6116 (catalog sales), 619/929-2555 (fax).
Price: $99.95.
Minimum Hardware Requirements: MPC: *IBM 386/compatible, DOS 3.1, Windows 3.1, 2MB RAM, 30MB minimum hard drive space, SVGA monitor, CD-ROM drive, audio board, speakers, mouse.*
Platform: *Macintosh, MPC.*
Documentation: *Four-page user guide in disc case.*
Technical Support: *619/929-2626.*
Curriculum: *Arts and Music.*
Grade Level: *Middle, Senior High.*

Jazz: a Multimedia History is a complete chronology of jazz music with text, photographs, video and selected recordings from 1923 to 1991. It is a comprehensive history of a uniquely American art form based on the college-level textbook, *Jazz: From Its Origins to the Present*, published by Prentice-Hall.

Installation is easy and, in minutes, the opening screen with four menu items appears, offering Text, Pictures, Music, and Information. The Text section is 24 chapters, four appendices, glossary, bibliography, and discography. The text covers the history of jazz from its birth in late 19th century New Orleans to the 1992 debut of the latest Tonight Show band, which features saxophonist Branford Marsalis and pianist Kenny Kirkland.

The multimedia version contains the linear text and 120 musical examples displayed in musical notation. Click on the musical score and hear a few minutes of the jazz piece played by the authors to illustrate musical concepts. Click on the photograph icon in the left margin of the screen to see it enlarged. Some photos have several enlarged views. Both pictures and music can be accessed separately in the Pictures gallery and Music gallery.

The Picture gallery is divided into two sections, photographs and video clips. Each section can be sorted—photographs by artist, date and chronology, and video clips by artist name, song title, date and manuscript order. There are many quality photographs but, unfortunately, only six video clips, only enough to whet the appetite.

The Video for Windows clips feature legendary figures like Louis Armstrong, Duke Ellington, Count Basie, Charlie Parker, Dizzy Gillespie, Miles Davis, John Coltrane, Billie Holiday with Ben Webster and Lester Young. Click on the Music gallery in the main menu to sort the music gallery by artist

name, song title, date or manuscript order. The last menu choice, Information, is the help section and offers technical advice for using MIDI clips of the music samples on the disc.

Navigating the program is easy and printing or saving of text is featured along with a search history. Students researching jazz will find this an excellent resource.

JFK Assassination: A Visual Investigation

Medio Multimedia Inc., P.O. Box 2949 Redmond, WA 98073-9964; 800/788-3866, 206/885-4142 (fax).
Price: $49.95.
***Minimum Hardware Requirements: MPC:** 386 IBM/compatible, 2MB RAM VGA with 256 color, Windows 3.1, DOS 3.1, CD-ROM drive, audio board with speakers, mouse.*
***Platform:** MPC.*
***Documentation:** None.*
***Technical Support:** 206/867-5500.*
***Curriculum:** Social Studies.*
***Grade Level:** Middle, Senior High.*

Ask anyone over forty where they were on November 22, 1963—the day John F. Kennedy was shot. Most can remember their exact location and thoughts. It's an historical event that stopped time.

JFK Assassination: A Visual Investigation presents the facts of this wrenching drama. The program includes the full text of Jim Marrs' *Crossfire*, the *Warren Commission Report*, and *JFK Assassination: A Complete Book of Facts*. Multimedia elements include more than 20 minutes of narrated overview, full-motion clips of five films documenting the assassination (including the Zapruder film), 3D animation recreations of the assassination, a comprehensive photo library, and photo and witness maps of Dealey Plaza at the moment of the event.

Select Intro on the main menu to begin your investigation, which includes a video sequence giving the background of Kennedy's campaign trip to Dallas and a compelling local Dallas broadcast of the event. "Something has happened along the motorcade route...people are running...It's official, the president is dead."

The main menu presents four other choices including Overview, Dealey Plaza, Film and Photos, Analysis and Text. Each explores questions such as was there a plot to kill John F. Kennedy? Who was really involved? What are the conspiracy theories?

Click on Overview to continue the investigation of the disc, which includes biographical information on Kennedy, or on other menu choices, Dallas, Conspiracy Theories, Aftermath, and Conclusions. Going back one menu level, Dealey Plaza offers eyewitness maps and Analysis includes animated sequences recreating the angle of the bullets and the fatal attack on Kennedy based on the various theories, including the Zapruder View and Grassy Knoll View.

Searching is easy. A menu bar at the top of the screen offers options to go to the main menu, back one screen, view the index, search by keyword or see a search history. Keyword searches can be done by searching all categories or limiting to one or more of overview, Crossfire, Book of Facts or photo library. There are print, save and annotation functions on the tool bar at the top of the screen.

Both students and faculty are intrigued by this program. It allows them to collect the facts, look at the evidence, discuss the theories and draw their own conclusions. And, just after they think they have studied everything on the disc, they find screens listing more books and documentaries on JFK's assassination.

Just Grandma and Me
(*See* Living Books)

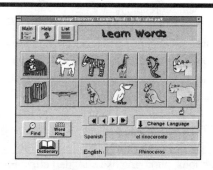

Language Discovery
Applied Optical Media Corporation, 1450 Boot Road, Building 400A, West Chester, PA 19380; 800/321-7259, 610/429-3701, 610/429-3810 (fax).
Price: $49.95.
Minimum Hardware Requirements:
Macintosh: System 7.0, 4MB RAM, 12-inch monitor with 512 VRAM, CD-ROM drive;
MPC: IBM 386/compatible, DOS 3.1, Windows 3.1, 2MB RAM, SVGA monitor, CD-ROM drive, audio board, speakers, mouse.

Platform: Macintosh, MPC.
Documentation: Four-page user guide in
disc case.
Technical Support: 800/321-7259.
Curriculum: Foreign Language.
Grade Level: Elementary, Middle.

....

Language Discovery is a delightful language exploration program featuring cartoon characters, colorful graphic screens
and the four languages of English, German,
French and Spanish.

The program begins when you choose
Learn Words on the main menu and then
select a specific environment, for example,
at school, camping, in the bedroom, in the
garden, in the kitchen, etc. Several objects
related to that place are illustrated in a
scrolling menu of icons. Click on the icon.
The foreign word is displayed on the screen
and pronounced in the language chosen at
the bottom of the screen. Click on the language button and hear the object spoken in
four different languages.

To practice finding words, select Find
Words from the main menu and choose the
same environment as in Learn Words. All
objects introduced in the first section are
shown in a colorful, well-designed illustration. Practice finding an object by clicking
on pictures to see and hear the foreign word.
Or, test your knowledge by trying to locate
the object after the word has been pronounced. If you are wrong, the program
pronounces the name of the incorrect object
and repeats the original request.

The Word King is another game to challenge and reinforce early language development. Object icons are displayed onscreen
and pronounced as you identify the foreign
word that describes the object. The level of

difficulty increases, becoming more chal-
lenging as the game progresses. The program also has a complete dictionary of all
of the words in the program to read and hear
pronounced.

Language Discovery is designed to
encourage foreign language development in
young children, concentrating on noun and
object identification—the basic vocabulary
necessary to begin learning a language. The
multilingual, interactive features make it a
delight to use.

LIFEmap Series
*Time Warner Interactive Group, 2210
West Olive Avenue, Burbank, CA 91506-
2626; 800/593-6334, 818/955-9999,
818/955-6499 (fax).*
Price: $39.99 per disc; set price $99.99.
Minimum Hardware Requirements:
*Macintosh II or LC; System 6.0.7; 5MB
RAM; color monitor; CD-ROM drive.*
Platform: Macintosh.
*Documentation: Ten-page booklet
in jewel case.*
Technical Support: 800/565-TWIG.
Curriculum: Science.
Grade Level: Senior High.

*(The series includes three CD-ROM titles:
Animals, Animals with Backbones, and
Organic Diversity.)*

....

Developed by the California Academy of
Sciences in San Francisco, these three discs
comprise an excellent introduction to the
"genealogy of the earth." According to the
developers, every organism on earth is related,
and these discs visually show how those
relationships can be traced. In the process of

finding the links for all relationships, the student will gain an understanding of what makes animal groups related, the common features showing a descent from a common ancestor, and how those features have changed over a long period of time.

Each disc in this series includes different groups of related organisms: Volume 1, Organic Diversity. Bacteria, algae, fungi, and land plants; Volume 2, Animals with Backbones. Fishes, amphibians, reptiles, and mammals; Volume 3, Animals. Spiders, insects, mollusks, and sea stars.

Cladistics is the study and use of branching family trees and is the primary tool used in these discs to show relationships between families and groups of organisms, as well as their link to ancestral groups. Descent with modification is the phrase used to describe the evolutionary process, and it can be observed everywhere: children are descended from their parents and may be similar physically, but they are not identical. A family tree shows the relationships between the child and the parent; the LIFEmap series puts together a family tree for all of the organisms on earth. A vast subject, it is manageable on these discs.

After loading the disc in the CD-ROM drive, double-click on the LIFEmap icon to begin. After an introduction, clicking anywhere on the screen will start the first interactive part of the program. At every level there is a help button that provides a tour of all functions on the current screen. There is a speaker icon to hear pronunciation of scientific names. A magnifying glass provides detailed descriptions of new features described at individual levels. There is a deliberate attempt to integrate all three discs into a cohesive unit, but each disc can be used alone.

These discs represent an authoritative and informative way of looking at man's relationship to every other creature on earth. The history of life on earth goes back about 3.5 billion years and CD-ROM technology goes back less than a decade, but they come together on this set of discs in a perfect match. They contain the information necessary to understand the evolution of the earth's creatures and the technology to make that information accessible to students. The visual links, the voice-over narration, and the connecting explanatory text combine with superb scholarship to make these discs well worth purchasing.

★ **Living Books**

Brøderbund Software, Inc., 500 Redwood Place, Novato, CA 94948; 415/382-4400.
Price: *$49.95 each.*
Minimum Hardware Requirements:
Macintosh: *LC/II series or Performa, System 6.0.7, 4MB RAM, 8-bit 256-color monitor;* ***MPC:*** *IBM 386/compatible 16MHz/compatible, DOS 3.3, Windows 3.0 with MSCDEX 2.0 or Windows 3.1, 4MB RAM, SVGA monitor, audio board, speakers, mouse.*
Print Equivalent: *Just Grandma and Me, by*

Mercer Mayer, Arthur's Teacher Trouble,
by Marc Brown (included with CD-ROM).
Platform: *Macintosh, MPC .*
Documentation: *User guide booklet.*
Technical Support: *415/382-4700.*
Curriculum: *Storybook.*
Grade level: *Primary, Elementary.*

(This series includes Just Grandma and Me
and Arthur's Teacher Trouble. Future titles
include New Kid on the Block by Jack
Prelutsky and a series of classics based on
Aesop's Fables.)

....

The Living Book series by Brøderbund is
the best example of a CD-ROM storybook
series published to date. It is easy to install
and a positive delight to use. Double-clicking
on the icon after inserting the disc brings up a
screen that lets the user select the language
version (English or Spanish in Arthur and
English, Japanese or Spanish in Grandma).
The user can then select whether or not to
"play" with the book or to listen to the story
read aloud. Charming animation and simple,
catchy tunes continue in the background
while the user makes a choice.

Just Grandma and Me is probably the number one storybook disc on the market today. It
is a charming and amusing story with one
scene per "page" describing Little Critter's
trip to the beach with his grandmother. Each
scene has multiple items to click and explore
for little bits of animation, song and funny
jokes. The story has one or two sentences per
page, which are read aloud by a good narrator in the chosen language, and individual
words are pronounced when clicked.

Nobody does cartoon animation on a
CD-ROM better than Brøderbund, and
Arthur's Teacher Trouble confirms this.

Arthur is a bespectacled little student who gets
into the dreaded Mr. Ratburn's class. He has
to study day and night to keep up, but in the
end he wins the great spelling bee and finds
that preparation is what really matters! This
disc is sure to entice all levels of students for
many reasons. Similar navigation tools, word
devices, catchy tunes, hidden surprises and
superb animation are available in both discs.

Aside from their sheer entertainment
value, Arthur and Grandma have much to
offer in terms of reading and word recognition. As the story is read aloud, the spoken
words are highlighted. Clicking on any word
in the text in the "play" or interactive mode
highlights it and the user will hear it spoken.

For their ease of installation and use,
excellent animation and sound, sheer pleasure of wonderfully written stories, and
skillful language lessons, discs in this series
are most highly recommended!

Long Hard Day on the Ranch
(*See* Discis Books)

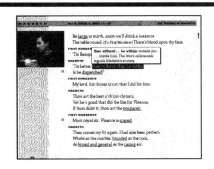

Macbeth
The Voyager Company, 578 Broadway,
New York, NY 10012; 212/431-5199,
212/431-5799 (fax). Also: One Bridge
Street, Irvington, NY 10533; 800/446-2001,
914/591-6481 (fax).

Price: $99.95.

Minimum Hardware Requirements:

Macintosh: Any color Macintosh (25MHz, 68030 recommended), System 7.0, 3.5MB available RAM, CD-ROM drive, color monitor.

Platform: Macintosh.

Documentation: 16-page user's guide.

Technical Support: 914/591-5500.

Curriculum: Language Arts.

Grade Level: Senior High.

....

This brand-new disc from the Voyager Company is a different approach to the presentation of a Shakespearean play. Using the full range of features available in a CD-ROM format, this is drama as it was never envisioned by the Bard!

Installation and operation are straightforward and easy. Complications set in when you try to decide which version of the play to listen to or watch. The entire play is presented in authentic-looking text, which can be read on the screen from start to finish. Words unclear to modern English speakers have instant definitions when you click on the word—no more tiny print and hard-to-find annotations. You can watch a QuickTime version of the play by the Royal Shakespeare Company (directed by Trevor Nunn) and then compare it to film versions by Orson Welles, Roman Polanski, or Kurosawa.

If you are unclear about the interpretation of a certain line or scene, Voyager has included a 24,000-word commentary by UCLA's David Rodes. A.R. Braunmuller, also of UCLA, wrote the annotations, did the textual analysis and wrote several

essays for this edition of Macbeth. Commentaries for the film clips were written by Michael Cohen.

Finally, there is the Macbeth Karaoke— where the user can select one of two scenes with just two players, Lord and Lady Macbeth. The first is from Act I, Scene 7, "If it were done...," and the second is the famous murder scene, Act 2, Scene 2. The user can read one part aloud while the other part is spoken by Lisa Harrow or Robert Thaler.

This is an excellent program that brings depth to the study of one of Shakespeare's masterpieces without being overwhelming in its details or pedantic in its attitude.

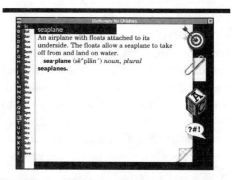

★ Macmillan Dictionary for Children—Multimedia Edition

Macmillan New Media, 124 Mount Auburn Street, Cambridge, MA 02138; 617/661-2955, 800/342-1338, 617/661-2403 (fax).

Price: $39.95.

Minimum Hardware Requirements:

Macintosh: LC System 6.0.7, 4MB RAM, 12-inch color monitor, CD-ROM drive; MPC: IBM 386/compatible, DOS 3.1, Windows 3.1, 4MB RAM, 2.5MB minimum hard drive space, VGA monitor, CD-ROM drive, audio board, speakers, mouse.

Platform: Macintosh, MPC.
Documentation: Four-page user guide in disc case.
Technical Support: 800/342-1338 between 9:00 a.m. and 5:00 p.m., Eastern time, Monday through Friday.
Curriculum: Reference & Interdisciplinary.
Grade Level: Primary, Elementary.

....

Macmillan Dictionary for Children—Multimedia Edition is one of the best multimedia titles. It actively involves children in language acquisition through the use of multimedia. Although it is recommended for ages seven to 12, it engages a far broader audience beginning with a narrated guided tour with Wendy and Zak, a pop-up animated character with a wonderful sense of humor. It provides the spoken version of any word by clicking on its pronunciation, multiple access paths to words and their definitions, three word games including Hangman, Words Within Words and Spelling Bee plus a notepad to personally select words.

Based on the print edition of *Macmillan Dictionary for Children,* the multimedia disc is a CD-ROM with nearly 12,000 word entries, 1,000 illustrations and 400 sound effects. The screen design is crisp and simple using well-designed icons.

Installation under Windows is easy. To locate words, users can type in a word, if they know how to spell it, or click on the letter in an alphabetic list on the left side of the page. If a child spells a word incorrectly, Zak offers his closest guess.

In addition, you can browse the dictionary by "page turning." Entries include definition, syllable division, pronunciation, part of speech and the plural. For most entries, the

definitions are followed by a simple sentence, showing the word in context. Some words have brief histories (for example, Easter is derived from the pagan festival Estre) and notes on usage (for example, Chile is pronounced the same as chilly and chili). Idioms, verb and adjective forms are also included. Clicking the right mouse button on a word in the definition gives you its meaning, making cross-referencing easy.

As you move through the dictionary, Zak, a red one-inch-square electronic gremlin, pops up to give his opinion about certain words. Zak blushes at "naked," runs from an "avalanche," giggles at "prank," groans at "earache," and yawns at the word "and." He adds a playfulness that gently encourages children to think about the word and its meaning and pronunciation. An added benefit is a notepad, My List, that encourages children to list their personal favorites. By clicking on the icon, this function can be easily reached from anywhere in the dictionary pages. Unfortunately, there is no provision to save My List as a file to be retrieved later.

This electronic dictionary is well worth the price, although it would be nice to see it run faster, offer print and save functions, and include multiple levels of difficulty in the games.

Magazine Article Summaries
EBSCO Publishing Inc., P.O. Box 2250, Peabody, MA 01960-7250; 800/653-2726, 508/535-8500, 508/535-8545 (fax).
Price: $799, quarterly; $1199, academic year; $1599, monthly.
Minimum Hardware Requirements: DOS: IBM 286/compatible: 640K RAM, DOS 3.2, MSCDEX 2.1, hard drive,

CD-ROM drive, monochrome monitor;
Macintosh: SE/30, System 6.05, 1.5MB
RAM, hard drive, CD-ROM drive.
Platform: *Macintosh, DOS.*
Documentation: *Installation guide,*
detailed 62-page user's guide, keyboard
basics template.
Technical Support: *800/758-5995.*
Curriculum: *Reference & Interdisciplinary.*
Grade Level: *Middle, Senior High.*

....

Magazine Article Summaries (MAS) indexes and provides abstracts for over 450 general interest magazines back to 1984 and the *New York Times* back to 1989. It includes the full text of thousands of book reviews from *Magill Book Review*. The abstracts average 50 words per citation. By survey, the magazines covered are those found most frequently in libraries. The annual subscription provides monthly updates.

There are two search modes in Magazine Article Summaries. The first level of searching is for the novice and provides three fields linked by an implicit AND. The second level of searching adds OR and NOT to the searching capabilities for more advanced users. All citations brought up by a search may be downloaded to a disk or printed. MAS can also produce bibliographies and generate interlibrary loan requests. It has excellent accounting features, such as magazine title field annotation, so you can limit searches to local holdings by tagging the title field. The software also can provide statistics on the number of times each title is used, as well as periodic use statistics.

Additional features school library media specialists will like are the free 60-day trial and no charge for LAN use within a school site.

Mammals:
A Multimedia Encyclopedia
National Geographic Society, 1145 17th
Street NW, Washington, DC 20036;
800/368-2728, 301/921-1575 (fax).
Price: *$99.*
Minimum Hardware Requirements:
Macintosh: *System 6.0.8, 4MB RAM, color*
or grayscale monitor; **IBM 286/compati-**
ble: *DOS 3.3, MSCDEX 2.1, 640K RAM,*
color monitor, CD-ROM drive, speakers.
Platform: *Macintosh, DOS.*
Documentation: *16-page booklet;*
large map.
Technical Support: *800/342-4460.*
Curriculum: *Science.*
Grade Level: *Elementary, Middle.*

....

Instead of just reading about mammals or looking at photographs, students can watch 45 full-motion clips, listen to 155 sound clips and test their knowledge about more than 150 warm-blooded vertebrate animals in a game called Project Classify. This CD-ROM, based on National Geographic's updated, two-volume *Book of Mammals*, includes 700 full-screen photos, 150 range maps, 150 fact screens, 150 vital statistics screens, 155 authentic vocalizations and essays equivalent to more than 600 pages of text.

The program is easy to navigate. The opening screen offers several options to begin exploring the world of mammals including Getting Started, About Mammals, Mammals A to Z, Orders of Mammals, Glossary, Game, and Credits. Click on About Mammals to read a series of essays, including topics like Homes & Habitat, Finding Food, Survival in Question, Season to Season, and Caring for Young. To study a specific mammal, choose Mammals A to Z. Each mammal has a screen with a color photo, information about the order, food, habits and status, breeds and species. Icons point the way to additional information, such as photos, range maps, textual information and vital statistics, including reproduction, lifespan, weight, height and size range.

When this program was first introduced four years ago, it was state-of-the-art and one of the first CD-ROMs to offer full-motion video. Educators were in awe! As with all ground-breaking products, it has been surpassed by newer, more innovative technology. Mammals still contains information needed by elementary students and it operates on minimum hardware requirements, but the slow delivery of full-motion video and limited sound capacity make it seem dated.

Mammals of Africa
(*See* ZooGuides)

Masterplots II CD-ROM

Salem Press Inc., 131 N. El Molino Avenue, Suite 350, Pasadena, CA 91101; 818/584-0106, 818/584-1525 (fax).
Price: $1295.
Minimum Hardware Requirements: DOS: IBM 286/compatible, DOS 3.2, 640K RAM, 5MB minimum hard drive space, CD-ROM drive.
Platform: DOS.
Documentation: 70-page manual.
Technical Support: 800/221-1826.
Curriculum: Language Arts.
Grade Level: Senior High.

Masterplots II CD-ROM contains the complete searchable text of the Masterplots II printed series—*American Fiction Series* (1986), *Short Story Series* (1986), *British and Commonwealth Fiction Series* (1987), *World Fiction Series* (1988), *Nonfiction Series* (1989), *Drama Series* (1990) and *Juvenile and Young Adult Fiction Series* (1991)—plus *Cyclopedia of World Authors II* (1989) and *Cyclopedia of Literary Characters II* (1990). More than 100 authors from *Cyclopedia of World Authors* are also included. Nearly 3,000 works are treated with detailed character profiles for over 1,400 works and more than 800 author biographies.

Each essay in Masterplots II typically presents the plot of the book, story or drama, followed by a short analysis of themes and characters, a review of critical comment on the work, source series, genre, type and time of plot, locale, first publication or production date. In addition, there are sources for further study, sometimes briefly annotated, and links to other entries and essays, such as character analysis or book review. This second series does not have works covered in the original Masterplots series, but rather concentrates on works of the twentieth century with a strong emphasis on works written since 1950.

The database can be searched by author, theme, subject, genre, country, historical setting, title, character name, date of publication or keyword. Searching is done through a Query Profile screen using fill-in-the-blanks. Full Boolean logic is supported and an on-disc tutorial is available for first-time users. Users can search at the beginner level with several screen display options and simplified field access through keyword, author, title, subject and locale. The advanced-level screen looks the same but adds two new fields, the genre and reference fields. In addition, the advanced query screen allows the searcher to connect results from previous searches to the current search. The expert level adds the ability to save searches.

Whole or partial sections of the text can be printed or downloaded to a disk. Context-sensitive help is provided on every screen. Special features include screen savers, display color choices and record-keeping. The usage statistics function records the number of searches performed, number of hits, number of documents printed, and other pertinent data.

This program is well-designed and has a powerful, easy-to-use search interface. Students will find it very useful for enhancing background knowledge and selecting titles for further research.

Mavis Beacon Teaches Typing

The Software Toolworks, Inc., 60 Leveroni Court, Novato, CA 94949; 800/231-3088, 415/883-3000, 415/883-3303 (fax).
Price: $59.95
Minimum Hardware Requirements:
MPC Level 1: IBM 386 25MHz/compatible, DOS 5.0, Windows 3.1, MSCDEX 2.21, 4MB RAM, CD-ROM drive, SVGA monitor, audio board and speakers, mouse.
Platform: Macintosh, DOS, MPC.
Documentation: 76-page owner's manual.
Technical Support: 415/883-3000.
Curriculum: General.
Grade Level: Middle, Senior High.

OK, all you hunt-and-peck artists, look out! Mavis is here and she doesn't mess around. Mavis Beacon, that is, and this CD-ROM is the latest evolution in one of the world's most successful typing tutorial programs. Everything that works well about CD-ROM products works well here, and if you need a program to build general office skills and typing skills, you won't go wrong with Mavis.

The installation is quick and easy, and double-clicking on the icon in Windows takes you directly into Mavis Beacon's classroom. Here you register and then Mavis keeps track of your skills, your scores, and your words-per-minute. The program remembers not only who you are, but where you were in the sequence of lessons when you return to it.

Each lesson builds on a typing skill, adding levels of complexity as it adds various key combinations. Each lesson can be followed on screen by a simulated pair of hands on a keyboard that type as you do, so you never need to look at your keyboard. Each individual lesson is tallied, and your ability level is reported. If you had trouble with the lesson, you are asked if you want to repeat it. Following each level is an exercise with a metronome and some other skill-builders, such as typing the words on a banner dragged across the screen by a small airplane.

The graphics of this program are excellent, and some of the exercises are like games—very imaginative and fun to do. The accompanying sounds are also relevant, with a choice in the level of chattiness you can select. For example, when I opened one of the skill-building units but decided not to try it, a voice-over asked, "Too tough for you, huh?"

The manual that accompanies the disc contains supplementary material about the history of the typewriter, plus general forms for business letters. It offers useful and interesting information to complement the typing lessons on the disc.

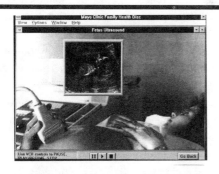

Mayo Clinic Family Health Book

IVI Publishing, 7500 Flying Cloud Drive, Minneapolis, MN 55344; 612/996-6000, 612/996-6001 (fax).
Price: $69.95.
Minimum Hardware Requirements:
Macintosh: Macintosh II or LC, System 6.0.6, 4MB RAM, CD-ROM drive; MPC: IBM 386/compatible, DOS 3.1, Windows 3.1, MSCDEX 2.2, 4MB RAM, VGA monitor, CD-ROM drive, audio board and stereo headphones or speakers, mouse.
Platform: Macintosh, MPC.
Documentation: One-page instruction sheet in jewel case.
Technical Support: 800/754-1484.
Curriculum: Health.
Grade Level: Senior High.

The Mayo Clinic Family Health Book is an interactive guide to the most useful and clinically-correct health information. It covers a complete range of topics, and has an excellent interface.

The program runs from the CD-ROM and needs only to have QuickTime, included with the disc, installed on the hard drive. The opening screen is a table of contents with a complete list of subject headings. These same general headings appear at the right of the screen and can be clicked at any time to move to that section.

At the bottom of the screen is a row of buttons for specialized functions. If the icon is not self-explanatory, the name of the button appears in a box to the left when the mouse pointer is moved over the icon. These functions are the Contents screen, a Notepad, Trail (history of where you've been so far in using the disc this time), Search, Dictionary, List of Illustrations, and a Return button. The Search button allows you to type in any term or combination of terms, and the program then displays a list of all sections, articles and illustrations that contain that term or terms. The Notepad lets you type in your own remarks, keep them, recall them, and print them.

The first main section on the disc is Anatomy, a series of cutaway illustrations showing various parts of the human body, such as skeleton, nervous system, muscles, etc. Subsequent sections deal with Lifecycles, First Aid/Safety, Keeping Fit, Diseases/Disorders, Skin Disorders, Modern Care and Appendices. The Appendices have definitions, lists of drugs and weights and measures conversions.

Technically, this disc is extremely well-done. It's not slow, even on a 150kbps CD-ROM drive, and changing from topic to topic is almost seamless. The quality of the audio portions is very high, and even using the internal speaker on a Macintosh computer, the quality was good and clear. The screen design and navigation controls are intuitive, and the guided tour introduction is good.

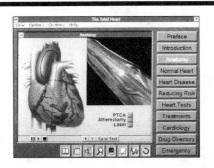

Mayo Clinic—The Total Heart

IVI Publishing, 7500 Flying Cloud Drive, Minneapolis, MN 55344; 612/996-6000, 612/996-6001 (fax).
Price: $59.95.
Minimum Hardware Requirements:
Macintosh: Macintosh II or LC, System 6.0.6, 4MB RAM, CD-ROM drive;
MPC: IBM 386/compatible: DOS 3.1, Windows 3.1, MSCDEX 2.2, 4MB RAM, VGA monitor, CD-ROM drive, audio board and stereo headphones or speakers, mouse.
Platform: Macintosh, MPC.
Documentation: Instruction card in jewel case.
Technical Support: 800/754-1484.
Curriculum: Health.
Grade Level: Senior High.

....

Mayo Clinic—The Total Heart is an excellent addition to any collection of health reference works. It contains well-done animation and graphics depicting the workings of the heart as well as an extensive text report on every conceivable topic relating to the heart and its place in our health and well-being.

The opening screen gives the user the option of searching or browsing through a variety of text-based sections. These sections include a preface and introduction, the anatomy of the heart, the normal heart, heart disease, reducing the risks of heart disease, treatments of heart disease, issues in cardiology, a drug directory, and what to do in an emergency. Each section has very solid, well-written and non-technical information, along with related labeled drawings, some half-hearted animated drawings, dictionary definitions and charts. All words in the text defined in the dictionary are shown in a different color, and all related topics are in another color and underlined for quick access.

At the bottom of the screen are several buttons that allow the user to go back to the Contents page, make notes, track the trail created through the information, check out the dictionary or illustrations or symptoms, or return to a previous screen.

The Total Heart has excellent information and a good interface. The user can browse or search on many different levels through different kinds of information. Getting lost is practically impossible, and gathering information by browsing and then making notes and printing the information is quick and easy. The only drawback to this disc is the quality of the animated illustrations. This is definitely a minor issue, and The Total Heart would be a good purchase for any home or library.

McGraw-Hill Multimedia Encyclopedia of Science and Technology

McGraw-Hill Inc., 11 West 19th Street,

New York, NY 10011; 800/722-4726,
212/337-4092 (fax).
Price: *$1300 for single version,*
$325 for update.
Minimum Hardware Requirements:
MPC: *386 IBM/compatible with 4MB*
RAM, 3MB available hard drive space,
VGA monitor, Windows 3.1, CD-ROM
drive, sound board and mouse.
Platform: *MPC*
Documentation: *Eight-page user guide.*
Technical Support: *800/643-4351.*
Curriculum: *Science*
Grade Level: *Senior High*

....

McGraw-Hill Multimedia Encyclopedia of Science and Technology contains the 20-volume seventh edition (1992) *McGraw-Hill Encyclopedia of Science & Technology* and the new fifth edition (1994) of the *McGraw-Hill Dictionary of Scientific and Technical Terms*, with 105,100 terms and 122,600 definitions. It includes more than 3,000 contributors including 21 Nobel laureates, 7,300 articles covering 81 major subject areas, every science and engineering discipline with thousand of hypertext links to related articles, 550 photos, line drawings, 22 geographic maps with almanac data, 45 sky maps and charts, including 100 newly created graphics, 39 full-color animations with narration covering astronomy, biology, earth science, physics and engineering, nearly 40 minutes of sound, and the full text and 250 biographies of historically important scientists with cross references to relevant articles.

The program has a powerful, user-friendly, graphical interface that takes full advantage of

Windows features. The program screen features a Menu Bar including File, Edit, Search, Text, Window, Document, Bookmark and Help to assist the user. The information stored on the CD-ROM is organized into eight databases that are available through a pull-down list in the Program Toolbar: Encyclopedia, Dictionary, Biographies, Study Guide, Maps, Sky Maps, Animations and Illustrations. The Toolbar also includes buttons for Search, Index, Tile and Print.

You can search the Encyclopedia database for specific terms in two ways: 1) by entering a search term in the Quick Search dialog box; or 2) by setting multiple search criteria in the Advanced Search dialog box using Boolean operators. Searches can be limited to any or include all topics: Agriculture/Forestry, Astronomy, Biology, Chemistry, Computer Science, Engineering, Mathematics, Medicine/Psychology, and Physics. To browse topics, click on Encyclopedia and a List Window will appear with an alphabetical listing of the available topics. As you scroll thorough the list, double-click on the item to view the encyclopedia article. When viewing an article a Windows Toolbar appears at the top and includes buttons. The buttons, which are displayed only when they are applicable for a given article, include options to view animations, illustrations, maps, photos, an outline of the article, cross references, or jump to a particular term.

The encyclopedia also includes extra features such as study guides for use with standard curriculum outlines in physics, chemistry, biology, geoscience, health and engineering with suggestions for relevant articles for each topic, phonetic chart with audible pronunciations, and interactive periodic chart and geographic maps with data about each country or element respectively. The full text of the encyclopedia can be saved to a disk or printed, as can most of the multimedia items.

This disc offers students and teachers a powerful yet flexible search engine to explore a wealth of scientific information quickly and efficiently. The Windows environment encourages students to explore, compare and contrast data making the process of research more engaging and enjoyable.

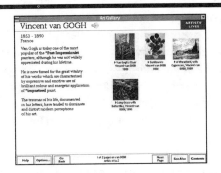

Microsoft Art Gallery

Microsoft Corporation, One Microsoft Way, Redmond, WA 98052; 800/426-9400, 206/936-7329 (fax).
Price: $79.
Minimum Hardware Requirements:
MPC: IBM 386/compatible, DOS 3.1, Windows 3.1, 4MB RAM, 1MB minimum hard drive space, VGA monitor, CD-ROM drive, audio board, speakers, mouse.
Platform: Macintosh, MPC.
Documentation: Six-page user guide in disc case.
Technical Support: 206/635-7172.

Curriculum: Arts and Music.
Grade Level: Middle, Senior High.

....

Microsoft Art Gallery contains the celebrated art collection of the National Gallery in London shown with color, sound and animation. The National Art Gallery was founded in 1824 and houses the United Kingdom's national collection of Western European paintings from the 13th century to the early 20th century. It includes 2,000 works by noted painters such as Monet, da Vinci, Titian, Raphael, Van Gogh, and Vermeer.

Art Gallery allows you to browse through the paintings exhibited in the National Gallery Collection in four different ways. Artists' Lives presents biographies of the artists and their paintings. Historical Atlas organizes the collection by place and time. Click on a geographic region or a time period to learn more about paintings from that time or place. Picture Types organizes the collection by type of work including Religious Imagery (Narrative, Allegory and the Nude), Portrait, Everyday Life, Views and Still Life.

Each broad category is further subdivided. Everyday Life contains Making Music, Courting and Brothels, Drinking, Leisure and Games, Education, Work, Soldiers, Smoking and Bubble Blowing, and Domestic Interiors. Six paintings, from 1620 to 1735, are explored in Education, ten in Leisure and Games, and 12 in Work.

Guided tours are also available. Four guided tours discuss important themes in art, with commentary and illustrations, including highlights from the Collection.

They include Composition and Perspective, Making Paintings, Paintings as Objects, and Beneath the Varnish.

All the graphics and text can be exported into the clipboard and then into word processing and paint programs to enhance a report or construct a personal version of the painting.

This program, along with the other Microsoft products, is extremely well-designed. It helps students explore the historical, geographical and social context of this remarkable collection. It provides the opportunity to experience masterpieces from one of the world's finest collections of art, discover the fascinating facts behind the paintings, witness the techniques of the painters and hear the names of the artists pronounced. It's a field trip students will enjoy and remember.

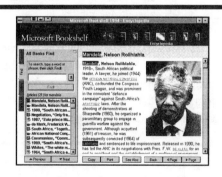

★ Microsoft Bookshelf 1994 Multimedia Edition

Microsoft Corporation, One Microsoft Way, Redmond, WA 98052; 800/426-9400, 206/936-7329 (fax).
Price: *$99.*
Minimum Hardware Requirements:
MPC: *IBM 386/compatible, DOS 3.1, Windows 3.1, 2MB RAM, 2MB minimum*

hard drive space, SVGA monitor, CD-ROM drive, audio board, speakers, mouse.
Platform: *Macintosh, MPC.*
Documentation: *22-page user guide in disc case.*
Technical Support: *206/635-7172.*
Curriculum: *Reference & Interdisciplinary.*
Grade Level: *Middle, Senior High.*

Originally released as an MS-DOS product in 1987, this classic reference has been updated again, incorporating new access paths and new and current information. Bookshelf includes seven popular reference works including *American Heritage Dictionary of the English Language*, Third Edition; *Original Roget's Thesaurus*; *Concise Columbia Encyclopedia*, Second Edition; *Hammond World Atlas*; *World Almanac and Book of Facts 1994*; a new book of quotations, *Columbia Dictionary of Quotations*; and a new addition to the collection, *People's Chronology*, a compendium of historical events illustrated with cultural, scientific and even culinary happenings. The seven reference works are linked to allow users to search the entire reference library at once or only the books of their choice. Access is also available from any other program running in Windows through a new feature, Quickshelf.

Using Bookshelf is easy and convenient. Words are pronounced, many illustrations are brought to life with animations, the full-motion video captures the historical moment, and the maps are current. A book bar on the top of the screen shows which book(s) are being searched. Typing the word "astronaut" and pressing <enter> brings up articles on "astronaut" in all seven books. Moving the mouse in the Table of

Contents area shows which books contain articles on the topic, such as the dictionary, thesaurus and encyclopedia. Searching "Anita Hill" retrieves a full-motion video clip of Hill's and Thomas's statements at the Senate hearings.

Topics can be searched and results imported to another program, such as a word processor or spreadsheet. Click on Quotations book in the book bar, type in Madonna, Salman Rushdie or Dan Quayle to locate recent quotes that can be copied and pasted right into Microsoft Publisher, Word or WordPerfect.

Bookshelf is both fun and informative, an easy path to typical reference information, quotes, fast facts, synonyms, pronunciations, maps, etc.

Microsoft Dangerous Creatures

Microsoft Corporation, One Microsoft Way, Redmond, WA 98052; 800/426-9400, 206/936-7329 (fax).
Price: $79.95.
Minimum Hardware Requirements:
MPC: 386SX IBM/compatible, 4MB RAM, 2.5MB hard drive space, VGA monitor, CD-ROM drive, sound board, mouse, DOS 3.1, Windows 3.1; Macintosh: Macintosh with color monitor, System 6.0.7, 4MB RAM, 1MB hard drive space, CD-ROM drive.
Platform: MPC, Macintosh.
Documentation: Six-page user guide in disc case.
Technical Support: 206/635-7172
Curriculum: Science.
Grade Level: Elementary, Middle, Senior High.

Microsoft Dangerous Creatures describes more than 250 of the wildest creatures on

earth using 800 detailed articles, hundreds of full-color photographs, more than 100 video clips, and hours of sounds and narration. Explore on your own or through twelve narrated tours from three expert guides—the amusing naturalist, the adventurous photographer or the magical storyteller. Each tour represents the guide's point of view.

The main menu or Contents screen offers the option to explore the creatures by location through the Atlas; by Weapons, as in jaws, venom and claws; by Habitats, Forest, Arctic, Desert, Ocean, Grassland, and Wetland; or through the alphabetic Index. Any choice will eventually lead to articles about specific animals. The articles contain hot links to related articles and videos for more detailed information. For example, opening the article on the wolf shows a screen of text plus hot spots that you can click, such as "eating hierarchy," "predator power," "wolf ways," "foxy cousins" and a video called "Making Tracks."

Any of the articles can be printed and images from the picture gallery can be saved as Windows wallpaper or copied to the clipboard for use in another program. Students are intrigued by this program. It involves and motivates them to explore and learn.

Microsoft Dinosaurs

Microsoft Corporation, One Microsoft

Way, Redmond, WA 98052; 800/426-9400, 206/936-7329 (fax).
Price: $79.95
Minimum Hardware Requirements:
MPC: IBM 386/compatible, DOS 3.1, Windows 3.1, 2MB RAM, 30MB minimum hard drive space, VGA monitor, CD-ROM drive, audio board, speakers, mouse.
Platform: Macintosh, MPC.
Documentation: Six-page user guide in disc case.
Technical Support: 206/635-7172.
Curriculum: Science.
Grade Level: Elementary, Middle, Senior High.

Microsoft Dinosaurs is an interactive exploration into the world of prehistoric animals. Like all of Microsoft's CD-ROM products, this title has an intuitive and attractive interface. From the first roar of the dinosaur in the opening screen through hours of discovery, this program educates, entertains and delights the user.

The main menu or contents screen offers six choices for your exploration including Atlas, Families, Timeline, Index, Guided Tour, and Dinosaur Movies. Each section takes you to a variety of options and each screen offers hyperlinks to more information.

Click on Families, for example. Dinosaurs are divided into two families, Saurischians and Ornithischians, with four and five subcategories of dinosaurs in each. Click on any of these subcategories to see a screen of 12 to 15 representative dinosaurs. You can then click on any of these individual dinosaurs to view a full screen exploring its habitat, eating habits, skeleton, etc. Each previous screen also has other "hot buttons" linking to more information—usually narrated with graphics and text.

There are six dinosaur movies on the disc, five of which are cartoon-style. Microsoft Dinosaurs also includes 16 narrated, guided tours. Each tour visits between nine and 16 articles with which your tour guide tells a little bit of the story. During the tour you can stop to explore each screen. Click on the guided tour button to continue. The tours are presented with humor and explore unique dinosaur attributes, facts and more.

Screens can be saved to the clipboard using the Options menu. Text, however, cannot be printed. The Options menu also offers dinosaur screen savers and a picture gallery you can use as a Windows wallpaper.

★ Microsoft Musical Instruments
Microsoft Corporation, One Microsoft Way, Redmond, WA 98052; 800/426-9400, 206/936-7329 (fax).
Price: $79.95.
Minimum Hardware Requirements:
IBM 386/compatible: 2MB RAM, sound board, SVGA monitor, mouse, speakers, DOS 3.1, Windows 3.1, MSCDEX 2.2 or higher.
Platform: Macintosh, MPC.
Documentation: 22-page user guide in disc case.

Technical Support: 206/635-7172.
Curriculum: Arts and Music.
Grade Level: Middle, Senior High.

....

Microsoft Musical Instruments is an encyclopedia of musical instruments that offers an interactive environment for users to explore the sights and sounds of more than 200 instruments from around the world. Included are more than 200 essays or articles, more than 500 photographs, historical and factual information, and 1,500 sound samples. It was produced in cooperation with Dorling Kindersley of London, publishers of the *Eyewitness Series*, highly illustrated, practical reference books produced for children and adults, and well-known by librarians.

As all with MPC titles, it installs easily. Users can explore the world of musical instruments by choosing one of four categories from the main menu including Families of Instruments, Musical Ensembles, A to Z of Instruments, or Instruments of the World.

Families of Instruments classifies the instruments according to Brass, String, Woodwinds, Keyboards, and Percussion. Click on any of these to find a screen filled with instruments of that type. The other three main sections offer additional information. Musical Ensembles features audio demonstrations of groups of instruments by playing samples of diverse musical styles. It looks at orchestras, steel bands, wind bands, jazz bands, rock bands, and chamber groups.

A to Z of Instruments organizes all subjects alphabetically from an accordion to a zurna. This index leads the user directly to a selected instrument for more information. Users can hear the pronunciation of the instrument's name and a sample of its music, as well as find facts about the instrument's origin and history.

Instruments of the World displays a world map. Click on any section, such as South East Asia or North America, and the screen zooms in to display instruments for that area, each with its own sound icon. What better way to learn about another culture than listening to and learning about its music? This title adds a new dimension to research in world cultures and global studies classes. Students' only complaint will be that the sound clips are not long enough.

Mixed-Up Mother Goose

Sierra On-Line, Inc., P.O. Box 53250, Bellevue, WA 08015-3250; 800/743-7725. 800/757-7707 (orders), 209/562-4317 (fax).
Price: $59.95.
Minimum Hardware Requirements: DOS: IBM PC/compatible, 512K RAM, 3MB minimum hard drive space, VGA monitor, CD-ROM drive, speakers, mouse, DOS 3.1, MSCDEX 2.1.
Platform: DOS.
Documentation: 14-page user guide in disc case.

Technical Support: 209/683-8989.
Curriculum: Language Arts.
Grade Level: Primary, Elementary.

....

Mixed-Up Mother Goose is an adventure game designed for children ages four and up. The object of the game is to help Mother Goose complete her mixed-up rhymes by locating the 18 missing characters and objects and bringing them back to their rightful owners. This interactive multimedia game includes full-color graphics, digitized sound, voices and music. The program can operate in Japanese, German, French, Spanish or English.

It is an MPC title and loads easily under Windows. In the opening section, the user chooses a "child" to help Mother Goose locate 18 nursery rhyme characters. The child moves around Mother Goose Land picking up lost objects that are randomly distributed and returning them to the appropriate nursery rhyme character, such as Mary's little lamb and Jack Sprat's ham.

Each time the game is played, the objects are in a different place. When the object is returned to the correct character, a golden egg is deposited in the Egg Carton icon on the bottom of the screen and the nursery rhyme character sings his/her rhyme as it is spelled out in large letters across the screen. When the icon is filled, the game is over and the child is returned home on the back of a goose.

The well-designed screen consists of a game window and various icons placed on the side and the bottom to give the user control. A lever icon sets the speed at which the child moves through the game. The Mouth icon allows characters to speak to each other. A Map icon shows the location of characters and allows the players to click on locations and see what item is missing or has been found. The Inventory shows the item the child has picked up.

Students will enjoy helping Mother Goose as they encounter fluttering butterflies, flower petals dropping from trees, ticking clocks, barking dogs and more. The program's interactivity enhances the enjoyment and fun of nursery rhymes. It serves as an excellent introduction to computer usage by teaching basic computer skills, such as using a mouse, navigating through windows, selecting icons, etc.

Moving Gives Me A Stomach Ache (*See* Discis Books)

Multimedia Animals Encyclopedia, Volume 1

Applied Optical Media Corporation, 1450 Boot Road, Building 400A, West Chester, PA 19380; 800/321-7259, 610/429-3701, 610/429-3810 (fax).
Price: $59.95.
Minimum Hardware Requirements:
***Macintosh:** System 7.0, 4MB RAM, 12-inch monitor, with 512 VRAM, CD-ROM drive;*

MPC: IBM 386/compatible, DOS 3.1, Windows 3.1, 2MB RAM, SVGA monitor, CD-ROM drive, audio board, speakers, mouse.
Platform: Macintosh, MPC.
Documentation: Six-page user guide in disc case.
Technical Support: 800/321-7259.
Curriculum: Science.
Grade Level: Middle, Senior High.

....

Multimedia Animals Encyclopedia contains almost 2,000 creatures selected from the 40,000 living species in the vertebrate branch of the Animal Kingdom including Amphibians, Birds, Mammals and Reptiles. In-depth information about each animal is easily located by choosing one of the five buttons on the main menu, including Animals, Bookshelf, Topics, Range Maps, or Help. Unique features, such as the pronunciation of every common name, class, order and scientific name, complex interlinking ability, and the opportunity to build your own private zoo make this program very powerful and especially useful in schools.

Installation is easy under Windows. The opening menu is clear and needs little instruction. The program's Help system provides complete context-sensitive descriptions of the procedures and options. Every screen includes the Main Menu button and the Back button at the upper left corner to retrace your steps or start over.

Users can go directly to Animals, choose a class and then a group or a specific animal with its common name or scientific name. The Results screen contains a detailed illustration showing important physical characteristics. Range Map shows the normal range of the species. Habitat provides a description and drawing of the typical habitat. Classification identifies the Class, Order and Family. Diet gives information about the major food of the animal. Size provides typical total length and tail traits. Sound offers audio clips of selected animal sounds. Description provides text presenting the important characteristics, behaviors and relationships to other species. And Conservation Status provides conservation information as determined by the International Union for Conservation of Nature and Natural Resources.

Other options are Bookshelf, Topics, or Range Maps. Bookshelf allows you to browse characteristics that can lead to similar groups of animals or specific species and hear the pronunciation of the common name, scientific name, Class, Order and Family of every animal. Topics provides a Glossary of approximately 200 words and Conservation, a complete listing of endangered, Indeterminate, Out of Danger, Rare, and Vulnerable animals. Topics also provides the ability to build your own zoo of the animals you have researched with Zoo. The final section, Characteristics, is a student favorite. When you choose a characteristic, such as Feeding, the program lists three to five animals and their unique feeding habits for comparison and enjoyment.

Animals are a popular topic at any age and this program encourages students to go beyond mere identification to explore the subject through classification and comparison. *Important:* This program does not have a print function: The next edition, due out in 1995, will include a print function so text can be printed.

Mud Puddle (*See* Discis Books)

Multimedia Beethoven, Multimedia Mozart, Multimedia Stravinsky

(Each title is sold separately.)
Microsoft Corporation, One Microsoft Way, Redmond, WA 98052; 800/426-9400, 206/936-7329 (fax).
Price: $79.95.
Minimum Hardware Requirements:
MPC: IBM 386/compatible, DOS 3.1, Windows 3.1, 2MB RAM, 30MB minimum hard drive space, VGA monitor, CD-ROM drive, audio board, speakers, mouse.
Platform: MPC.
Documentation: Six-page user guide in disc case.
Technical Support: 206/635-7172.
Curriculum: Arts and Music.
Grade Level: Senior High.

These three titles from Microsoft allow the novice or trained listener to explore and experience the symphonies of Beethoven, Mozart and Stravinsky in depth with freedom. Each title transports the user into the world of the composer to explore his music, learn about his life and take an in-depth look at the musical architecture of the symphony.

Beethoven, Mozart and Stravinsky are all similar in content and organization. Following the easy installation process, each of the opening menus offers a choice between learning about the composer's world through A Pocket Guide or A Close Reading. Mozart also includes The Instruments and Quartet Listening. Multimedia Stravinsky includes Rite Listening, The Rite as Dance, and Stravinsky's Orchestra.

Moving about the programs is intuitive. Most screens have buttons to click for moving within the program, starting and stopping musical passages and interacting with the program. All screens have Contents, Exit, and Help buttons. The Contents/Chapters button brings you back to the main menu.

Exploring the program is intriguing, entertaining and educational. The Pocket Guide maps the structure of the symphonies on a single screen, allowing the user to hear immediately, with the click of a mouse button, any section from the movements. The Composer's World uses text, pictures and music to describe the cultural, social and political background of his life. A Close Reading contains a continuous commentary on the entire work, synchronized to the music it describes.

Each program also contains a listening section, The Art of Listening, Rite Listening, or Quartet Listening, that begins with the simplest of concepts and explains the nuts and bolts of the composer's musical language, as well as the larger symbolism.

An entertaining, interactive game is included to challenge the user's knowledge of the symphony and its background. Multimedia Beethoven includes a glossary of musical and historical terms, explained in a clear, precise manner. Mozart and Stravinsky include bibliographies.

Although the programs contain similar elements, each is unique in design and content. All three combine high-quality audio, images and text into a well-integrated educational program and offer an exciting way to learn about these great composers and their music.

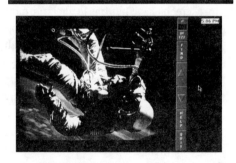

Murmurs of Earth:
The Voyager Interstellar Record
Time Warner Interactive Group, 2210 West Olive Avenue, Burbank, CA 91506-2626; 800/593-6334, 818/955-9999, 818/955-6499 (fax).
Price: $59.99 (2-disc set).
Minimum Hardware Requirements: Macintosh: Macintosh II or LC, System 6.0.5, 2MB RAM, color monitor, CD-ROM drive; DOS: IBM 286/compatible, 640K RAM, VGA monitor, CD-ROM drive. (The same discs play on either platform, and the sound tracks are playable on any CD-Audio player.)

Platform: Macintosh, DOS.
Documentation: Ten-page booklet in jewel case, which contains a complete listing of musical selections; 265-page softcover book with the same title by Carl Sagan, et al.
Technical Support: 800/565-TWIG.
Curriculum: Science.
Grade Level: Senior High.

....

Murmurs of Earth is a unique disc and book combination. The book documents the work of a committee, headed by Carl Sagan, to select pictures and messages to be sent on the Voyager space flight. This cosmic time capsule posed extraordinary problems and generated enormous intellectual and cultural interest among the mission's scientists, politicians and organizers. The committee's selections are contained on these two discs. The first disc contains illustrations and photographs, and the second disc has the recorded greetings and music. The book explains the choices and reproduces all of the pictures and illustrations. Because the audio disc is also playable on a CD-audio drive, it is not necessary to have a CD-ROM drive to enjoy this project.

As a generator of ideas and cross-cultural studies, these two discs are without equal. For example, the selection on the discs includes greetings in 55 different languages, recorded during two sessions at Cornell University in 1977. The transcription of those greetings is in the book in the original languages showing the name of the language, its English translation, the speaker's name, the countries where that language is used, the total number of speakers and their percentage of the world population. The discs also include 116 digital color photographs and 90 minutes of digitally-recorded sounds of the earth, musical selections and even a whale song!

Like tossing a message in a bottle into the ocean, this digital message launched into a galactic ocean represents the best effort of a group of brilliant and concerned people to identify and describe the planet Earth, its people and its history. As a resource for schools, the discs should generate fascinating discussions and serve as a model for individual or group projects.

The Musical World of Professor Piccolo

Opcode Systems Inc., 3950 Fabian Way, Suite 100, Palo Alto, CA 94303; 415/856-3333, 800/557-2633 (orders), 415/494-1113 (fax).
Price: $69.95.
Minimum Hardware Requirements: MPC: IBM 386/compatible, 4MB RAM, hard drive, SVGA monitor, sound board, CD-ROM drive, mouse, speakers, Windows 3.1.
Platform: MPC.
Documentation: Ten-page user guide in disc case.
Technical Support: 415/494-9393.
Curriculum: Arts and Music.
Grade Level: Elementary, Middle, Senior High.

This delightful interactive music program offers a general overview of musical topics, including music theory, music notation, music styles and their history. Beginning with the first screen the program is friendly and inviting, asking for your name and offering a range of fun places to visit.

Visit Professor Piccolo's Music Town and stop at the Symphony Hall to learn about instruments and the evolution of the orchestra. Go to the Jazz Club to learn about instruments and the evolution of jazz music. Visit the Rock Club to learn about instruments and rock music, and the Church to learn about instruments of the church and its influence on music. Drop into the Library to research specific musical terms or musical instruments or click on Games to play some fun musical games.

In each section nine icons are available to navigate and research additional information. Visit the Rock Club and listen to the entire rock band or just a single instrument, such as the electric guitar, drum set or voice synthesizer. In addition, the history, instrument ranges screen, musical form screen and instrument family diagrams are available. The text can also be read aloud.

Ready for a challenge? Pick a game. Sound Off challenges you to recognize the sounds of the instruments in an orchestra. Musical Pursuit is a game of trivia on different musical topics including classical, jazz, rock, church and music theory. Pitch Adventure is a game to recognize melody patterns, and Rhythm Risk is a rhythm game loosely based on the popular game Simon. The games are designed for multiple users and easily adaptable for classroom use. There is a user's database to save individual students' lessons.

Screens are well-designed and the program is easy to navigate. Printing is available, as is the ability to set a bookmark to a particular screen. According to the developers, the program is meant to be an introduction to types of music and music theory with the hope that it will inspire the user to continue learning. This program will do that and more!

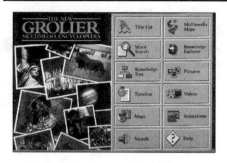

The New Grolier Multimedia Encyclopedia

Grolier Electronic Publishing, Inc.,
Sherman Turnpike, Danbury, CT 06816;
203/797-3530, 800/356-5590,
203/797-3130 (fax).
Price: $395.95.
Minimum Hardware Requirements:
Macintosh: Macintosh Plus, System 6.0.5,
4MB RAM, CD-ROM drive; if color and
QuickTime animations are desired, the
minimum requirement is System 6.0.7 and
a color monitor; MPC: IBM 286
10MHz/compatible, DOS 3.3, Windows 3.0,
MSCDEX 2.1, 2MB RAM, 1MB minimum
hard drive space, VGA monitor, CD-ROM
drive, audio board and speakers, mouse;
DOS: IBM PC/compatible, DOS 3.1,
MSCDEX 2.1, 640K RAM, 1MB minimum
hard drive space, VGA monitor, CD-ROM
drive, audio board and speakers.
Platform: Macintosh, DOS, MPC.
Documentation: 70-page manual.
Technical Support: 800/356-5590, Monday

through Friday, 8:30 a.m. to 4:30 p.m.
Eastern Time.
Curriculum: Reference & Interdisciplinary.
Grade Level: Elementary, Middle,
Senior High.

The New Grolier Multimedia Encyclopedia is a good choice for school libraries. It has an easy-to-use interface, plenty of depth to its information, and a lot of ways to access the information.

This is the electronic version of *Grolier's Academic American Encyclopedia* with over 33,000 articles, 300 pictures, 250 maps, 50 digitized movies and 30 minutes of sound. Most articles and records are accessible with a single mouse click, reducing the time spent hunting through multiple volumes of a major encyclopedia.

When the encyclopedia opens, the screen shows a Title Index of all of the articles included. Clicking on an article title brings up the article right away. You can scroll through the list and look at all the titles, or you can type the first few letters of the article you are looking for. The Index goes directly to the entries that begin with those letters.

If you click Open to read the article you have highlighted, you can scroll up and down through the text. At the top of the screen are various icons that indicate what other features or resources are available with this article. Examples of these features are outlines, sound recordings, animations, photographs, etc.

To narrow down or refine a search in the encyclopedia, you can use the Word Search feature. There are two other ways to search for information in the encyclopedia—with the Word Index and the Knowledge Tree.

The Index lists every word in the encyclopedia with the number of articles in which it appears and the number of times it occurs. The Knowledge Tree displays a hierarchical list of topics, starting with six main branches of knowledge including Arts, Geography, History, Science, Society and Technology.

There is a Notepad, an electronic file for the user to keep notes in while working, and Bookmarks, which enable the user to tag or mark certain articles, sections or features to come back to later. Any article, picture or map can be printed, as well as the Notepad; and articles can be saved to disk for later use in a word processing program. All material that is printed from the encyclopedia has a copyright date and citation on it.

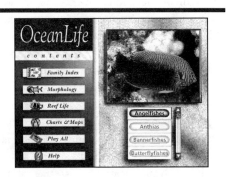

OceanLife: Volume 2: Micronesia

Sumeria, 329 Bryant Street, Suite 3D, San Francisco, CA 94107; 415/904-0800, 415/904-0888 (fax).
Price: *$49.95.*
Minimum Hardware Requirements:
Macintosh: *System 7.0, 6MB RAM, 256 color monitor, CD-ROM drive;* ***Windows:*** *IBM 386 33MHz/compatible, DOS 5.0,*

Windows 3.1, 6MB RAM, VGA monitor, audio board, CD-ROM drive.
Platform: *Macintosh, Windows.*
Documentation: *Eight-page booklet in jewel case.*
Tech. Support: *415/904-0800.*
Curriculum: *Science.*
Grade Level: *Senior High.*

OceanLife: Micronesia is the second in a series of CD-ROMs dealing with the world of tropical fish. Volume 1 is Western Pacific and Volume 3 is Hawaii. Micronesia is a two-disc set, each containing stunningly beautiful underwater photographs and videos of more than 150 species of fish that inhabit the waters from Ponaphei to Palau.

Each disc opens with a screen that offers several choices. All the fish on the disc are listed alphabetically by their family names, and clicking on the name moves to a screen with a photograph and accompanying text about the species, and then on to individual fish.

Another screen shows the morphology of a fish with all of its parts named. Another takes you to a series of maps including world political, topographic or world relief. Certain areas on each map can be enlarged, and you can scroll the maps by clicking on the compass points of the icon in the corner. By dragging two "tacks" to different locations on the map, you can get the approximate distance between them in miles and kilometers.

Another button is called Fishes by Family, and lets the viewer select a family of fish, and then view branches of the family, and finally individual fish in each family.

These are the zoological classifications of fish and provide another level of information and expertise.

The vivid fish illustrations, photographs and videos, plus the astonishing variety of size and type of fish, the delightful and curious names of some of the fish (Thick-lipped Wrasse, Sergeant-major Damsel, and Convict Tang, just to name a few) and the general quality of this disc make it hard to resist. The only deciding factor should be if such a limited topic fits into your school curriculum or home needs.

Oceans Below

The Software Toolworks Inc., 60 Leveroni Court, Novato, CA 94949; 415/883-3000, 800/231-3088, 415/883-3303 (fax).
Price: $49.95.
Minimum Hardware Requirements:
Macintosh: System 6.0.7, 4MB RAM, 13-inch screen, 256-color monitor, CD-ROM drive; IBM 386/compatible: DOS 3.1, Windows 3.1, 2MB RAM, 2MB minimum hard drive space, SVGA monitor, CD-ROM drive, audio board, speakers, mouse.
Platform: Macintosh, DOS, MPC.
Documentation: One-page card.
Technical Support: 415/883-3000.

Curriculum: Science.
Grade Level: Middle, Senior High.

Oceans Below explores 17 scuba diving spots, such as the Galapagos Islands, the Caribbean, Australia's Great Barrier Reef, the Red Sea, Hawaii and the California Coast. It contains more than 200 video clips of marine life, plant life and undersea sites, among them ship wrecks and occasional buried treasure, along with 125 photographs, narration and original music to give you the feel of scuba diving.

This is not a diving simulation, but you can learn the elements of scuba diving, including narrated information about each piece of diving equipment, water temperature, currents, marine life, ocean conservation, dive safety, dive organizations and visibility. A map shows diving locations around the world. Once you select your site and dive, you take an interactive tour by pressing hot buttons.

Click on any plant, animal or occasional buried treasure, and a short video, disguised in a diving mask, explains the item you have chosen. A Sea Life Chart accesses information on native fish in each dive location. A list of marine life and its location is given in Site attractions in the world Map. A student would learn that soft coral is located in Palau and the manatee can be found in Belize.

Visit one of the hottest places on earth and one of the most beautiful spots undersea, the Red Sea. First check the Sea Life Chart to learn about the Turkey fish, the Blue Spotted Ribbon Tailed Ray, the Masked Butterfly fish. A narrated introduction presents you with the dive conditions. The dive is in warm water with 40 feet visibility. We'll go down about 70 feet along a 60-foot sand bar and see some incredible sights, including a ship wreck. Press the Descend button when you are ready to go down. Happy diving.

The icon bar at the bottom of the screen allows the user to control the program. Depending on your position, different icons appear to help you navigate, such as those for Dive Info, World Map, Treasure Chest, Site Attractions, Sea Life Chart, Regional Map, Begin Dive, Topside Information, Descend, and Ascend. A help button and exit button are on every screen.

Oceans Below will encourage students to explore the undersea world. Its interactive nature and the narration will hold their attention. The information is not presented via text, but through narration and video. All the help is given with context-sensitive audio explanations.

Orchestra:
The Instruments Revealed

Time Warner Interactive Group, 2210 West Olive Avenue, Burbank, CA 91506-2626; 800/593-6334, 818/955-9999, 818/955-6499 (fax).
Price: $79.98.

Minimum Hardware Requirements:
Macintosh: System 6.0.5, 2MB RAM, 4.5MB minimum hard drive space, speakers or headphones.
Platform: Macintosh.
Documentation: Ten-page booklet in jewel case.
Technical Support: 800/565-TWIG.
Curriculum: Arts and Music.
Grade Level: Elementary, Middle, Senior High.

....

The Orchestra contains the full digital recording of "The Young Person's Guide to the Orchestra," composed by Benjamin Britten. The audio part of the CD-ROM is also playable on any compact disc player. The caliber of the musical recording is excellent and, depending on the audio playback equipment used, is well worth listening to. If you wish to just listen, be sure to access track two on the disc to avoid the data noise from track one.

In addition to the music, the CD-ROM has several sections that allow full exploration and understanding of the composer's work. The Theme and Variations section includes musical notation of key parts of the score and provides complete annotation to different parts of the piece.

The Instrument Catalog is a special section that illustrates and describes every instrument in the orchestra and gives the history of each. A musical sample by each instrument can be heard by clicking on the appropriate icon.

Another section is A Conducting Lesson, which allows the user to simulate picking up a baton and follow diagrams and examples for conducting an orchestra. In the Orchestration Lab, the user can choose a section of music and the instruments that will play it, then listen to the result. The final interactive section is the Arcade, a musical instruments quiz. Individual instruments play short musical examples and the listener tries to identify the instruments.

Installing the CD-ROM involves moving a copy of HyperCard 2.1 from the disc to the hard drive, and copying the Orchestra folder to the hard drive. Because the disc cannot play digital music at the same time a HyperCard stack is running, the stacks must run from the hard drive. This solution takes up a little space on the hard drive, but it allows the program to move forward much more efficiently.

The HyperCard interface allows quick and easy access to all parts of Orchestra. Moving from place to place is never a problem. If you are unfamiliar with HyperCard, there is a guided tour of the entire program through all of its sections. Open this tour directly from the CD-ROM itself. There is a separate Notebook for recording notes and a help file accessible from almost every part of the program.

Orchestra would be an invaluable part of any music curriculum. The quality of the sound, the interface, the screen design and the depth of content make this a very good disc for your collection.

The Oregon Trail

MECC, 6160 Summit Drive North, Minneapolis, MN 55430-4003; 800/685-6322, 612/569-1500, 612/569-1551 (fax).
Price: *$69.95; $79, classroom version.*
Minimum Hardware Requirements:
Macintosh: *System 7.0, 4MB RAM, CD-ROM drive, color monitor highly recommended.*
Platform: *Macintosh, MPC.*
Documentation: *Four-page booklet in jewel case. The classroom version comes with a teacher's binder containing lesson plans, activities, suggestions and more detailed operating instructions. There is also a printable 17-page user's guide on the CD-ROM*
Technical Support: *612/569-1678.*
Curriculum: *Social Studies.*
Grade Level: *Elementary, Middle, Senior High.*

....

The Oregon Trail has been one of the most successful educational programs since its introduction in 1975. This new CD-ROM version has many additional features, thanks to the amount of storage space available in the CD-ROM format.

Students use this program as a simulated wagon train trip from the Midwest to the Willamette Valley in Oregon, along a trail used by hundreds of real people in the 1800s. Actual towns, rivers, forts and other landmarks are incorporated into the program so that a knowledge of geography as well as history is important. Songs about the settlements along the trail can be played, and the maps and illustrations used in the program are taken from old photographs, paintings, lithographs and personal accounts.

Purchasing equipment and supplies at the start of the trail, bartering along the way, calculating miles traveled and the economics of food supplies and remaining bullets all combine to create valuable lessons in arithmetic as well as in critical thinking and decision-making. The student has a chance to stop and think about the consequences of any action plus assess the tools available to solve problems that occur. Since the simulation can be played with one player or several, it can be a tutorial or a collaborative group activity.

Above all, the simulation is fun. Things are happening all the time and there are so many variables that an individual or group of students can play many times with many different outcomes.

Organic Diversity
(*See* LIFEmap Series)

Our Earth (*See* Wonders of Learning CD-ROM Library)

Paper Bag Princess
(*See* Discis Books)

★ Picture Atlas of the World
The Software Toolworks Inc., 60 Leveroni

Court, Novato, CA 94949; 415/883-3000, 800/231-3088, 415/883-3303 (fax).
***Price:** $99.00.*
***Minimum Hardware Requirements:** DOS: IBM 286/compatible, DOS 4.0, MSCDEX 2.1, 2MB RAM, VGA monitor, CD-ROM drive, speakers, mouse.*
***Platform:** DOS.*
***Documentation:** 18-page user guide.*
***Technical Support:** 415/883-3000.*
***Curriculum:** Reference & Interdisciplinary.*
***Grade Level:** Elementary, Middle.*

....

The Picture Atlas of the World is a multimedia exploration of the countries of the world containing over 1,200 photographs, video clips, interactive maps, audio clips of native speakers, plus music, animation and text. With multimedia, a one-dimensional information resource becomes interactive and addictive.

Navigating Picture Atlas is easy. As the program opens, a friendly voice offers to lead a guided tour. This narrated journey guides you through the menus and offers suggestions for further exploration, indicating how one menu connects to another.

The main menu presents choices including Mapping Our World, World Map, Countries A-Z, Index, and Credits. Mapping Our World divides into three sections, Where in the World?, Round Earth on Flat Paper, and Spinning Through Day and Night. Together they provide an understanding of the concepts of mapping, longitude, latitude and time zones.

The World Map is an overview of the world's population, climates, continents and nations. Click on any continent to access the full screen shot of that continent and its countries. In turn, click on individual countries to narrow your search. At the country level, icons are used to access comprehensive articles about the country, a photo tour, full-motion video clips, traditional music, vital statistics, economic, cultural and demographic information—even railroad routes.

Scroll through the easy Countries A-Z listing and click on Germany, to learn about the Mosel Valley where Riesling grapes are harvested by hand for its famous wine. After a unique video of the cows' traditional autumn return to town from Bavaria's high mountains, a second video features the Mosel Valley.

An added benefit to the Picture Atlas is that in addition to saving or printing the text, the graphics, music and full-motion video clips can be saved to a disk and imported into a multimedia authoring program such as Linkway Live! for student use. Although Picture Atlas is designed for elementary and middle-school children, it can be used successfully with older students to involve them in learning about other countries. Watch out—it is truly addictive. Students will want to visit every country and listen to the language, check out the statistics, watch the videos and visit a national attraction or two.

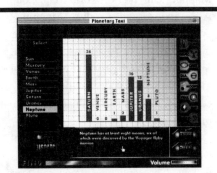

Planetary Taxi

The Voyager Company, 578 Broadway, New York, NY 10012; 212/431-5199, 212/431-5799 (fax). Also: One Bridge Street, Irvington, NY 10533. 800/446-2001, 914/591-6481 (fax).
Price: *$39.95.*
Minimum Hardware Requirements:
Macintosh: *Macintosh II, LC, System 7.0, 2.2MB available RAM, CD-ROM drive, color monitor.*
Platform: *Macintosh.*
Documentation: *Ten-page user's guide.*
Technical Support: *914/591-5500..*
Curriculum: *Science.*
Grade Level: *Elementary, Middle.*

....

Planetary Taxi is the second volume in the Visual Almanac Series from Apple's Multimedia Lab. It uses a game format to teach concepts of space, size and interplanetary relationships.

There are several facets to this program that should make it very popular with students trying to learn about the planets and their relationship to each other and to Earth.

First, there are some supplementary documents on the CD-ROM that can be opened with Excel, a spreadsheet program, and Word, a word processing program. One document describes the planets and some fascinating facts and puzzles about each one. Two documents let students calculate the relative size of the planets. The spreadsheet has all the calculations built in. For example, all you have to do is enter a size in inches for the Sun, and the program displays the relative sizes for all the other planets and the distance in feet and paces apart that they are.

The main part of Planetary Taxi is a game with three kinds of taxis to be driven around the galaxy. Picking up passengers and taking them places means knowing the answers to some questions such as, "Which planet has years that are shorter than Earth years?" or "Which distance is shorter—from Uranus to Mars, or Pluto to Saturn?" Answering questions correctly results in a trip through the galaxy, a happy passenger who tips well and the chance to get more passengers. All the action is coordinated by the dispatcher, a New York lady named Rita.

To help find the correct answer, there is a Planetary Info screen (also called the Postcard Rack, standing next to Rita's booth) with detailed information about each planet. There are graphs and charts to show comparative distances, sizes, moons, lengths of days and years, temperatures and so on. In addition, there are video clips, satellite and telescope photographs and narrated information about the planets.

The graphics are clever, bright, colorful and easy to read and understand. It would be hard to imagine any student not having fun with this program and learning a great deal about the solar system at the same time.

★ **Prehistoria**

Grolier Electronic Publishing, Inc.,

Sherman Turnpike, Danbury, CT 06816; 203/797-3530, 800/356-5590, 203/797-3130 (fax).
Price: *$69.95.*
Minimum Hardware Requirements:
Macintosh: *Macintosh LC/II, System 6.0.7, 2MB RAM, CD-ROM drive, 4MB minimum hard drive space, 256 color monitor;*
MPC: *386 20MHz/compatible, DOS 5.0, Windows 3.1, MSCDEX 2.21, 4MB RAM, VGA monitor, audio board, mouse.*
Platform: *Macintosh, MPC.*
Documentation: *Registration booklet in jewel case.*
Technical Support: *800/356-5590, Monday through Friday, 8:30 a.m. to 4:30 p.m. Eastern Time.*
Curriculum: *Science.*
Grade Level: *Middle, Senior High.*

....

Prehistoria is a superb disc that makes an excellent addition to any collection. It is difficult to cite any one element over any other, but clearly one of the major advantages is the identification of its source material. It can be very difficult sometimes to know where the contents of a CD-ROM come from, and this should be a concern for teachers and librarians who are using the material in an educational setting. Quality of data is of primary importance, and it is helpful to see the source of the Prehistoria content and a full list of names and credits. The source is the *Macmillan Illustrated Encyclopedia of Dinosaurs and Prehistoric Animals*, published by Marshall Editions Ltd. in England.

Using Prehistoria is easy, satisfying and intuitive. It is easy to install, only requiring that QuickTime (for the Mac version) and the program application are on the hard drive before beginning.

The opening screen of the program offers seven choices (or Features). The first is Gallery, which groups and displays similar types of animals. Here you can see at a glance the families of dinosaurs and prehistoric creatures, starting with seven basic groups. Clicking on a family leads to subgroups within each family until you arrive at a selection of individual animals. The screen for each individual animal is clearly laid out. The name with its meaning is across the top, with a speaker icon to click if you want to hear the name pronounced. There is a large, well-drawn picture of the animal and a tiny palette icon to click for another view of the animal. Another icon leads to the animal's zoological classification, and four icons at the left of the screen provide a view of other animals of the same type, the animal's position on a timeline, location of its fossil remains, its size relative to modern man and text to describe the animal more fully.

There are eleven major time periods in Prehistoria. By clicking on Time Tracker, you can go to any era and find the animals that lived in that era. Simulated maps of the world show an interesting progression of continental drift and the changing world.

Another Feature is a Search screen where the user can enter any word or combination of words to find an animal or more on any given topic. The fourth Feature is the Grolier Museum, which has eight "rooms." Each room can be explored and investigated. One room, for example, is the Baby Dinosaur room where there are such items as a video clip of scientists doing a cat scan on a fossilized dinosaur egg. The rooms have a combination of photographs, video clips, explanatory text and essays on various topics.

The Classifications Feature depicts each animal in its complete zoological hierarchy. Its class, order and family are given as well as the meaning of the animal's name. It summarizes and graphically depicts the information in a succinct manner.

The final Feature is the Creature Show, in which all 500 of the animals in Prehistoria are shown one after the other. It is like the grand finale of the circus, where all of the performers come out and parade before the audience. Each has a full-color illustration and detailed text description. The user can stop the show at any time to focus on an individual animal.

The color and sound, individual illustrations, skill used in moving the user from place to place, and depth of content combine to give this CD-ROM our very highest recommendation.

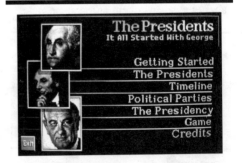

The Presidents:
It All Started With George

National Geographic Society, 1145 17th Street NW, Washington, DC, 20036; 800/368-2728, 301/921-1575 (fax).

Price: $99.

Minimum Hardware Requirements: DOS: *IBM 286/compatible, DOS 3.3, MSCDEX 2.1, 640K RAM, VGA monitor, CD-ROM drive, audio board, speakers, mouse.*

Platform: *DOS.*

Documentation: *16-page user guide.*

Technical Support: *800/342-4460.*

Curriculum: *Social Studies.*

Grade Level: *Elementary, Middle, Senior High.*

....

The Presidents is a multimedia presentation of the history about the presidency of the United States. It covers presidents, elections, political parties and the functions of the executive office. The program includes over 1,000 captioned images, 33 video clips, a multimedia timeline, famous presidential speeches, narrated photo essays, a presidential trivia game, a political party index, pop-up glossary, election facts, figures and maps.

The opening screen of The Presidents offers six options including Getting Started, The Presidents, Timeline, Political Parties, the Presidency, Game, and Credits. The first option, Getting Started, offers a narrated guided tour of the program, explains the button and makes suggestions for later navigation of the program.

Click on The Presidents to access an alphabetical list of presidents, then choose a president to see his title screen. Each president screen has a full-color picture, a characteristic quote, his term of office, political party, vice president and an interesting fact about the man. The user can click on an asterisk after the quote, the political party, and vice president to find more information.

Each title screen also has ten buttons to further navigate the program or to find more information about the president. Choices include options to go back to the main menu, the A-Z list of presidents, view photos of the president, look at his election record, listen to speeches, visit the multimedia timeline, read the president's biographical and historical information, view full-motion video clips or play the game.

The three sections, Timeline, Political Parties and The Presidency work together coherently to complement the presidents section, giving students a well-rounded view of the presidency and the men who held this office. The timeline begins with Washington and runs through George Bush. The menu bar on the top of the screen identifies which president was in office during the span of years listed on the bottom of the screen. The timeline has "hot spots" where the arrow cursor turns into a hand, designating an area to click on for more information. Clicking on these brings up video clips, more photographs and text about the event.

Political Parties lists the major political parties including Democratic, Democratic-Republican, Federalist, Republican, Whig and Third Parties, which includes all others, totaling over 50 parties. This is an excellent resource for identifying the lesser known political parties, such as Greenback, National Unity, Workers' World, Anti-Masonic or Free Soil.

Searching and navigating is easy, and buttons are consistent and allow the user to move seamlessly from one section to another. Students will find it fun to navigate this program to locate in-depth information about presidents and the presidency and to test their knowledge playing the game.

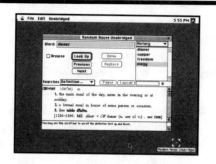

Random House Unabridged Dictionary, Second Edition

Random House Electronic Publishing, Third Floor, 201 E. 50th Street, New York, NY 10022-7703; 212/751-2600, 212/572-8700 (fax).
Price: *$79; $105, Canada.*
Minimum Hardware Requirements:
Macintosh: *SE/30, System 6.0.7, 2MB RAM, CD-ROM drive;* ***DOS:*** *IBM AT/compatible, DOS 3.3, 450K RAM, CD-ROM drive;* ***Windows:*** *IBM 286/compatible, 2MB RAM, Windows 3.1, MSCDEX, CD-ROM drive.*
Platform: *Macintosh, DOS, Windows.*
Documentation: *Four-page installation booklet in slip case.*
Technical Support: *801/228-9918, DOS; 801/226-9919, Windows; 801/228-9917, Mac, 7:00 a.m. to 6:00 p.m. Mountain Time.*
Curriculum: *Reference & Interdisciplinary.*
Grade Level: *Elementary, Middle, Senior High.*

....

The printed *Random House Unabridged Dictionary* has long been a favorite of big dictionary users. With over 315,000 words and definitions, it can answer nearly everything for the word fancier—everything, that is, until the CD-ROM version is tried for the first time!

The electronic version of the *Random House Unabridged Dictionary* loads quickly and easily onto a Macintosh or IBM/compatible computer. Versions for all the platforms are on the same CD-ROM disc. In the Macintosh version, the dictionary is available through the Apple menu, making it accessible to a user anytime during the use of another program. Since the dictionaries included with most word processors are considerably smaller, it adds quite a bit to those applications.

There are several notable features in the dictionary, in addition to its size and accessibility. The user can type any word, and the definition appears in a box on the lower half of the screen. If the word was typed incorrectly, the dictionary suggests a list of possible words. A wildcard feature lets the user type any word with missing letters, using a question mark (for one character) or an asterisk (for up to 30 characters). The dictionary shows every word that fits the request—a boon for poor spellers and crossword puzzle fans! An interesting feature is the Anagram function where users can type in any word and the dictionary provides a list of every word that can be formed from that single word.

About the only thing this dictionary does not do is pronounce the words. With that exception, it is comprehensive, easy-to-use and provides a myriad of search and look-up features that will please all levels of users.

Readers' Guide Abstracts

The H.W. Wilson Company, 950 University Avenue, Bronx, NY 10452; 800/367-6770,

718/588-8400, 718/590-1617 (fax).
Price: $1495 annual subscription.
Minimum Hardware Requirements:
DOS: *IBM 286/compatible, 640K RAM,*
DOS 3.1, MSCDEX, CD-ROM drive,
monochrome monitor. ***Macintosh:*** *Version*
due out Fall 1994.
Platform: *DOS.*
Documentation: *Wilsondisc teaching*
guide, user aid reference set, database
descriptions, quick reference guide.
Technical Support: *800/367-6770,*
Ext. 6004.
Curriculum: *Reference & Interdisciplinary.*
Grade Level: *Middle, Senior High.*

....

Readers' Guide Abstracts (RGA) indexes and abstracts about 240 periodicals—the same periodicals that are covered in the *Readers' Guide to Periodical Literature.* There are 67,000 abstracts added annually, with monthly updates. RGA also contains indexed and abstracted articles from the *New York Times* from 1983 to the present. Periodical coverage begins in January, 1983 for indexing and September, 1984 for abstracting.

The *Wilsondisc Teaching Guide*, which comes with Readers' Guide Abstracts (RGA), includes installation and customizing instructions, as well as how to use and teach with RGA. Wilson allows users to keep all out-of-date discs, and there is no additional charge for networking the discs in a single school district. For a nominal sum (telecommunications costs), users can search Readers' Guide online to get the latest information between updates.

The disc offers three levels of searching. First, a menu-driven level searches by single

subjects with an onscreen thesaurus. A fill-in-the-blanks, multiple keyword subject search is made with Boolean operators, including searching the abstract field. There is also an advanced command-driven search mode.

The H.W. Wilson Company has been in the indexing and abstracting business a long time and has refined and honed its information access skills over many years. The print index has existed since 1904, and the extension of that expertise into the electronic world is worthwhile. All data can be downloaded to a disc or printed, and titles can be tagged to indicate local holdings. The abstracts that accompany each entry are about 250 words in length, substantially more than in other indexes. A free 90-day trial offer is available, or a 60-day trial offer with a hardware loan.

Resource/One

University Microfilms International, (UMI),
300 N. Zeeb Road, Ann Arbor, MI 48106;
800/521-0600, 313/761-4700, 313/761-
1204 (fax).
Price: *$799 (quarterly), $1199 (school*
year), $1599 (monthly).
Minimum Hardware Requirements:
IBM 286/compatible: *640K RAM, DOS*
3.2, MSCDEX 2.1, hard drive, CD-ROM
drive, monochrome monitor.
Platform: *DOS.*
Documentation: *User's guide, keyboard*
template, point-of-use cards, controlled
vocabulary list.
Technical Support: *800/521-0600,*
Ext. 2513.
Curriculum: *Reference & Interdisciplinary.*
Grade Level: *Middle, Senior High.*

....

Resource/One indexes articles in more than 130 general-interest magazines, and the *New York Times Currents Events Edition* since 1988 and *USA Today* since 1991. Short abstracts are also provided for each citation and the discs are updated monthly.

It offers two levels of searching, providing ease of access for the beginner and more sophisticated access for the experienced user, with features such as word truncation and proximity. Both levels have access to Boolean search operators, AND, OR and NOT. There is a keyword index, and all twenty fields are labeled and searchable. Individual titles can be tagged to indicate local holdings. All citations can be downloaded to disc or printed.

Microfiche is available for full text of indexed articles. There is no extra charge for up to four network users.

★ The San Diego Zoo Presents...The Animals!

The Software Toolworks Inc. 60 Leveroni Court, Novato, CA 94949; 415/883-3000, 800/231-3088, 415/883-3303 (fax).
Price: $119.95.
Minimum Hardware Requirements:
Macintosh: *Mac II or Quadra, System*

6.0.7 4MB RAM, 12-inch RGB monitor, CD-ROM drive; ***MPC:*** *IBM 386/ compatible, DOS 3.1, Windows 3.1, 2MB RAM, SVGA monitor, CD-ROM drive, audio board, speakers, mouse.*
Platform: *Macintosh, DOS, MPC.*
Documentation: *32-page booklet.*
Technical Support: *415/883-3000, 6:00 a.m. to 5:00 p.m., Pacific Time.*
Curriculum: *Science.*
Grade Level: *Elementary, Middle.*

The San Diego Zoo Presents...The Animals! is a colorful collection of animal sounds, sights and statistics presented in the concept of biomes, a combination of biological, geographical and climate features. Targeted to younger children, it explores the delicate relationship between animals, man and the environment using multimedia. It contains 80 video clips with synchronized sound, totaling more than 60 minutes of motion video, two and a half hours of audio, over 1,300 color photographs and more than 2,500 pages of animal and habitat description, articles and scientific data. Biome organization of the zoo helps emphasize three important issues in the world today; that is, all life is connected, people affect habitats and many species are endangered.

The program's main menu is a map of the zoo's different exhibits, such as Biome exhibits, Kid's Corner, Storybook Theater, Nursery, Zoo Gardens, and Center for Reproduction of Endangered Species, and Guided Tours. For example, by clicking on the Tundra biome, you are taken to the zoo's tundra exhibit to hear and learn about the region and the animals that live in that biome. Each exhibit has Exploration buttons offering additional information to view at your present site or you can jump to its home exhibit. As the mouse slides over a button, its purpose is highlighted in a small pop-up window.

There are multiple ways to travel around the zoo. You can navigate from one exhibit to the next within any biome, tour another location, press buttons to walk through the exhibits in order, or press the exhibit jump button to move instantaneously to any exhibit. Location labels in the upper left corner of each exhibit help you remember your present location.

Installation is easy; the Windows version takes only a few minutes. A narrated guided tour offers an explanation of how to navigate and explains general features of the program.

The Animals! is an exciting place to visit— from the amazing video of a giraffe's birth to the tender story of raising Gordy Gorilla— nature comes alive! The San Diego Zoo's commitment to natural habitats and reverence for animals, as well as its mission to educate young people in these beliefs, is clearly demonstrated in this delightful CD-ROM.

Scary Poems for Rotten Kids
(*See* Discis Books)

Scribner's Writers Series

Charles Scribner Sons, 866 Third Avenue, New York, NY 10022; 212/702-9691, 800/257-5755 (orders).
Price: *$595.00.*
Minimum Hardware Requirements:
Windows: *IBM 386/compatible, DOS 3.3, Windows 3.1, 2MB RAM, 1MB minimum hard drive space, VGA monitor, mouse.*
Platform: *DOS, Windows, Macintosh.*
Documentation: *141-page manual; reference cards.*
Technical Support: *800/342-1338.*
Curriculum: *Language Arts.*
Grade Level: *Senior High.*

The Scribner's Writers Series on CD-ROM contains 510 essays about well-known literary figures taken from *Scribner's Writers Series.* The full texts of *American Writers* and *British Writers* are included plus limited selections from *European Writers* (about 88 entries), *Latin American Writers* (about 16 entries), *Modern American Women Writers* (33 entries), *African-American Writers* (16 entries), *Ancient Writers* (18 entries), *Science Fiction Writers* (95 entries) and *Supernatural Fiction Writers* (two entries). The essays contain biographical information and critical commentary on individual authors.

The program runs under Windows, which allows easy installation. The opening screen offers several choices to search the contents including Name, Genre, Time Period, Nationality, and Quick Start. Click on any of the first four choices to view an alphabetical list. The Genre button divides the authors into the categories of autobiography/memories, children's/juvenile, criticism, essay, journalism, nonfiction, novels, philosophy, plays, poetry, religion and short stories. The

Time Period button lists writers by the century in which they wrote. The Nationality button lists authors according to their country of origin. There are 37 nationalities listed.

You can also find writers by clicking on the Index button on the menu bar at the top of the screen. A window of All Topics opens. Begin typing the author's name and the index moves to that location. You can limit your search by genre, language, nationality, race, sex and time period. Users can also search by word or phrase and can perform more complex searches using Boolean operators or combining category and keyword searches.

The author entry screen is attractive with easy-to-read large type, which includes links to other articles and bibliographies. Selecting Bookmark holds the reader's place within articles. Annotate allows users to enter notes as they read and mark annotated articles with a special icon for future use. A full topic or a part of it can be printed or saved to disk.

The program features in-depth, well-written essays that have always been used by teachers and students in print format. Now in electronic version, the information is more available and easily accessible, especially through a network.

Time Warner Interactive Group, 2210 West Olive Avenue, Burbank, CA 91506-2626; 800/593-6334, 818/955-9999, 818/955-6499 (fax).
***Price:** $79.99.*
Minimum Hardware Requirements:
Macintosh:** Macintosh II or LC, System 6.0.7, 4MB RAM, CD-ROM drive.* ***DOS: *IBM 286 16MHz/compatible, Windows 3.0, MSCDEX, 4MB RAM, CD-ROM drive; VGA Plus monitor, audio board and speakers, mouse.*
***Platform:** Macintosh, DOS.*
***Documentation:** Eight-page booklet in jewel case.*
***Technical Support:** 800/565-TWIG.*
***Curriculum:** Social Studies.*
***Grade Level:** Senior High.*

....

Seven Days in August is an interactive documentary that describes the week in August 1961 when the Berlin Wall was built. Particularly relevant for today's students because of the wall's recent demise (and the accompanying events that signaled the end to the Cold War), Seven Days in August provides a thorough look at critical events that shaped the next thirty years in world history.

The disc is easily loaded and requires no software installation on the hard drive. Opening the program leads to a screen with six choices. The user can look at authentic photographs of the building of the wall. The section called Berliners shows the effects of that enterprise on the people of Berlin, in both the eastern and western sections of the city. Profiles describes seven key political leaders of the time, from John F. Kennedy to Willy Brandt.

Seven Days in August

The final main section is called Roundtable and has several well-known news commentators discussing the events and their after-effects. These commentators were on the scene or reporting the events during the building of the wall and subsequently at its demise.

Seven Days in August is another example of a CD-ROM that takes a thorough and complete look at a very small segment of history, encouraging complete understanding of an era.

Seven Natural Wonders, Volume Two

InterOptica Publishing Limited, 300 Montgomery Street, Suite 201, San Francisco, CA 94104; 415/788-8788, 415/ 788-8886 (fax)
Price: *$99.95*
Minimum Hardware Requirements:
Macintosh II or LC, System 6.0.7, 4MB RAM, CD-ROM drive, color monitor.
Platform: *Macintosh, Windows.*
Documentation: *None.*
Technical Support: *212/941-2988.*
Curriculum: *Science.*
Grade Level: *Middle, Senior High.*

Seven Natural Wonders is a Sierra Club Electronic Guide that provides information in the form of text, photographs and drawings, animated guides, and maps about seven of the world's most amazing natural features or animals. From Mt. Everest to the Blue Whale, this disc describes the history and ecology of each natural wonder.

The disc loads quickly and easily, requiring only that you drag the folder to the hard disk and launch the program from the hard disk. The opening screen shows a map with the name of each wonder located, along with its icon. The seven wonders are Mt. Everest, the Blue Whale, the Wildebeest Migration, the Indian Monsoon, the Great Barrier Reef, the Grand Canyon and the Amazon Rainforest. This list, though somewhat unusual—not all animals nor all natural features—does show a nice balance of large-scale natural phenomena. Users may choose a guided tour, a geologic timeline to locate each of the wonders in its time frame, or a multimedia quiz.

Each natural wonder has many different areas to explore, including an Overview, Facts and Figures, Geography, Video, Animation, Maps, and Glossary. Each also has sections relating specifically to the wonder, such as Climatology for the Indian Monsoon, and Biology and Predators for the Wildebeest Migration.

Presumably because of the Sierra Club influence, there is a decided environmental perspective to this disc, with repeated reminders of the importance of the seven wonders and their role on our planet.

A Silly Noisy House
The Voyager Company, 578 Broadway,

New York, NY 10012; 212/431-5199,
212/431-5799 (fax). Also: One Bridge
Street, Irvington, NY 10533.
800/446-2001, 914/591-6481 (fax).
Price: *$59.95.*
Minimum Hardware Requirements:
Macintosh: *System 6.0.7, 2MB RAM,*
color monitor, hard disk, amplified
speakers or headphones; ***Windows:***
IBM 486, 25MHz/compatible, DOS 5.0,
Windows 3.1, MSCDEX, 4MB RAM,
SVGA monitor, audio board, speakers.
Platform: *Macintosh, Windows.*
Documentation: *Seven-page booklet*
in jewel case.
Technical Support: *914/591-5500.*
Curriculum: *Storybook.*
Grade Level: *Primary, Elementary.*

....

Based on a story by Peggy Weil, A
Silly Noisy House is a delightful tour
through a house full of surprises—songs,
animation, rhymes, sound effects and a
myriad of special effects, including secret
passageways! There is no text in the main
program at all, which means even the
youngest non-reader can explore the Silly
Noisy House. Installation is simple—
copy the folder "A Silly Noisy House" to
the hard disk. Launch the program by
double-clicking on the Silly Noisy House
icon on the hard disk.

When the program opens, the user is outside the house. Clicking the mouse moves
you to the door of the house, into the front
hall and then into all the rooms of the house.
Random events occur when various objects
are clicked. The same event does not
always occur, so the element of surprise is
always present. Objects can sing, recite

nursery rhymes, tell little stories and riddles
or lead you into secret passageways.

You can move around a room by clicking
at the edge of the picture where the sideways arrow appears. You can go outside the
house by clicking on a window, and you
can return to the front of the house from any
point by clicking on any house, even if it's
a picture of a house on a bath towel in the
bathroom!

The quality of sound throughout the disc
is superb, as is the color and caliber of
drawing. The sheer number of events hidden throughout A Silly Noisy House keeps
the attention of every user, not just small
children. This animated storybook has set a
high standard for others to follow and
should be a favorite family and classroom
treasure for years to come.

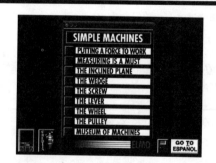

Simple Machines

Science for Kids, Inc., 9950 Concord
Church Road, Lewisville, NC 27023;
910/945-9000, 910/945-2500 (fax).
Price: *$199.*
Minimum Hardware Requirements:
Macintosh II or LC, System 6.0.7, 2.5MB
RAM, CD-ROM drive, color monitor.
Platform: *Macintosh, MPC.*
Documentation: *Teacher's Edition*

includes a 56-page teacher's manual, student science journal pages (black line masters), and a science lab kit.
Technical Support: *910/945-9000.*
Curriculum: *Science.*
Grade Level: *Elementary, Middle.*

....

Simple Machines is an introduction to the physical sciences for children aged 8-14. This very complete package includes teacher's materials as well as some simple lab tools—a spring scale, carrier, pulley, and weighing pan. The CD-ROM uses a group of cartoon young people to work on various scientific problems.

When the disc is launched, ELMO (Electronic Learning Module) greets the user to offer choices. ELMO is a personal digital assistant that looks like a large remote control unit. ELMO has a digitized voice and can guide you through choices and often gives background information on the current subject.

To begin, the user can select any of the six simple machines that are covered in these lessons: inclined plane, wedge, screw, lever, wheel and axle, or pulley. Simple drawings with simple animations explain the basic principles of each machine, and objects are shown that use that machine. For example, in a room full of objects, clicking on one of them shows its internal workings and how the machine works in that object (like a piano uses levers to activate the hammers to sound the tones when the keys are pressed).

The user can also look at ancient tools and machines and see the development history of each of these simple machines. Within the story of each machine is its own history and

where it was developed, building in a subtle geography and history lesson.

The supplementary materials that are included in Simple Machines gives teachers, parents and students plenty to work with in a classroom, lab, library setting or at home. The lessons on the disc are also accessible in either English or Spanish, so it would make a nice tutorial program for students in a bilingual program.

Simple Machines is created in Macromind Director, software with excellent animation and graphics capabilities, and there are nice touches in the program as a result of those capabilities. Color, sound and graphics are all very good. This disc, like many others having extensive multimedia capabilities, will run better on a CD-ROM drive rated at 300kps or higher.

SIRS Researcher
SIRS, P.O. Box 2348, Boca Raton, FL 33427-2348; 407/994-0079, 407/994-4704 (fax).
Price: *$ 1,250.*
Minimum Hardware Requirements:
DOS: *IBM 386/compatible, DOS 3.3, MSCDEX 2.0, 512KB RAM, VGA monitor.*
Platform: *DOS.*

Documentation: 40-page manual; reference cards.
Technical Support: 800/426-7477.
Curriculum: Reference & Interdisciplinary.
Grade Level: Middle, Senior High.

....

SIRS, a collection of thousands of full-text articles from over 800 domestic and international newspapers, magazines, journals and U.S. government documents, covers important events and issues in the physical and social sciences. In addition, some articles include charts, tables, graphs, maps and other graphics. Taken from the popular print edition of *SIRS*, it contains articles published in *Social/Critical Issues and Science* volumes since 1989 and the *Global Perspectives* volume since 1991. When full text is not available, abstracts are provided by the SIRS staff.

The opening screen includes choices for Library of Congress Subject Headings, Article Title Search, Keyword Search or Quit. The choice of Library of Congress Subject Headings offers an alphabetical listing of headings. The user can tag articles to print bibliographic citations, print partial or full text or download a section or full article to a disk. Article line numbers help pinpoint specific information and can be removed by a toggle function.

Choosing Article Title Search brings up a list of general topics that correspond to the SIRS print volumes. Keyword Searches displays an input screen to develop Boolean searches, AND, OR, NOT for up to three words. Help screens are available by pressing the function key, <F1>, and include a section on how to cite articles in SIRS according to Turabian, MLA and APA formats.

SIRS Researcher is a popular reference title for students due to its full-text content coverage and easy search mechanism. The topics are right on target for student research, including Aging, AIDS, Crime, Ethnic Groups, Drugs, Health, Human Rights, Sports, Sexuality, Death and Dying, Pollution, Technology, World Affairs and more.

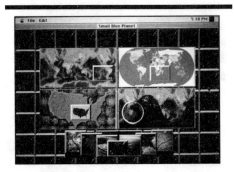

Small Blue Planet:
The Electronic Satellite Atlas

Now What Software, 2303 Sacramento Street, San Francisco, CA 94115; 800/322-1954, 415/885-1689, 415/922-1265 (fax).
Price: $79.95.
Minimum Hardware Requirements:
Macintosh: Macintosh II or LC; System 6.0.7; 4MB RAM; CD-ROM drive.
Platform: Macintosh, MPC.
Documentation: Six-page booklet in jewel case.
Tech. Support: 818/992-8484.
Curriculum: Reference & Interdisciplinary.
Grade Level: Middle, Senior High.

....

The Small Blue Planet is an electronic atlas that uses real-life photographs to show the earth in different configurations. Opening the atlas requires dragging the application to the hard disk so that the program can run from the hard disk while the images are taken from the CD-ROM. From then, it's easy to click on the appropriate tool to select different map configurations and settings. The Control Panel, which comes up at the right of the screen, includes buttons for accessing annotations, latitude and longitude readouts, compass directions, magnifying images on the screen, and more.

The available maps in Small Blue Planet include a Global Relief Map, a World Political Map, the Chronosphere, and the USA Relief Map. There is also a Satellite Gallery, which includes images gathered by remote-sensing devices.

The Global Relief Map was created by the National Oceanic and Atmospheric Administration (NOAA). It can be displayed side by side with the Political Map to compare features and locations. This is done using the Inset Button on the Control Panel. The World Political Map is up to date as of January 1, 1993. When the Inset Button is pressed in this map view, atlas statistics, ecological and landscape information, and historical information for each country are displayed.

The USA Relief Map provides aerial views of all parts of the United States, and the Red Dot Button will bring up aerial photographs of metropolitan areas. Atlas, landscape, and historical information can then be displayed for each city.

The Chronosphere is a unique feature that allows the viewer to see an entire day and night across the entire globe. The map across the background moves, with day and night reflected as shadows across the map. A spinning globe in the foreground repeats the same information in a slightly different way. From

any point on the map, the viewer can select the time of day and see what time it is in any other part of the world at the same moment. It automatically adjusts for Daylight Savings Time and can also display nighttime artificial illumination as seen by a satellite.

The wealth of information available in this atlas combined with its ease of use and added features, such as the Chronosphere, make it a useful reference tool.

Software Toolworks World Atlas

The Software Toolworks, Inc., 60 Leveroni Court, Novato, CA 94949; 800/231-3088, 415/883-3000, 415/883-3303 (fax).
Price: *$69.95*
Minimum Hardware Requirements:
Macintosh: *Macintosh II or LC, System 6.0.7, 4MB RAM, hard drive, CD-ROM drive, RGB monitor;* **DOS:** *386 16MHz/ compatible, DOS 5.0, MSCDEX 2.2, 1MB RAM, CD-ROM drive, SVGA monitor, audio board and speakers, mouse;* **MPC Level 1:** *386 25MHz/compatible, DOS 5.0, Windows 3.1, MSCDEX 2.21, 4MB RAM, CD-ROM drive, SVGA monitor, audio board and speakers, mouse.*
Platform: *Macintosh, DOS, MPC.*
Documentation: *Online manual included on the disc.*

Technical Support: 415/883-3000.
Curriculum: Reference & Interdisciplinary.
Grade Level: Middle, Senior High.

....

The Software Toolworks World Atlas is a basic atlas with maps of each section of the world, country and state information, national flags and anthems, and photographs and video footage from each country.

Each section or area of the world can be displayed as a political map or a topographical map with colors clearly delineating various geographic features. The information about each country—or capital city—appears in a separate text window that can be printed out. It is a little confusing that you can print only from the main window and not from the text window, even though there is a file menu on the text window. The information describes people, health, politics and government, travel, the economy, language and currency for each country.

There are usually ten photographs for each country and a short video clip of highlights in that country. The resolution and clarity of the photographic and video images depends on the caliber of your hardware and system—if you have an older CD-ROM drive, the video footage is very slow and jerky.

One of the most interesting features of World Atlas is its ability to create "statmaps," maps showing statistical information of the area under investigation. Characteristics such as population density, agricultural products, and GNP can be graphically depicted by showing pertinent areas on a map in different colors or shades of color. A similar feature is the graphing

capability of World Atlas. You can select from a list of economic, political, agricultural, or statistical topics and build graphs showing the top 15 countries or areas. This kind of visual information leads to greater exploration and arouses curiosity about similar topics. Who grows the most cocoa? Which country has the highest birth rate?

For basic country information, World Atlas is a complete and well put-together package. The enhancements (photographs, video, statmaps, and graphs) make it a worthwhile product.

Space Shuttle

The Software Toolworks, Inc., 60 Leveroni Court, Novato, CA 94949; 800/231-3088, 415/883-3000, 415/883-3303 (fax).
Educational/Library Edition available from Follett Library Book Company, 4506 Northwest Highway, Routes 14 & 31, Crystal Lake, IL 60014-7393. 815/455-1100, 815/477-9303 (fax).
Price: $49.95; $99.95, Educational/Library Edition.
Minimum Hardware Requirements:
Macintosh: *Macintosh II, LC, System 6.0.7, 4MB RAM, hard drive, CD-ROM drive, RGB monitor;* ***DOS:*** *386 16MHz/compatible, DOS 5.0, MSCDEX*

2.2, 1MB RAM, CD-ROM drive, SVGA monitor, audio board and speakers, mouse; **MPC Level 1:** *386 25MHz/compatible, DOS 5.0, Windows 3.1, MSCDEX 2.21, 4MB RAM, CD-ROM drive, SVGA monitor, audio board and speakers, mouse.* **Platform:** *Macintosh, DOS, MPC.* **Documentation:** *Educational/Library Edition contains Space Shuttle, by Bill Yenne, and an educator's resource guide.* **Technical Support:** *415/883-3000, The Software Toolworks; 800/323-3397, Follett.* **Curriculum:** *Science.* **Grade Level:** *Middle, Senior High.*

....

Space Shuttle is a complete look at the U.S. space program, with detailed information about the space program, all 53 manned space flights, astronaut preparation and training, and space orbiting vehicles. It is well done, with a straightforward interface, good NASA photographs and video segments, and excellent simulations of the actual training programs and space flights.

The opening sequence of Space Shuttle sets the tone for the program. A "tour" begins at Mission Control in Houston, Texas. As a control to change screens or to move from one section of the program to another, the Personal Digital Assistant (PDA) is a nice touch. This control has the look and feel of a sophisticated remote control, such as ones used to control television sets and VCRs. Selecting the Overview or Training buttons on the PDA lets you see the Mission Control facilities and training rooms, with classes in session. Since QuickTime videos are usually shown on a

small section of the monitor screen, this is disguised in Space Shuttle by showing the QuickTime videos on a "projection screen" in the training room itself. There are discussions of the equipment used during flights, the training requirements and topics such as weightlessness, working in space and various crew duties.

The student can also select any one of the 53 space flights and see video clips of the flight, listen to broadcasts from crew members and Mission Control, and read about scientific experiments or projects conducted during each flight. Clicking another button moves directly to drawings and illustrations of the different Shuttles or Orbiting Vehicles (O-V). Cut-away views show all areas and functions of the spacecraft.

The Educational/Library edition comes with two books, *Space Shuttle*, by Bill Yenne, and an educator's resource guide. Space Shuttle is a large, four-color book with excellent photographs of the shuttle flights and personnel. The educator's resource guide has nine lessons and worksheets for students, with an answer key for teachers. It also contains indexes to all of the space shuttle information and a list of resources for further reading and research.

Aside from the interest students have in the space program and the actual space flights, there is a lot of information on this disc. Calculations, projections and evaluations can all be a part of the learning process as students research, plan and assess the space flights and the work that was accomplished during each. It would make an interesting counterpart to a disc such as the Oregon Trail, in which students are asked to make decisions about the materials needed for that long trip.

Sports Illustrated 1994 Multimedia Sports Almanac

StarPress Multimedia, Inc., 303 Sacramento Street 2nd Floor, San Francisco, CA 94111; 415/274-8383.
Price: $60.
Minimum Hardware Requirements:
MPC: IBM/386 compatible, 33MHz, 4MB RAM, SVGA monitor, sound board, CD-ROM drive, Windows 3.1, DOS 5.0.
Macintosh: Macintosh II Series or Performa, System 7.0, 4MB RAM, color monitor, CD-ROM drive.
Platform: Macintosh, MPC.
Documentation: Eight-page user guide in disc case.
Technical Support: 900/555-7827 (first minute is free).
Curriculum: Sports.
Grade Level: Middle, Senior High.

....

Remember the sports highlights of 1993? Dallas demolished Buffalo in the Super Bowl. Jordan led the Bulls to their third straight title. Soccer fever kicked in as U.S. planned to host the '94 World Cup, and Brett, Ryan and Fisk retired from baseball and headed for the Hall of Fame. These stories and many more are presented in text, video, sound and graphics in the 1994 Multimedia Sports Almanac.

Sports Illustrated 1994 Multimedia Sports Almanac reviews the past 12 months of sports in-depth. It includes the full text of 1993 *Sports Illustrated* magazine (minus the swimsuit issue), the 1,200-page SI 1994 Sports Almanac, more than 450 color photos, year-in-review video segments and tons of statistics.

The main menu offers five choices: to search the full-text of *Sports Illustrated*; to view the Year in Review, a video recap of the year's sports events; to search the library, which contains the indexes of photos, videos and articles; to play the Ultimate Sports Trivia Challenge with over 300 questions to test your knowledge; to search for sports information.

Icons are positioned across the top of the screen to exit the program, select the sound level or turn animation on or off, print an article, chart or list, get help and search for a specific player or team. The Search function allows you to search all the articles and tables for the occurrence of any word or name. A compass icon indicates your location in the program. Click to jump to another screen. Foot tracks icon provides a list of previously viewed screens.

Sports enthusiasts will love this disc, as will students researching sports figures, teams and events

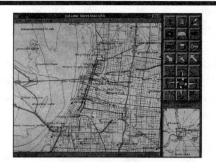

Street Atlas

DeLorme Mapping, Lower Main Street, P.O. Box 298, Freeport, ME 04032; 207/865-1234, 800/452-5931, 207/865-9291 (fax).

Price: $125, direct; $169, retail.
Minimum Hardware Requirements:
*Windows: IBM 286/compatible, Windows
3.0, 2MB RAM, VGA monitor, CD-ROM
drive, mouse.*
Platform: *Macintosh, Windows.*
Documentation: *Six-page fold-out booklet.*
Technical Support: *207/865-7098.*
Curriculum: *Reference & Interdisciplinary.*
Grade Level: *Middle, Senior High.*

....

Street Atlas USA is a comprehensive, detailed street-level map of the entire United States including highways, state routes, streets, back roads and their names, lakes, ponds, rivers and streams. It contains over one million maps based on the Census Bureau's TIGER (Topological Integrated Geographic Encoding and Reference) maps, embellished with contracted and in-house data sources. Locations can be found by place name, telephone exchange or by zip code. Once a site is on the screen, scroll around the area, zooming to see street names. Or, copy a map to a word processor or graphics program.

The opening screen displays a color map of the United States. Using a mouse, you zoom in on your selected area. Scroll around by clicking on different compass points. Zoom in and out using different levels of magnitude displayed on the side button. One click finds a location by area code and exchange, zip code or place name, and displays a map in full color. For example, type in 10607 and you'll view the southwest section of White Plains, New York. Type 914 area code and limit it to the 723 exchange, and the program zooms in on Scarsdale, New York. From there you can

search the specific street name you want. Almost all the streets searched are there, except sometimes in a newly developed area. DeLorme Mapping plans to continually update the program.

Buttons on the side of the screen allow the user to navigate the program easily. With a little help from teachers, even young students can learn to locate their streets, neighborhoods or towns to support social studies activities.

Tale of Benjamin Bunny
(*See* Discis Books)

Tale of Peter Rabbit
(*See* Discis Books)

Talking Storybook Series
*New Media Schoolhouse, Box 390, 69
Westchester Avenue, Pound Ridge, NY
10576; 800/672-6002, 914/764-0104 (fax).*
Price: *$69 each.*
Hardware Minimum Requirements:
Macintosh: *System 6.0.7, 2MB RAM, 8-bit
color monitor;* **DOS:** *IBM PC/compatible,
DOS 3.1, MSCDEX 2.1, 640K RAM, VGA
monitor.*
Platform: *Macintosh, MPC (Beauty & the*

Beast, Wind in the Willows are Macintosh only.)
Documentation: *Eight-page booklet in jewel case.*
Technical Support: *800/672-6002.*
Curriculum*: Language Arts, Storybook.*
Grade Level*: Primary, Elementary, Middle, Senior High.*

(Series includes 20,000 Leagues Under the Sea, Adventures of Pinocchio, Beauty and the Beast, and Wind in the Willows.)

This series of talking storybooks includes some all-time classics and old favorites. Each story shows sequences in pictures across the top of the screen with the text below, while explanatory material (if requested) appears at the bottom of the screen. In the text under the pictures there are words in gray italics. A click on a gray word retrieves a definition, causes the word to be pronounced and the definition read. Each storybook has a different number of words defined in the context of the story, ranging from 100 in Wind in the Willows to over 450 in Pinocchio and 20,000 Leagues.

There are animation sequences in the pictures. For example, in Wind in the Willows, there are animations hidden on every one of the 30 pages. Beauty and the Beast and Pinocchio have "Living Pages," which contain a number of hidden animated surprises. The reader can access a Living Page directly from the Chapters menu or just wait for it to come along in sequence. In 20,000 Leagues Under the Sea, the Living Page is actually an underwater sequence in which the reader can follow the diver and look at the special fish encountered. Clicking the

mouse activates four choices labeled Nomenclature, Physical Description, Habitat, and Natural Selection. Choosing one of these gives information about that particular fish. This adds an unusual educational dimension to this storybook.

Finally, there is a quiz (called "Questions" in Pinocchio) for reading comprehension at the end of each story. There are multiple-choice questions for each section or chapter in the story.

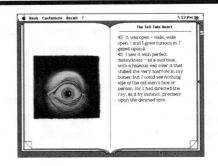

The Tell-Tale Heart

Discis Knowledge Research Inc., 45 Sheppard Avenue East, Suite 410, Toronto, Ontario M2N 5W9, Canada; 800/567-4321, 416/250-6537, 416/250-6540 (fax).
Price: *$59.95.*
Minimum Hardware Requirements:
Macintosh: *System 6.0.5 (including System 7), 1MB RAM for black and white, 2MB RAM for color, CD-ROM drive, keyboard and hard disk not required.*
Platform: *Macintosh.*
Documentation: *12-page booklet in jewel case. A separate teacher handbook is available for $34.95, as well as the combination of disc and handbook for a special price of $89.95.*

Technical Support: 800/567-4321.
Curriculum: Language Arts.
Grade Level: Middle, Senior High.

....

This is the classic story by Edgar Allen Poe, with all the features we have come to expect from a Discis product. Installation is quick and easy, and the program runs with the easiest of interfaces, not even requiring a keyboard.

There are two separate and complete readings of the story—one a complete dramatic reading, and the other also a complete reading of the story but with added questions and commentary to stimulate thinking and group discussion.

The program's complete text is in English, but the phrased reading of the book can be customized to Spanish, and the grammar and parts of speech can also be in Spanish.

All Discis Books have default settings that enable the student to work with the text in various ways. For example, a single click on a word results in its pronunciation. A double-click also brings up the pronunciation, but it is divided into syllables. Pressing and holding the mouse button down results in the pronunciation and an explanation (or definition) of the word. Each of these three actions also results in the word being added to the Recall list, so that a teacher, parent or the student can review the selected words. Similar effects are used for clicking on pictures, page corners and sentence speakers. All these features can be customized to the user's own needs.

This disc is a good tool to introduce students to the short story format, to Poe's works in general or to study this story in considerable detail. Discis does stories

about as well as anyone in the market today, and this classic horror story is no exception.

Thomas' Snowsuit
(*See* Discis Books)

★ Time Almanac 1993
Compact Publishing Inc., 5141 MacArthur Boulevard NW, Washington, DC 20016; 800/964-1518, 202/244-6363, 202/244-6363 (fax).
Price: $99.95.
Minimum Hardware Requirements: MPC: IBM 386/compatible, DOS 3.1, Windows 3.1, 3MB RAM, 1MB minimum hard drive space, SVGA monitor, CD-ROM drive, audio board, speakers, mouse; Macintosh: LC System 7.0, 4MB RAM, color monitor.
Platform: Macintosh, DOS, MPC.
Documentation: 25-page user guide; teacher activity booklet.
Technical Support: 800/964-1518.
Curriculum: Reference & Interdisciplinary.
Grade Level: Middle, Senior High.

....

Time Almanac, a news and current events reference source, contains 20,000 articles, more than 60 minutes of video and 1,000 charts, photos, covers and maps. The 1993 edition features the full text of *TIME Magazine* from 1989 through January 4, 1993, selected articles from 1983 through to 1989, plus the 1992 *CIA Factbook* and the new directory of the 103rd Congress.

The Contents screen or main menu offers several topical choices to navigate the program including Weekly Issues, Portraits, Newsquest and more.

Forty-two short full-motion videos highlight major *TIME* stories from 1989 to 1992, including Bill Clinton Campaigns for President, Police Acquitted in Rodney King Case, the Los Angeles Riots, Germans Celebrate Reunification, Tiananmen Square, Berlin Wall and Gulf War Victory.

The Multimedia Portraits section features famous *TIME* cover story profiles and includes John F. Kennedy, Martin Luther King, Richard Nixon, Albert Einstein, Adolph Hitler, Henry Ford, Dwight Eisenhower, as well as Women of the Year. These in-depth portraits contain videos, photos and *TIME* magazine articles. Nixon's portrait features two videos, the "Checkers" Speech and his resignation, eighteen captioned photos and a series of 18 articles covering his political career.

Menus and buttons make locating information easy and keywords can be combined to search for specific articles. A list appears with links to additional information in video, photos, covers, charts and maps. The menu bar at the top of the screen provides access to the features of the program. The toolbar offers easy mouse access to commonly-used Menu Bar functions, such as close, print, save, copy, annotate, search, put a bookmark, as well as navigation buttons.

Newsquest challenges users' knowledge of people and events in the news. Each quiz consists of 20 questions drawn from articles in *TIME Magazine* from 1989 to 1992. Getting the answers to the questions right is only part of the challenge. The ultimate goal for each quiz is to identify the source of the *TIME Magazine* quote, which is revealed letter by letter in the Quote box at the bottom of the screen.

"Researching with the *TIME Almanac*" is an activity guide for students, teachers and librarians, that contains 30 short lesson plans incorporating *TIME Almanac* into the curriculum.

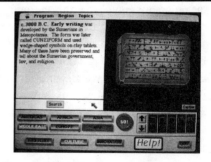

Time Traveler CD: A Multimedia Chronicle of History

New Media Schoolhouse, Box 390, 69 Westchester Avenue, Pound Ridge, NY 10576; 800/672-6002, 914/764-0104 (fax).
Price: $159.
Hardware Minimum Requirements:
Macintosh: System 6.0.7, 2MB RAM, eight-bit color monitor, CD-ROM drive; MPC: IBM 386/compatible, DOS 5.0, Windows 3.1, MSCDEX 2.1, 4MB RAM, audio board and speakers, SVGA monitor, CD-ROM drive, mouse.

Platform: Macintosh, MPC.
Documentation: Eight-page booklet in
jewel case.
Technical Support: 800/672-6002.
Curriculum: Social Studies.
Grade Level: Middle, Senior High.

....

Time Traveler CD is a wide-ranging disc that covers famous events and people from 4000 BC to 1992. It does not deal in depth with any topic, but provides an overview of significant events in the history of the world. Its primary attraction is an ability to slice history through a variety of planes, not just by period, but by geography and subject.

Clicking on the Time Traveler CD icon brings up the main window, from which all searches are conducted. The Control Panel is a convenient way to select the desired slice of history. Buttons can be clicked to select a topic in the general areas of History, Culture, or Innovation. Geographical regions can also be determined, such as Americas, Middle East, Africa, Europe, or Asia. A button labeled Map can also be clicked to bring up a map of the region specified. A Date box allows the user to type in a specific date or to select a date by clicking on up or down arrows to move forward or backward in time from the date in the box.

Program material is in several forms. A text window has brief descriptions of the event or person prominent in the region, topic or time period selected. Scroll arrows allow the user to read the text. There is also a picture window in which an illustration or map is displayed. If there are multiple illustrations for the region, topic or time period chosen, then arrows appear to select further images.

If the user knows an exact event or person's name, a Search button under the text window can be clicked to bring up a box where text can be entered. A Help! button brings up a screen that explains all buttons and windows.

Time Traveler CD is a good program that presents many famous events and people. Without being comprehensive or highly detailed, it nevertheless offers students a good way to access information about the past on several levels of interest.

TOM General Reference System

Information Access Company (IAC), 362
Lakeside Drive, Foster City, CA 94404;
800/227-8431, 415/378-5200, 415/358-
4769 (fax).
Price: $1195.
Minimum Hardware Requirements:
DOS: IBM 286/compatible, 640K RAM,
DOS 3.3, MSCDEX, CD-ROM drive,
monochrome monitor; Macintosh: SE/30,
System 6.05, 2MB RAM, CD-ROM drive.
Platform: DOS.
Documentation: 50-page manual and
introduction to TOM videotape guide.
Technical Support: 800/227-8431.
Curriculum: Reference & Interdisciplinary.
Grade Level: Middle, Senior High.

....

TOM General Reference is InfoTrac's high school edition and provides indexes and short abstracts to articles in 154 general-interest magazines. Its cumulative index covers January 1985 to the present, and the full text of over 100 articles on CD-ROM goes back two years. Each annual subscription comes with monthly updates during the school year months of August through May.

The Expanded Search feature enables searchers to expand any topic to find additional information. Unfortunately there is no word truncation feature, so all searches must be more precise. An onscreen thesaurus subject search simplifies the searching process for beginners. Options are highlighted in boxes on the screen. Citations can be downloaded to disk or printed.

TOM comes with a print index to InfoTrac programs along with other helpful aids such as gummed key caps, newsletters, information packets and a keyboard template. There is a 24-hour customer line, 800/775-5667 and an InfoTrac News hotline, 800/788-NEWS.

TOM can be networked. There is no charge on the Mac platform, but networking costs $400 for the first year on the IBM platform, decreasing in cost in the second year. Old discs must be returned when the new ones are received.

TriplePlay Spanish

Syracuse Language Systems, 719 East Genesee Street, Syracuse, NY 13210; 315/478-6729, 315/478-6902 (fax).
Price: $69.95.
Minimum Hardware Requirement: MPC: IBM/386 compatible, 4MB RAM, 3MB minimum hard drive space, SVGA monitor, CD-ROM drive, DOS 3.1, Windows 3.1, sound board, mouse.
Platform: MPC.
Documentation: 50-page booklet.
Technical Support: 800/688-1937.
Curriculum: Foreign Language.
Grade Level: Elementary, Middle, Senior High.

TriplePlay is a multimedia language immersion program that employs interactive games to teach beginning-to-intermediate Spanish (or English or French; each language is a separate CD-ROM). The user chooses from three levels and six subject categories, Food, Numbers, Home & Office, Places & Transportation, and People & Activities to play games structured to immerse students in language acquisition. Level I focuses on training the ear and perfecting pronunciation as you learn nouns, verbs and simple phrases; Level II focuses on vocabulary; and Level III immerses you in realistic dialog in various scenarios. The program emphasizes hearing the language spoken correctly, motivating the student to learn and discovering that learning language is fun.

The opening screen is cleverly designed with icons to represent the six subject areas and three levels of language study. Each level teaches more than 1,000 words and phrases and each one builds on topics previously learned. Click on the topic and the corresponding game icon available for each level is highlighted. Click on the specific game icon to move to the play environment. Games on the first two levels have a practice mode to allow you to explore the vocabulary. The conversational games on the third level let you hear dialog spoken normally or at a deliberately slow rate to hear the nuances of foreign pronunciation. After practicing, play to see how much you have learned. Choose from an assortment of games including bingo, Concentration, matching cards, maps, jigsaw puzzles and more. At the third level, record your own voice to compare it to the native speaker.

TriplePlay takes the drudgery out of learning a language—the program motivates students to learn a language while encouraging them to have fun at the same time.

Twelve Roads to Gettysburg

Ebook, Inc., 32970 Alvarado-Niles Road, Suite 704, Union City, CA 94587; 510/429-1331, 510/429-1394 (fax).
Price: $69.95.
Minimum Hardware Requirements:
Macintosh: Macintosh II, System 6.0.7, 4MB RAM, 256-color monitor, CD-ROM drive; MPC: IBM 286 16MHz/ compatible, Windows 3.0, MSCDEX, 4MB RAM, CD-ROM drive, audio board and speakers, mouse.
Platform: Macintosh, MPC.
Documentation: Four-page booklet in jewel case.
Technical Support: 510/713-8904.
Curriculum: Social Studies.
Grade Level: Middle, Senior High.

This disc demonstrates the value of CD-ROM in studying a single event in U.S. history. The depth and breadth of the information about this three-day battle enables anyone to achieve a greater understanding of the event and the people and forces behind it.

The disc is divided into five sections. Each section has text, illustrations, maps and some audio material, including songs of the period, posters and Matthew Brady photographs. In Campaigns and Strategies, the military tactics of both sides are described and discussed. In The Battle, original and source documents are linked to maps and photographs of the area, while a narrator explains the progress of the battle and simple, animated maps show the advance and retreat of different armies.

The two sections of Armies and Leaders show organizational charts of military troops, give biographies of Confederate and Union military leaders as well as regimental histories and describe military weapons and uniforms.

The final section shows Gettysburg as it is today with maps and access routes, national park and monument locations, hours and fees.

The Battle of Gettysburg has been described as one of the most important single events in the history of our country. This disc is a giant first step along the road to understanding its background, players and impact.

20,000 Leagues Under the Sea
(*See* Talking Storybook Series)

VideoHound Multimedia
Visible Ink Software, 835 Penobscot Building, Detroit, MI 48224-0748; 800/735-HOUND.
Price: $79.95.

Minimum Hardware Requirements:
MPC: IBM/386 compatible, Windows 3.1,
DOS 3.1, 2MB RAM, 30MB hard drive
space, VGA monitor, sound board,
CD-ROM drive.
Platform: MPC.
Documentation: 20-page user guide in
disc case.
Technical Support: 800/877-4253,
Ext. 6021.
Curriculum: Arts and Music.
Grade Level: Middle, Senior High.

....

VideoHound contains reviews and details about 52,000 videos, including more than 20,000 movies, 3,500 portraits of stars and directors, 600 full biographies from the Hollywood Who's Who, 400 scene photos from motion picture classics, 14,000 images of movie stills, sound effects, and color box art for thousands of video movies. The database includes not only popular movies but also nine video guides covering a wide range of subject areas.

VideoHound's main menu offers the choice to implement searches, select a particular title or view and maintain customized video files. After you have chosen one of the nine video guides, you can quickly locate videos by title, individual criteria or a combination of criteria. From the contents screen click on one of the following: Title, to search by title, keyword from title, or browse; Star or Cast Member or Director to search by name; Category, to search by over 1,000 standard categories (Drama, Science Fiction, Comedy, etc.) or special interest categories (Killer Plants, Apartheid, Books to Film, Tear-A-

Plenty, etc.); Awards, to search for major awards in twenty categories with subcategories and descriptions; Multimedia Gallery, to look at Cast Images, Director Images, Box Art Images, Category Images, Category Sound Effects, Biographies; Videos Guides, to search through nine databases; List Maker, to create and save your own customized searches; and Other Search Options which include, Format, Year Released, MPAA Rating, Closed-Captioned, Color or Black and White, and VideoHound Rating.

The powerful search engine allows you to locate videos by combining categories such as Romantic Drama with a VideoHound Rating of excellence ("four bones"), and then narrow the list by choosing additional criteria, such as Director, MPAA rating, format, etc.

After a title is selected, a screen appears giving basic details about the movie: MPAA rating, tint, close captioned, silent film, format, running time, release year, VideoHound Rating and the categories it included. In addition, it offers access to film details such as film synopsis, videographies, awards list and photographs. All of the choices are hyperlinked, allowing you to explore the entire database from any title detail screen. For example, even though you were looking at Westerns, click on Anti-Heros in the category list of Butch Cassidy and the Sundance Kid, and a list of more than 30 titles in that genre will be displayed.

An added feature of VideoHound is the ability to create your own customized lists. You can add, remove, view and print your lists. This is a helpful feature for both faculty and students. Media specialists could develop customized lists to support class-room curriculum or term paper topics.

The breadth and depth of information on this disc makes it a valuable item for school libraries, but it is also great fun.

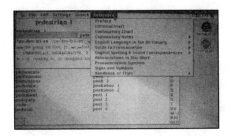

Webster's Ninth New Collegiate Dictionary, 1992 Edition

Highlighted Data, Inc., 6628 Midhill Place, Falls Church, VA 22043; 703/533-1939, 703/533-2039 (fax).
Price: *$199.95.*
Minimum Hardware Requirements:
Macintosh: *Macintosh Plus: 800K disk drive, 1MB RAM.*
Platform: *Macintosh.*
Documentation: *29-page user's manual included.*
Technical Support: *703/516-9211, 9:00 a.m. to 5:00 p.m., Monday through Friday*
Curriculum: *Reference & Interdisciplinary.*
Grade Level: *Elementary, Middle, Senior High.*

....

A complete dictionary for use with the Macintosh computer, Webster's Ninth contains almost 160,000 entries and 200,000 definitions. Words are searchable in several ways—by alphabet, cross-referencing and direct typing. Each entry is dated, and individual words can also be pronounced. Print size can be enlarged, definitions printed and categories (such as biographical and geographical names) searched.

Installation is easy—the software to access the dictionary comes on a separate floppy disk. Run the dictionary from the floppy or copy the software to the hard disk.

The dictionary opens at the first page of the letter A. Words are listed without definitions. Double-click on any word to bring up its definition. Use the alphabetic listing at the right side of the screen to find another part of the dictionary. Click on the turned-up page corner at the bottom left to flip through the dictionary one page at a time. Using the menu or the <Command><F> key combination brings up the Search dialog box. Any word can then be typed into the box to retrieve its definition.

The information in the definition window for each word includes its phonetic spelling, etymology, the date it first came into use and all forms of definitions and combining forms. There are also over 1000 illustrations in the dictionary. Entries with illustrations can be searched through the Search menu.

Each entire entry in the dictionary can be printed. Definitions can also be cut or copied to the scrapbook or another document. Any definition printed or pasted also carries the copyright notice, so that the source is correctly identified. This is a good feature for teaching correct use of citations in report writing.

Anyone with a CD-ROM drive should seriously consider this product. It has all the standard dictionary features and provides electronic enhancements—sound and search capabilities—sure to help students in the learning process.

Whales and Dolphins

Media Design Interactive, The Old Hop Kiln, 1 Long Garden Walk, Farnham, Surrey, GU9 7HP, England; 011/44/252 737630, 011/44/252/710948 (fax).
Price: $69.95.
Minimum Hardware Requirements: MPC: IBM 386/ compatible 4MB RAM, hard drive, SVGA monitor, sound board, CD-ROM drive, mouse, speakers, Windows 3.1.
Platform: MPC.
Documentation: Four-page user guide in disc case.
Technical Support: 800/654-8802.
Curriculum: Science.
Grade Level: Middle, Senior High.

....

Investigate the world of sea-dwelling mammals and learn how they live, breed and feed. Whales and Dolphins explores these warm-blooded mammals through full-motion video, narrations, sound effects, color illustrations and photographs, full species index and distribution maps.

As the program opens to the table of contents, you are greeted by whale sounds. The program is organized into two main sections. The chapters offer an overview and background on the mammals, and the index names 79 individual whales, dolphins and porpoises. The chapters are Intro, Life Cycle, Body Plan, Ecology, and Species. Each major heading is sub-divided into three additional categories.

The A-Z Index includes the choice to search by families including Mysticeti, Odontoceti and an illustrated look at all the major whale, dolphin and porpoise families. Click on the individual cetacean or the families icon. In either case you retrieve a screen showing a graphic of the cetacean, a few paragraphs of information, including location, length, color, body description, food preferences and social characteristics. Three icons present multimedia information, full-motion video, photos and world map, depicting geographic locations. Not all the cetaceans have all three available, but all have at least one photo and world map showing their habitat.

A menu bar on the top of the screen allows you to move to any section in the program. The organization is well-planned and the information will interest students and adults. It does lack a print function.

Click on Regulating Buoyancy under Body Plan to listen to the Sperm Whale and learn some fascinating facts about this creature. The Sperm Whale's head contains wax that is liquid at its normal body temperature but hardens when it cools so as the whale dives it increases in density, thereby helping to decrease its buoyancy. Did you know that blubber can be as thick as one foot or that there is a distinct difference between the humpback whale's and the killer whale's songs?

Whales and Dolphins
(*See* ZooGuides)

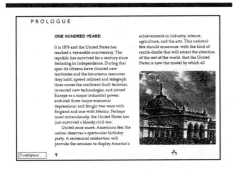

Who Built America?

The Voyager Company, 578 Broadway, New York, NY 10012; 212/431-5199, 212/431-5799 (fax). Also: One Bridge Street, Irvington, NY 10533. 800/446-2001, 914/591-6481 (fax).
Price: $99.95; $350, Education Edition.
Minimum Hardware Requirements:
Macintosh: *Macintosh II, LC, System 7.0, 6.2MB available RAM, CD-ROM drive, color monitor.*
Platform: *Macintosh.*
Documentation: *Eight-page user's guide. Education version includes five copies of the CD-ROM plus a teaching guide, lesson plans, student activities and suggestions for using the program in various classes.*
Technical Support: *914/591-5500*
Curriculum: *Social Studies.*
Grade Level: *Senior High.*

Covering U.S. history from 1876 to 1914, Who Built America? is based on the American Social History Project at Hunter College (City College of New York) directed by Steve Brier. It includes the entire text of the two-volume history by the same name but has added vast numbers of primary documents, period photographs and illustrations, old film footage and sound recordings from that era.

The disc is easy to install and operate, but requires quite a bit of hard disk space. Who Built America? is an invaluable resource for the study of this segment of U.S. history. The chance to see illustrations, old films, authentic newspaper advertisements and to read letters and memoirs from people who lived through those years enhance the study of history as print alone cannot possibly do. There is even a sound recording of a young boy's eyewitness account of a lynching in rural Florida in 1902. The biggest regret about this disc is that it covers only 38 years of history!

The CD-ROM is arranged like the printed volumes, with table of contents and printed chapters covering almost 400 pages. On each page of text, there may be an illustration or button to click for an explanation or added enhancement. Underlined place names, when clicked, bring up a U.S. map with the location of the place highlighted and blinking. A timeline presents key events for the 38 years covered by the project.

The searching and navigating tools are powerful and abundant, but may not be completely obvious to HyperCard novices. For example, pressing and holding the mouse button while the pointer is on the current chapter name brings up an entire list of all chapters and subheadings. If you press and hold the mouse button while the pointer is on a single word, it brings up a dialog box in which you can select other occurrences of the same word.

The amount of material contained on this disc is astonishing. Who can resist recordings of 1,911 love songs or the first published crossword puzzle?

Wind in the Willows
(*See* Talking Storybook Series)

Wonders of Learning CD-ROM Library

National Geographic Society, 1145 17th St. NW, Washington, DC 20036; 800/368-2728, 301/921-1575 (fax). Co-produced with Discis Knowledge Research, Inc.
Price: *$89.95 per disc; set of all five titles is $395.*
Minimum Hardware Requirements:
Macintosh Plus: System 6.0.5 or 6.0.7, 2MB RAM, color monitor recommended.
Platform: *Macintosh.*
Documentation: *User's guide, poster and color booklets (including text and pictures on the CD-ROM) for each product. Also includes catalog cards.*

Technical Support: *800/342-4460, 800/437-4383 (Canada).*
Curriculum: *Social Studies, Science.*
Grade Level: *Primary.*

(Series includes A World of Animals, Our Earth, The Human Body, A World of Plants, and Animals and How They Grow.)

Each of these titles contains a set of books in print and on the CD-ROM. (A World of Animals and Our Earth were reviewed for this book. It is assumed the other three products in this series are similar in format, design and content.) A World of Animals contains Butterflies, Farm Animals, Spiders, Whales, and Dinosaurs: Giant Reptiles. Our Earth contains Discovering Maps, Why Does It Rain?, What Air Can Do, and Our Planet Earth. In both formats, these books are full of beautiful color photographs with easy-to-understand text. The CD-ROM has music and sound effects to accompany the story, picture buttons for children to push and explore and a tutorial or help screen that provides word definitions and explanations in English or Spanish.

A teacher or parent can customize each program for the child's own reading needs. The volume, size and style of type, line spacing and settings for clicking or selecting can all be changed or adjusted. In addition to enlarging the type size for a beginning reader, for example, you can also lengthen the pause between phrases so that the sentences are read more slowly. In the tutorial, you can adjust the settings so that a word is pronounced in English, then in Spanish, and again in English, all with a single mouse click. The Customize menu can be hidden from the reader by holding down the Command key and then pressing the Delete key. It can be restored with the same keystroke combination.

The Recall List will track up to 32 words the reader has clicked on during the session. The teacher or parent can review those words to see which words are causing problems or to see if the reader has learned those words after a session. The Recall List can also be hidden from the reader's view by the same keystroke combination used to hide the Customize menu.

Each CD-ROM also contains an Activity Guide with ideas for follow-up projects, discussion ideas and suggestions for curriculum integration. Parents and teachers can benefit from the ideas in the Activity Guides, which can be printed or saved to a floppy disk.

This is an excellent series for the primary grades, for beginning readers and for exploring some of the basic sciences and geography.

Word Tales

Time Warner Interactive Group, 2210 West Olive Avenue, Burbank, CA 91506-2626; 800/593-6334, 818/955-9999, 818/955-6499 (fax).
Price: $59.99

Minimum Hardware Requirements:
Macintosh: *Macintosh II or LC; System 6.0.7; 4MB RAM with 2.2MB available on hard drive; CD-ROM drive.* ***MPC: IBM/ 386 16MHz/compatible; Windows 3.1; 4MB RAM; CD-ROM drive; VGA Plus monitor; audio board and speakers; mouse.***
Platform: *Macintosh, MPC.*
Documentation: *Six-page booklet in jewel case.*
Technical Support: *800/565-TWIG.*
Curriculum: *Language Arts.*
Grade Level: *Primary, Elementary.*

....

Word Tales is a disc for beginning readers. Full of good animation and clever games, it will help teach the letters of the alphabet in a most delightful way. It is easy to install and run, although not completely easy to launch. It requires adult supervision to begin, but once it is up and running it requires only clicking on objects and pictures to make things happen.

Word Tales consists of a series of cartoon pictures that ask for the correct letter to begin the word depicted on the screen. Several other letters can be used to complete the word, but only the right letter makes the word match the picture. After completing the word, the program moves to a picture of a room with many objects that begin with the same letter. When each correct object is clicked, its word is added to the list at the right of the screen. Each word is also pronounced aloud. When the list is competed, a hidden, animated sequence celebrates with the user.

The user is led through all of the sequences by Milo, a bright green and very engaging character. When each Word Tale is complete, the user gets to play an arcade game with a little robot and a brick floor that keeps disappearing.

Word Tales is a bright, easy-to-use, entertaining program for young and beginning readers.

A World Alive

The Voyager Company, 578 Broadway, New York, NY 10012; 212/431-5199, 212/431-5799 (fax). Also: One Bridge Street, Irvington, NY 10533; 800/446-2001, 914/591-6481 (fax).
Price: $49.95.
Minimum Hardware Requirements:
Macintosh: Macintosh II, LC, System 7.0, 2.2MB RAM, CD-ROM drive, color monitor.
Platform: Macintosh.
Documentation: Eight-page user's guide.
Technical Support: 914/591-5500.
Curriculum: Science.
Grade Level: Senior High.

....

The Voyager Company is known for making quality discs, and A World Alive is no exception. This disc features over 100 different animals in several major categories (habitat, classification and geography) with clear easy-to-read fact sheets on each individual animal. The animal's common name, Latin name, diet, lifespan and gestation period are listed, along with a brief description, a drawing to show comparative size, and a button that describes the animal's current status (prolific, endangered, etc.).

A World Alive also has a 30-minute video documentary about all of the animals. Narrated by James Earl Jones, the video is

the work of Sea Studios and the St. Louis Zoo. Another feature of the disc is an educational game called What is That? (WIT), that poses questions based on the information about the animals. The disc also includes a search capability so that the user can enter any word or combination of words, and the section of the program containing the search terms is displayed.

From the opening footprints across the title screen to the final moments of the video, A World Alive is a pleasure to watch and provides valuable information in an easy format.

A World of Animals
(*See* Wonders of Learning CD-ROM Library)

A World of Plants (*See* Wonders of Learning CD-ROM Library)

World Vista

Applied Optical Media Corporation, 1450 Boot Road, Building 400A, West Chester, PA 19380; 800/321-7259, 610/429-3701, 610/429-3810 (fax).
Price: $59.95.
Minimum Hardware Requirements:
MPC Level 1: 386 25MHz/compatible, DOS 5.0, Windows 3.1, MSCDEX 2.21, 4MB RAM, CD-ROM drive, SVGA monitor, audio board and speakers, mouse.
Platform: Macintosh, MPC.
Documentation: Four-page booklet in jewel case.
Technical Support: 800/321-7259.
Curriculum: Social Studies.
Grade Level: Middle, Senior High.

....

This is another in-depth atlas from Applied Optical Media (see also American Vista). It covers every country in the world and a wide variety of topics. You can search by topic and then select a country or city, or you can select a country first and then look at all of the information about that country. Topics include data about the water supply, principal cities, islands, mountains or rivers, as well as thematic maps.

One interesting feature is the list of languages spoken throughout the world. Each language is listed with the places where it's spoken, and at the bottom of the screen are five or six key phrases. When clicked, each phrase is spoken aloud in the language selected.

Fifty of the world's major cities are included on the disc with interesting and pertinent information about each one. Color photographs are provided for all countries and cities on the disc.

The maps and historical data are from Rand McNally, and the music from the Smithsonian Institute. This CD-ROM atlas disc has a great deal of information on it, all accessible and easy to use. It will be a worthwhile addition to your school library media center.

REMedia, Inc., 13525 Midland Road, Poway, CA 92064; 619/486-5030.
Price: *$55.95.*
Minimum Hardware Requirements:
Macintosh: *Macintosh II, LC, System 6.0.7, 4MB RAM, hard drive, CD-ROM drive, eight-bit color monitor.*
Platform: *Macintosh.*
Documentation: *Two-page booklet in jewel case.*
Technical Support: *619/486-5030.*
Curriculum: *Science.*
Grade Level: *Middle, Senior High.*

(Series includes Volume 1: Butterflies, Volume 2: Whales and Dolphins, Volume 3: Mammals of Africa, Volume 4: The Rainforest.)

Each of the three volumes reviewed covers a group of animals. Volume 1: Butterflies was released first and has a significant number of problems that have been solved in later volumes. On this disc the narrator is distinctly British and uses British speech patterns that may be confusing to U.S. students. The text was obviously translated from British to American English, but the job was not well done. Hence you see "color" and "coloured dust" on the same screen. The QuickTime videos on Volume 1 have no controls and cannot be stopped or started at will. These flaws have been corrected on Volumes 2 and 3 and should pose no problem for anyone. The final caveat for these discs is that the narrated text and the written text on the screen do not match. On Volume 1, this is very confusing as they happen at the same time. On Volumes 2 and 3, the spoken

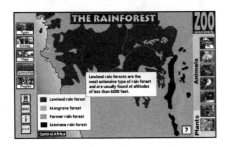

ZooGuides Series

text can be started by the viewer and serves to expand on the written text. There is less overlap, so it is less confusing.

Each disc is divided into parts, corresponding to the study of individual animal groups. These sections are Introduction, Life Cycles, Body Plan, Ecology, and Species. Each section contains written text, a map showing species distribution, common and Latin names, biological classification and a brief video. The color and quality of the images are excellent, and on Volume 2: Whales and Dolphins, some of the underwater scenes are extraordinary.

CHAPTER 7
SUPPLEMENTARY LIST OF SUGGESTED CD-ROMs FOR SCHOOLS

This chapter is an alphabetical compilation of 201 CD-ROM titles that are currently available and applicable for school use. This list should be used to supplement the Core Collection of titles reviewed in Chapter 6.

Descriptive and producer information is given for each title, along with a recommended grade level and curriculum. Titles in this chapter are included in Chapter 8, CD-ROM Titles by Curriculum and Grade Level, along with the 100 Core Collection titles.

about Cows
Quanta Press Inc.
1313 Fifth Street, Suite SE 223A
Minneapolis, MN 55414
612/379-3956
Fax: 612/623-4570
Price: $29.95
Platform: Macintosh, DOS
Grade Level: Elementary, Middle, Senior High School
Curriculum: Social Studies
Description: Pictures, poems, photographs and information about every bovine topic you can imagine.

A.D.A.M.
A.D.A.M. Software
1600 Riveredge Parkway, Suite 800
Atlanta, GA 30328
800/755-ADAM
404/980-0888
Fax: 404/955-3088
Tech. Support: 404/953-2326
Price: Library-dependent; write for information
Platform: Macintosh
Grade Level: Senior High School
Curriculum: Science
Description: Very expensive and very comprehensive CD-ROM and software application for the study of anatomy. Incorporates dissection techniques, animation and other multimedia aids.

Advanced Spelling Tricks
BrightStar
3380 146th Place SE, Suite 300
Bellevue, WA 98007
206/649-9800
Fax: 206/649-0340
Price: $49.95
Platform: Macintosh
Grade Level: Elementary, Middle
Curriculum: Language Arts
Description: Yobi, the wise and magical, leads the user on an adventure-filled journey that moves forward only when words are spelled correctly.

Adventures
Deep River Publishing
P.O. Box 9715-975
Portland, ME 04104
800/643-5630
207/871-1684
Fax: 207/871-1683
Tech. Support: 207/871-1684
Price: $49.95

Platform: MPC
Grade Level: Middle, Senior High School
Curriculum: Reference & Interdisciplinary
Description: A comprehensive yet simple to use travel resource. Option to search by category, country, state, province or custom search. Each search generates a list of selections for you to browse through and select a specific type of adventure.

Aesop's Fables
Ebook Inc.
32970 Alvarado-Niles Road, Suite 704
Union City, CA 94587
510/429-1331
Fax: 510/429-1394
Tech. Support: 510/713-8904
Price: $29.95
Platform: MPC
Grade Level: Primary, Elementary
Curriculum: Storybook
Description: Aesop's wise and witty tales told through an interactive story program. Includes narration and graphics.

African American Experience
Globe Fearon Educational Publisher
P.O. Box 2649
Columbus, OH 43216
800/848-9500
Fax: 614/771-7361
Price: $99, school
Platform: Macintosh, DOS
Grade Level: Senior High School
Curriculum: Social Studies
Description: An electronic textbook that tells the history of African-Americans beginning in the African homeland. Includes the African continent explorers, freedom fighters, politics, biographies, culture and social life.

Allie's Playhouse
Opcode Systems Inc.
3950 Fabian Way, Suite 100
Palo Alto, CA 94303
800/557-2633 (orders)
415/856-3333
Fax: 415/494-1113
Tech. Support: 415/494-9393
Price: $59.95
Platform: Macintosh, MPC
Grade Level: Primary
Curriculum: Storybook
Description: An interactive educational program to encourage children to explore and experiment, make decisions, take risks, make mistakes, succeed and, most importantly, learn.

Amanda Stories
Voyager
1 Bridge Street
Irvington, NY 10533
800/446-2001
Fax: 914/591-6481
Tech. Support: 914/591-5500
Price: $59.95
Platform: Macintosh, Windows
Grade Level: Primary, Elementary
Curriculum: Storybook
Description: Ten stories of Inigo and Your Faithful Camel. Full-color animations, sound and charming story plots. Interactive component allows user to select path of adventure.

Amazing Universe
Hopkins Technology
421 Hazel Lane
Hopkins, MN 55343-7116
800/397-9211
Fax: 612/931-9377

Tech. Support: 800/397-9211
Price: $79.95
Platform: Macintosh, DOS, Windows
Grade Level: Senior High School
Curriculum: Science
Description: A collection of photographs
of outer space objects taken from satellites
and earth-based observation. One hundred-
one images of planets, galaxies, comets
and the Sun.

America Adventure
Knowledge Adventure
4502 Dyer Street
La Crescenta, CA 91214
800/542-4240 (orders)
818/248-0166 (bulletin board)
Fax: 818/542-4205
Tech. Support: 818/249-0212
Price: $79.95
Platform: DOS, Windows
Grade Level: Middle, Senior High School
Curriculum: Social Studies
Description: A multimedia adventure of
America's people and places, past and
present. Watch movies, learn about
regional foods and play the states game.

American Heritage: Illustrated
Encyclopedia Dictionary
XIPHIAS
8758 Venice Boulevard
Los Angeles, CA 90034
800/421-9194 (sales)
310/841-2790
Fax: 310/841-2559
Price: $39.95
Platform: DOS, MPC
Grade Level: Senior High School
Curriculum: Reference & Interdisciplinary
Description: A multimedia reference of

over 180,000 definitions and thousands of
colorful pictures, with the ability to look
up words without knowing the spelling
or use a hot word to call up all definitions
associated with the word.

The American Indian:
A Multimedia Encyclopedia
Facts on File Inc.
460 Park Avenue South
New York, NY 10016-7382
800/322-8755
212/683-2244
Fax: 212/683-3633
Tech. Support: 800/322-8755
Price: $295
Platform: DOS
Grade Level: Senior High School
Curriculum: Social Studies
Description: A complete and comprehen-
sive source of information on the native
peoples of the North American continent;
includes full text of rare documents and
treaties from the National Archives, 1,100
images and sound bites of authentic
American Indian songs and colorful stories
and legends.

Animal Alphabet
REMedia Inc.
13525 Midland Road
Poway, CA 92064
619/486-5030
Tech. Support: 619/486-5030
Price: $39.95
Platform: Macintosh
Grade Level: Primary
Curriculum: Language Arts
Description: Each letter in the alphabet is
represented by an animal cartoon with a
page of spoken text and a video sequence.

Barron's Complete Book Notes
World Library Inc.
2809 Main Street
Irvine, CA 92714
800/443-0238
714/756-9500
Fax: 714/756-9511
Tech. Support: 714/756-9550
Price: $49.95 (Prices due to change
Summer '94)
Platform: Macintosh, DOS, Windows
Grade Level: Senior High School
Curriculum: Language Arts
Description: Complete unabridged text of
101 literary guides including plot summaries,
discussions, analyses and author biographies.

Baseball's Greatest Hits
Voyager
1 Bridge Street
Irvington, NY 10533
800/446-2001
Fax: 914/591-6481
Tech. Support: 914/591-5500
Price: $59.95
Platform: Macintosh
Grade Level: Middle, Senior High School
Curriculum: Sports
Description: Sixty-five of baseball's greatest
moments with introductions by Mel Allen,
the radio announcing of the actual event,
and video clips when available. Hundreds of
photos, player statistics, team histories and
rosters; includes a baseball trivia game.

Beethoven Symphony #9
Voyager
1 Bridge Street
Irvington, NY 10533
800/446-2001
Fax: 914/591-6481

Tech. Support: 914/591-5500
Price: $99.95
Platform: Macintosh
Grade Level: Senior High School
Curriculum: Arts & Music
Description: Five-part exploration of one of
the world's greatest symphonies. Examines
the musical score, individual instruments
and the life and times of the composer.

Beyond the Wall of Stars
Creative Multimedia
514 NW 11th Avenue, Suite 203
Portland, OR 97209
800/262-7668
503/241-4351
Fax: 503/241-4370
Tech. Support: 503/241-1530
Price: $49.99
Platform: Macintosh, MPC
Grade Level: Middle, Senior High School
Curriculum: Language Arts
Description: This grand quest, the first in a
trilogy, leads you into a problem solving
voyage of discovery that lets you direct the
future to save planet Celadon through 3D
animation images, sound and text. You
read, decide and solve your way through
the Wall of Stars.

Billie Holiday
Ebook Inc.
32970 Alvarado-Niles Road, Suite 704
Union City, CA 94587
510/429-1331
Fax: 510/429-1394
Tech. Support: 510/713-8904
Price: $29.95
Platform: MPC
Grade Level: Senior High School
Curriculum: Arts & Music

Description: The music, biography and background of one of jazz's musical greats.

Biography and Genealogy—
Master Index
Gale Research Inc.
835 Penobscot Building
Detroit, MI 48226-4094
800/877-GALE
313/961-2242
Fax: 313/961-6083
Tech. Support: 800/877-4253, Ext. 6021
Price: $1250
Platform: DOS
Grade Level: Senior High School
Curriculum: Language Arts
Description: A comprehensive index to current and retrospective biographical dictionaries and who's who. Containing more than 8.8 million citations, provides access to more than 2,000 volumes and editions of over 675 biographical reference sources.

Biology Digest on CD-ROM
NewsBank, Inc.
58 Pine Street
New Canaan, CT 06840-5426
800/762-8182
203/966-1100
Fax: 203/966-6254
Tech. Support: 800/762-8182
Price: $300; back files $600
Platform: DOS
Grade Level: Senior High School
Curriculum: Science
Description: Extensive summaries of articles from over 170 scientific journals and science-related periodicals worldwide. Over 3,000 articles per year cover the areas of Viruses, Microflora and Plants,

Animal Kingdom, Human Organism, Infectious Diseases, Population and Health, Cell Biology and Biogenesis, Environment Quality and Biology Education.

Books in Print Plus
Bowker Electronic Publishing
121 Chanlon Road
New Providence, NJ 07974-1154
800/323-3288
Price: By subscription
Platform: Macintosh
Grade Level: Senior High School
Curriculum: Reference & Interdisciplinary
Description: Bibliographic information on all books currently published in the U.S. Searchable by title, author, ISBN, publisher, grade level and keyword.

Busytown
Paramount Interactive
700 Hansen Way
Palo Alto, CA 94304
415/813-8030
Fax: 415/813-8055
Tech. Support: 415/813-8030
Price: $39.95
Platform: Macintosh, DOS
Grade Level: Primary
Curriculum: Language Arts
Description: Based on the work of Richard Scarry, Busytown features twelve interactive "playgrounds" for children from three to seven years old. Includes music and accompanying parent's guide and teacher's guide.

Canadian Catalog of Media Resources
Innotech Multimedia
2001 Sheppard Avenue E., Suite 118
North York, Ontario, Canada M2J 4Z7

416/492-3838
Fax: 416/492-3843
Tech. Support: 416/492-3838
Price: $117.83
Platform: Macintosh, DOS
Grade Level: Senior High School
Curriculum: Reference & Interdisciplinary
Description: A collection of film and
video catalogs.

Career Opportunities
Quanta Press Inc.
1313 Fifth Street, Suite SE 223A
Minneapolis, MN 55414
612/379-3956
Fax: 612/623-4570
Price: $69.95
Platform: Macintosh, DOS
Grade Level: Senior High School
Curriculum: Reference & Interdisciplinary
Description: Features U.S. Department
of Commerce texts with information
about employment. Includes addresses,
scholarships and such areas as benefits,
salary ranges and work environment.

CD Calculus
John Wiley and Sons Inc.
605 Third Avenue
New York, NY 10158
212/850-6172
Fax: 212/850-6799
Price: $49.95
Platform: DOS
Grade Level: Senior High School
Curriculum: Mathematics
Description: The entire text of *Calculus
with Analytic Geometry* 4th Ed. by
Howard Anton.

CD Coreworks
Roth Publishing Inc.

185 Great Neck Road
Great Neck, NY 11021
800/899-7684
Fax: 516/829-7746
Tech. Support: 800/899-7684
Price: $475
Platform: DOS
Grade Level: Senior High School
Curriculum: Language Arts
Description: Integrates four poetry indexes
in a single disc, providing a definitive index
to more then 140,000 poems and over
25,000 essays, 4,000 short stories and
850 plays in the English language.

"CELL"EBRATION
Science for Kids Inc.
9950 Concord Church Road
Lewisville, NC 27023
910/945-9000
Fax: 910/945-2500
Tech. Support: 910/945-9000
Price: $289
Platform: Macintosh
Grade Level: Primary, Elementary
Curriculum: Science
Description: An interactive multimedia
science learning system that includes les-
son guides, teacher's manual, hands-on
activities, microscope, magnifying glass
and 15 slides.

CIA World Fact Book
Quanta Press Inc.
1313 Fifth Street, Suite SE 223A
Minneapolis, MN 55414
612/379-3956
Fax: 612/623-4570
Price: $49.95
Platform: Macintosh, DOS
Grade Level: Middle, Senior High School

Curriculum: Social Studies
Description: A reference disc of the U.S. government's own almanac containing 249 countries, territories and islands around the world.

Coate's Art Review: Impressionism
Quanta Press Inc.
1313 Fifth Street, Suite SE 223A
Minneapolis, MN 55414
612/379-3956
Fax: 612/623-4570
Price: $79.95
Platform: Macintosh, DOS
Grade Level: Senior High School
Curriculum: Arts & Music
Description: A comprehensive look at all major artists and artworks of the Impressionist era. Includes background information as well as museum and collection data.

The College Handbook
Macmillan New Media
124 Mount Auburn Street
Cambridge, MA 02138
800/342-1338
617/661-2955
Fax: 617/661-2403
Tech. Support: 800/342-1338
Price: $39.95
Platform: DOS
Grade Level: Senior High School
Curriculum: Reference & Interdisciplinary
Description: More than 2,700 colleges to help pinpoint the right college.

**Complete Guide to
Special Interest Videos**
Quanta Press Inc.
1313 Fifth Street, Suite SE 223A

Minneapolis, MN 55414
612/379-3956
Fax: 612/623-4570
Price: $49.95
Platform: Macintosh, DOS
Grade Level: Senior High School
Curriculum: Social Studies
Description: A listing of over 9,000 videos, organized by title and by subject, with an order form included for any of the videos.

Complete HOUSE
Deep River Publishing
P.O. Box 9715-975
Portland, ME 04104
800/643-5630
207/871-1684
Fax: 207/871-1683
Tech. Support: 207/871-1684
Price: $39.95
Platform: Macintosh, MPC
Grade Level: Senior High School
Curriculum: Arts & Music
Description: Features House Design—an in-depth look at the relationship of homeowner, environment and house. Also, Kitchen and Bath Design—gets right down to plan and construction of kitchen. CAD/FP as a drawing package includes 20 complete floor plans.

Composer Quest
Opcode Systems Inc.
3950 Fabian Way, Suite 100
Palo Alto, CA 94303
800/557-2633 (orders)
415/856-3333
Fax: 415/494-1113
Tech. Support: 415/494-3331
Price: $69.95
Platform: DOS

Grade Level: Senior High School
Curriculum: Arts & Music
Description: Offers a unique and revolutionary way to learn music history through investigating the work of the great composers, spanning the years from 1600 to the present.

Compton's Interactive Encyclopedia
Compton's NewMedia Inc.
2320 Camino Vida Roble
Carlsbad, CA 92009
800/862-2206
800/216-6116 (catalog sales)
619/929-2500
Fax: 619/929-2555
Tech. Support: 619/929-2626
Price: $149.95
Platform: Macintosh, Windows
Grade Level: Elementary, Middle
Curriculum: Reference & Interdisciplinary
Description: All 26 volumes of *Compton's Encyclopedia* including 9 million words in 32,000 articles, 13,000 images, maps and graphs, 5,000 charts and diagrams, 43 animated sequences and 60 minutes of music, speech and other sound.

Consumer Information
Quanta Press Inc.
1313 Fifth Street, Suite SE 223A
Minneapolis, MN 55414
612/379-3956
Fax: 612/623-4570
Price: $49.95
Platform: Macintosh, DOS
Grade Level: Senior High School
Curriculum: Reference & Interdisciplinary
Description: Most of the books and publications currently available from the Federal Government Consumer

Information Center at Pueblo, Colorado. It covers subjects ranging from children to travel, and anything in between.

Contemporary Authors
Gale Research Inc.
835 Penobscot Building
Detroit, MI 48226-4094
800/877-GALE
313/961-2242
Fax: 313/961-6083
Tech. Support: 800/877-4253, Ext. 6021
Price: Single User—$3500; Updates 2x/year—$650; Lease/year—$795.
Platform: DOS
Grade Level: Senior High School
Curriculum: Language Arts
Description: An authoritative source of biographical and bibliographical information on important authors of our time. Includes the full text of *Contemporary Authors*, Vol. 1-40, *Contemporary Authors New Revision Series*, Vol. 1-41 and *Contemporary Authors Permanent Series*, Vol. 1-2.

Countries of the World
Bureau for Electronic Publishing
141 New Road
Parsippany, NJ 07054
800/828-4766 (orders)
201/808-2700
Fax: 201/808-2676
Tech. Support: 201/808-2700, Ext. 22
Price: $495
Platform: Macintosh, DOS
Grade Level: Senior High School
Curriculum: Social Studies
Description: Detailed information on population, society, environment, foreign relations, geography, religion, agriculture,

economy, etc., taken from 106 different *U.S. Army Country Handbooks*. Update was due out in June 1994.

Creepy Crawlies
Media Design Interactive
The Old Hop Kiln, 1 Long Garden Walk
Farnham, Surrey, GU9 7HP England
011-44-252-737630
Fax: 011-44-252-710948
Tech. Support: 800/654-8802
Price: $69
Platform: Macintosh, MPC
Grade Level: Middle, Senior High School
Curriculum: Science
Description: The world of bugs designed for kids. Also defines and classifies lower animals according to biological taxonomy.

Crossword Cracker and Margana
Nimbus Information Systems
P.O. Box 7427
Charlottesville, VA 22906
804/985-1100
Fax: 804/985-4625
Price: $24.45
Platform: DOS
Grade Level: Senior High School
Curriculum: Language Arts
Description: A word analysis system designed to crack that elusive crossword clue.

Dinosaur Adventure
Knowledge Adventure
4502 Dyer Street
La Crescenta, CA 91214
800/542-4240 (orders)
818/248-0166 (bulletin board)
Fax: 818/542-4205
Tech. Support: 818/249-0212
Price: $39.95

Platform: DOS
Grade Level: Elementary, Middle
Curriculum: Science
Description: An interactive book, this CD-ROM is a complete resource on dinosaurs for elementary students—what dinosaurs ate, where they lived and how they interacted. Also includes information on the explorers who found dinosaur fossil remains.

Dinosaur Safari
Creative Multimedia
514 NW 11th Avenue, Suite 203
Portland, OR 97209
800/262-7668
503/241-4351
Fax: 503/241-4370
Tech. Support: 503/241-1530
Price: $69.99
Platform: MPC, Macintosh
Grade Level: Elementary, Middle, Senior High School
Curriculum: Science
Description: Travel back in time to the Mesozoic Era with this dinosaur adventure game while learning about dinosaurs, geography, flora, fauna and geology. Three-hundred-ten locations in five time periods, 100 species of Mesozoic plants and 60 live action, animated creatures are included.

Distant Suns
Virtual Reality Labs Inc.
2341 Ganador Court
San Luis Obispo, CA 93401
805/545-8515
Fax: 805/781-2259
Tech. Support: 805/545-8515
Price: $149.95

Platform: Macintosh, MPC
Grade Level: Senior High School
Curriculum: Science
Description: Take a trip on a spaceship offering earth views of the solar system, lunar phase guide and planet position guide. View up to 9,100 stars, 450 galaxies, reproduce eclipses, see lunar phases and read detailed information on the past and present solar system.

Doctor's Book of Home Remedies
Compton's NewMedia Inc.
2320 Camino Vida Roble
Carlsbad, CA 92009
800/862-2206
800/216-6116 (catalog sales)
619/929-2500
Fax: 619/929-2555
Tech. Support: 619/929-2626
Price: $29.96
Platform: DOS, Windows
Grade Level: Middle, Senior High School
Curriculum: Health
Description: Over 2,300 home remedies containing thousands of tips and techniques that everyone can use for healing everyday health problems.

Don Quixote
Ebook Inc.
32970 Alvarado-Niles Road, Suite 704
Union City, CA 94587
510/429-1331
Fax: 510/429-1394
Tech. Support: 510/713-8904
Price: $29.95
Platform: MPC
Grade Level: Middle, Senior High School
Curriculum: Language Arts
Description: Don Quixote and his faithful companion, Sancho Panza, set out to rid the world of the Devil. This classic tale of humanity comes to life with vivid illustrations, music and lively narration.

Electricity and Magnetism
Cambrix Publishing
6269 Variel Avenue, Suite B
Woodland Hills, CA 91367
818/992-8484
Fax: 818/992-8781
Tech. Support: 818/992-8484
Price: $49.95
Platform: DOS
Grade Level: Senior High School
Curriculum: Science
Description: An interactive disc with hundreds of animations, photographs and diagrams of the world of electricity and magnetism. Users can activate animations which show how electrical current flows around a circuit or how a lightning conductor works.

Electronic Dewey
OCLC Forest Press
6565 Frantz Road
Dublin, OH 43017
800/848-5878 (orders)
614/764-6000
Fax: 614/764-6096
Tech. Support: 800/848-5800
Price: $400
Platform: DOS
Grade Level: Senior High School
Curriculum: General
Description: A computerized version of the Dewey Decimal Classification that lets you search the D.D.C. quickly and efficiently while assigning classification numbers as part of the cataloging process.

Electronic Encyclopedia of WWII
Marshall Cavendish Corp.
2415 Jerusalem Avenue, P.O. Box 587
North Bellmore, NY 11710
800/821-9881
Fax: 516/785-8133
Tech. Support: 800/643-4351
Price: $379.95, single users; $895, network
50 users
Platform: DOS
Grade Level: Senior High School
Curriculum: Social Studies
Description: A chronological and comprehensive history of the Second World War.
Includes the full text of the print
Encyclopedia of World War II.

Electronic Eugenean
400 E. 19th Avenue
South Eugene, OR 97401
South Eugene High School
Eugene, OR 97401
503/687-3201
Price: $25
Platform: Macintosh
Grade Level: Senior High School
Curriculum: General
Description: A unique high school yearbook created by the students, depicting
pictures and maps of the school, photographs of the students and faculty and
detailed events of the school year.

EPS PRO 1
Wayzata Technologies
2515 East Highway 2
Grand Rapids, MI 55744
800/377-7321
218/326-0597
218/326-2939 (bulletin board)
Fax: 218/326-0598

Tech. Support: 800/377-7321
Price: $149
Platform: Macintosh, Windows, DOS
Grade Level: Senior High School
Curriculum: Arts & Music
Description: A collection of over 800 fully
resizable Encapsulated PostScript images in
30 categories to use with desktop publishing. The CMD Collection consists of design
elements, T-Shirts, alphabetic designs for
color pieces, covers and backgrounds.

EPS PRO 2
Wayzata Technologies
2515 East Highway 2
Grand Rapids, MI 55744
800/377-7321
218/326-0597
218/326-2939 (bulletin board)
Fax: 218/326-0598
Tech. Support: 800/377-7321
Price: $149
Platform: Macintosh, Windows, DOS
Grade Level: Senior High School
Curriculum: Arts & Music
Description: Over 600 Encapsulated
PostScript images which are fully resizable
and can easily be edited. Easy to browse
images with QuickTime Slide Show or
printed catalog of all images.

European Monarchs
Quanta Press Inc.
1313 Fifth Street, Suite SE 223A
Minneapolis, MN 55414
612/379-3956
Fax: 612/623-4570
Price: $79.95
Platform: Macintosh, DOS
Grade Level: Senior High School
Curriculum: Social Studies

Description: Historical database of information related to the monarchs of Europe. Contains records of Kings and Queens from over 20 European nations (past and present). Also includes 16 black and white sketches of selected monarchs.

Everywhere USA Travel Guide
Deep River Publishing
P.O. Box 9715-975
Portland, ME 04104
800/643-5630
207/871-1684
Fax: 207/871-1683
Tech. Support: 207/871-1684
Price: $59.95
Platform: Macintosh, MPC
Grade Level: Middle, Senior High School
Curriculum: Reference & Interdisciplinary
Description: Thousands of U.S. tourist sites with an easy interface for viewing attractions.

The Family Doctor
Creative Multimedia
514 NW 11th Avenue, Suite 203
Portland, OR 97209
800/262-7668
503/241-4351
Fax: 503/241-4370
Tech. Support: 503/241-1530
Price: $79.99
Platform: Macintosh, MPC
Grade Level: Middle, Senior High School
Curriculum: Health
Description: Over 240 color images illustrating human anatomy, diseases, common medical procedures and brand name drugs. The full-text "Family Doctor" column covers 1,500 common questions. Also included is a consumer guide to 1,600 prescription drugs showing uses and side effects.

Federal Grants/ Funding Locator
Staff Directories Ltd.
P.O. Box 62
Mount Vernon, VA 22121-0062
703/739-0900
Fax: 703/739-0234
Tech. Support: 703/739-0900, Ext. 218
Price: $295
Platform: DOS, Windows
Grade Level: Senior High School
Curriculum: General
Description: Provides detailed information on every grant or funding program by a federal agency, over 1,400 programs covering topics from AIDS to Zoology with funds for individual schools, non-profit, etc.

Food/Analyst PLUS
Hopkins Technology
421 Hazel Lane
Hopkins, MN 55343-7116
800/397-9211
Fax: 612/931-9377
Tech. Support: 800/397-9211
Price: $199
Platform: DOS
Grade Level: Senior High School
Curriculum: Health
Description: A complete nutritional analysis program which reports food calories, fat, sugar, protein, cholesterol, vitamins and more. Contains 23,000 foods with 100 nutrients.

FracTunes
Quanta Press Inc.
1313 Fifth Street, Suite SE 223A
Minneapolis, MN 55414
612/379-3956
Fax: 612/623-4570
Price: $49.95

Platform: DOS
Grade Level: Senior High School
Curriculum: Arts & Music
Description: Helps the viewer add an
entirely new visual dimension to music
creating a new art form. It provides a
musical kaleidoscope driven by music data.

Freshe Arte
Quanta Press Inc.
1313 Fifth Street, Suite SE 223A
Minneapolis, MN 55414
612/379-3956
Fax: 612/623-4570
Price: $99.95
Platform: Macintosh, DOS
Grade Level: Senior High School
Curriculum: Arts & Music
Description: Public domain clip art—
over 1,500 images in 600dpi, royalty
free; includes a section of art created by
children.

From Alice To Ocean
Claris Corporation
5201 Patrick Henry Drive
Santa Clara, CA 95052
800/325-2747
Fax: 408/987-3932
Price: $49.95
Platform: Macintosh
Grade Level: Elementary, Middle, Senior
High School
Curriculum: Reference &
Interdisciplinary
Description: Book and CD-ROM combi-
nation that describes the incredible and
beautiful journey of a lone woman
(except for the photographer) and her
camels as they journeyed from central
Australia to the coast.

Front Page News—Plus Business
Buckmaster Publishing
Route 4 Box 1630
Mineral, VA 23117
800/282-5628
703/894-5777
Fax: 703/894-9141
Tech. Support: 800/282-5628
Price: $149.95, subscription; $650,
annually
Platform: MPC
Grade Level: Middle, Senior High School
Curriculum: Social Studies
Description: Over 200,000 news articles.
The articles may range in length from a
paragraph to over 3,000 words. All articles
contain a headline, data, source and the
full text of the article. Updated service
every three months.

Gale's Literary Index
Gale Research Inc.
835 Penobscot Building
Detroit, MI 48226-4094
800/877-GALE
313/961-2242
Fax: 313/961-6083
Tech. Support: 800/877-4253, Ext. 6021
Price: $149
Platform: DOS
Grade Level: Senior High School
Curriculum: Language Arts
Description: Combines various indexes
from 32 literary series including
*Contemporary Authors, Nineteenth
Century Literary Criticism* and
Contemporary Literary Criticism. The disc
indexes biographies and criticisms of over
110,000 authors and 120,000 titles.

Games in Japanese
(Playing with Language Series)

Syracuse Language Systems
719 East Genesee Street
Syracuse, NY 13210
315/478-6729
Fax: 315/478-6902
Tech. Support: 800/688-1937
Price: $39.95
Platform: MPC
Grade Level: Elementary, Middle
Curriculum: Foreign Language
Description: Multimedia games offering students an exciting way to practice, learn and use language.

Goferwinkel's Adventure
Ebook Inc.
32970 Alvarado-Niles Road, Suite 704
Union City, CA 94587
510/429-1331
Fax: 510/429-1394
Tech. Support: 510/713-8904
Price: $29.95
Platform: Macintosh, MPC
Grade Level: Elementary
Curriculum: Language Arts
Description: A journey through Lavender Land, a magical place where anything can happen. Will Goferwinkel ever find his way home?

The Grammy Awards
Compton's NewMedia Inc.
2320 Camino Vida Roble
Carlsbad, CA 92009
800/862-2206
800/216-6116 (catalog sales)
619/929-2500
Fax: 619/929-2555
Tech. Support: 619/929-2626
Price: $59.95
Platform: DOS

Grade Level: Middle, Senior High School
Curriculum: Arts & Music
Description: The 34-year history of the most prestigious awards in the music industry, as well as information on every nominee and winner.

Great Cities of the World Vol. 1
InterOptica Publishing Ltd.
300 Montgomery Street, Suite 201
San Francisco, CA 94104
800/708-7827 (orders)
415/788-8788
Fax: 415/788-8886
Tech. Support: 212/941-2988
Price: $49.95
Platform: Macintosh, Windows
Grade Level: Middle, Senior High School
Curriculum: Social Studies
Description: Covers Bombay, Cairo, London, Los Angeles, Moscow, New York, Paris, Rio de Janeiro, Sydney and Tokyo plus climate, currency, local times, phrases, culture, sights, transport, shopping, entertainment, recreation, restaurants, hotels and travel planner.

Great Cities of the World Vol. 2
InterOptica Publishing Ltd.
300 Montgomery Street, Suite 201
San Francisco, CA 94104
800/708-7827 (orders)
415/788-8788
Fax: 415/788-8886
Tech. Support: 212/941-2988
Price: $49.95
Platform: Macintosh, Windows
Grade Level: Middle, Senior High School
Curriculum: Social Studies
Description: Covers Berlin, Buenos Aires, Chicago, Jerusalem, Johannesburg, Rome, San Francisco, Seoul, Singapore and Toronto.

Great Literature Plus
Bureau for Electronic Publishing
141 New Road
Parsippany, NJ 07054
800/828-4766 (orders)
201/808-2700
Fax: 201/808-2676
Tech. Support: 201/808-2700, Ext. 22
Price: $99
Platform: Macintosh, DOS, MPC
Grade Level: Senior High School
Curriculum: Language Arts
Description: The full text of 943 classic
works of literature. It includes 31 biogra-
phies, journals, letters, 21 literary criticisms,
32 historical documents, 75 essays, 461
poems, 199 fictional works, 10 religious doc-
uments and 27 science and education books.

Great Wonders of the World Vol. 1
InterOptica Publishing Ltd.
300 Montgomery Street, Suite 201
San Francisco, CA 94104
800/708-7827 (orders)
415/788-8788
Fax: 415/788-8886
Tech. Support: 212/941-2988
Price: $99.95
Platform: Macintosh, Windows
Grade Level: Middle, Senior High School
Curriculum: Social Studies
Description: Man-made wonders of the
world such as the Empire State Building,
Angkor Wat, Great Wall of China, Inca
Ruins, Panama Canal, Pyramids, Taj
Mahal, trans-Siberian Railway, and Venice.

Great Wonders of the World Vol. 2
Natural Wonders
InterOptica Publishing Ltd.
300 Montgomery Street, Suite 201

San Francisco, CA 94104
800/708-7827 (orders)
415/788-8788
Fax: 415/788-8886
Tech. Support: 212/941-2988
Price: $99.95
Platform: Macintosh, Windows
Grade Level: Middle, Senior High School
Curriculum: Social Studies
Description: Over 350 illustrations, maps
and photographs. 500 pages of text for
Natural Wonders of the World such as
the Great Barrier Reef, Indian Monsoon,
Mount Everest, Grand Canyon, Amazon
Rain Forest, Wild Beast Migration, and
the Blue Whale.

Heart: The Engine of Life
Updata Publications Inc.
1736 Westwood Boulevard
Los Angeles, CA 90024
800/882-2844
Fax: 310/474-4095
Tech. Support: 800/882-2844
Price: $99
Platform: DOS
Grade Level: Middle, Senior High School
Curriculum: Health
Description: An animated color tutorial
that interacts with the user. Everything you
ever wanted to know about the heart and
how it functions.

The Herbalist
Hopkins Technology
421 Hazel Lane
Hopkins, MN 55343-7116
800/397-9211
Fax: 612/931-9377
Tech. Support: 800/397-9211
Price: $99.95

Platform: Windows
Grade Level: Senior High School
Curriculum: Health
Description: Introduces the skilled use of herbal medicines within a holistic approach. Includes details on over 180 herbs.

History of the World
Bureau for Electronic Publishing
141 New Road
Parsippany, NJ 07054
800/828-4766 (orders)
201/808-2700
Fax: 201/808-2676
Tech. Support: 201/808-2700, Ext. 22
Price: $79.95
Platform: Macintosh, DOS
Grade Level: Senior High School
Curriculum: Social Studies
Description: Based on two best-selling textbooks from Harper Collins, this title spans the history of the world from Caesar to Apollo space mission.

Illustrated Facts: How the World Works
XIPHIAS
8758 Venice Boulevard
Los Angeles, CA 90034
800/421-9194 (sales)
310/841-2790
Fax: 310/841-2559
Price: $39.95
Platform: Macintosh, MPC
Grade Level: Senior High School
Curriculum: Social Studies
Description: A compilation of 70 video clips that takes an entertaining look at man's endeavors in the areas of justice, warfare, money, media, lifestyle, enterprise and government.

Illustrated Facts: How Things Work
XIPHIAS
8758 Venice Boulevard
Los Angeles, CA 90034
800/421-9194 (sales)
310/841-2790
Fax: 310/841-2559
Price: $39.95
Platform: Macintosh, MPC
Grade Level: Middle
Curriculum: Science
Description: A compilation of 70 video clips that looks at man's endeavors in areas of transportation, computation, tools, communication, time measurement, weapons and sensory extensions.

Interactive Storytime, Volumes 1 and 3
Interactive Publishing Corporation
300 Airport Executive Park
Spring Valley, NY 10977
800/472-8777 (orders)
914/426-0400
Fax: 914/426-2606
Tech. Support: 914/426-0400
Price: $49.95
Platform: Macintosh, DOS
Grade Level: Primary, Elementary
Curriculum: Storybook
Description: Each disc in the series contains several stories, with good animation and music. Each story can be printed out in black and white line drawings, as a coloring book.

Introductory Chemistry CD-ROM
Falcon Software
P.O. Box 200
Wentworth, NH 03282
603/764-5788
Fax: 603/764-9051

Tech. Support: 617/235-1767
Price: $695
Platform: MPC
Grade Level: Senior High School
Curriculum: Science
Description: Covers the laboratory, lecture and textbook topics of a first year general chemistry course. Includes over 200 interactive lessons, approximately 110 hours of instruction.

John Schumacher's
New Prague Hotel Cookbook
Quanta Press Inc.
1313 Fifth Street, Suite SE 223A
Minneapolis, MN 55414
612/379-3956
Fax: 612/623-4570
Price: $29.95
Platform: DOS
Grade Level: Senior High School
Curriculum: Reference & Interdisciplinary
Description: Discusses Chef Schumacher's childhood to his professional progress as a chef. Recipes range from Eastern European dishes to traditional American.

KGB World Factbook
Quanta Press Inc.
1313 Fifth Street, Suite SE 223A
Minneapolis, MN 55414
612/379-3956
Fax: 612/623-4570
Price: $49.95
Platform: Macintosh, DOS
Grade Level: Senior High School
Curriculum: Social Studies
Description: World data collected from open Soviet literature (unclassified).

Kid's Zoo
Knowledge Adventure

4502 Dyer Street
La Crescenta, CA 91214
800/542-4240 (orders)
818/248-0166 (bulletin board)
Fax: 818/542-4205
Tech. Support: 818/249-0212
Price: $79.95
Platform: DOS, Windows
Grade Level: Primary, Elementary
Curriculum: Science
Description: An introduction to the world of baby animals. Learn animal names, letter sounds, footprints, and what fur and feathers look like. Read along with a 30-page electronic book.

Learn to Speak English
HyperGlot Software Co. Inc.
P.O. Box 10746
Knoxville, TN 37939-0746
800/949-4379
615/558-8270
Fax: 615/588-6569
Tech. Support: 800/949-4379
Price: $99
Platform: Macintosh, MPC
Grade Level: Middle, Senior High School
Curriculum: Foreign Language
Description: Based on a course developed and used by the U.S. Foreign Service. A complete first year language course with extensive sound on two CDs. Thirty-six context-driven lessons with strong emphasis on understanding spoken language.

Learn to Speak French
HyperGlot Software Co. Inc.
P.O. Box 10746
Knoxville, TN 37939-0746
800/949-4379
615/558-8270

Fax: 615/588-6569
Tech. Support: 800/949-4379
Price: $99
Platform: Macintosh, MPC
Grade Level: Middle, Senior High School
Curriculum: Foreign Language
Description: A complete first year language course with extensive sound on two CDs. Thirty-six context-driven lessons with strong emphasis on understanding spoken language.

Lenny's Music Toons
Paramount Interactive
700 Hansen Way
Palo Alto, CA 94304
415/813-8030
Fax: 415/813-8055
Tech. Support: 415/813-8030
Price: $39.95
Platform: Windows
Grade Level: Elementary
Curriculum: Arts & Music
Description: Meet Lenny, a world renowned musician, adventurer and collector of clever devices, who familiarizes children with music and exposes them to elements of music composition as well as sight reading and memory games.

Let's Go 1993 California and Hawaii
Compton's NewMedia Inc.
2320 Camino Vida Roble
Carlsbad, CA 92009
800/862-2206
800/216-6116 (catalog sales)
619/929-2500
Fax: 619/929-2555
Tech. Support: 619/929-2626
Price: $24.95
Platform: Macintosh, DOS, MPC

Grade Level: Middle, Senior High School
Curriculum: Social Studies
Description: 1993—The Budget Guide to California and Hawaii including Reno, Las Vegas, Grand Canyon, and Baja California.

Let's Go 1993 USA
Compton's NewMedia Inc.
2320 Camino Vida Roble
Carlsbad, CA 92009
800/862-2206
800/216-6116 (catalog sales)
619/929-2500
Fax: 619/929-2555
Tech. Support: 619/929-2626
Price: $24.95
Platform: Macintosh, DOS, MPC
Grade Level: Middle, Senior High School
Curriculum: Social Studies
Description: 1993—The Budget Guide to USA including Canada, Quebec, Ontario, British Columbia, and Yukon (maritime provinces).

Library of the Future Series
World Library Inc.
2809 Main Street
Irvine, CA 92714
800/443-0238
714/756-9500
Fax: 714/756-9511
Tech. Support: 714/756-9550
Price: $299
Platform: Macintosh, DOS, Windows
Grade Level: Senior High School
Curriculum: Language Arts
Description: The complete text with illustrations of over 950 titles from over 500 works of literature, philosophy, drama, poetry, science and religion.

Lingua ROM 3
HyperGlot Software Co. Inc.
P.O. Box 10746
Knoxville, TN 37939-0746
800/949-4379
615/558-8270
Fax: 615/588-6569
Tech. Support: 800/949-4379
Price: $999
Platform: Macintosh
Grade Level: Senior High School
Curriculum: Foreign Language
Description: Complete interactive set for learning Chinese, French, German, Italian, Russian and Spanish.

MACnificent 7.0 Education and Tales
Wayzata Technologies
2515 East Highway 2
Grand Rapids, MI 55744
800/377-7321
218/326-0597
218/326-2939 (bulletin board)
Fax: 218/326-0598
Tech. Support: 800/377-7321
Price: $59
Platform: Macintosh
Grade Level: Elementary, Middle
Curriculum: Reference & Interdisciplinary
Description: Over 5,000 files, including System 7.1 games and educational shareware, plus commercial demos, sounds and sound stacks. Includes The Librarian, which provides searching access to all of this information. All files are indexed and described.

Magazine Articles Summaries Elite
EBSCO Publishing Inc.
P.O. Box 2250
Peabody, MA 01960-7250
800/653-2726

508/535-8500
Fax: 508/535-8545
Tech. Support: 800/758-5995
Price: 4x/yr., $2399; 10x/yr., $2799; 12x/yr., $3199
Platform: Macintosh, DOS
Grade Level: Senior High School
Curriculum: Reference & Interdisciplinary
Description: 125 magazines full text plus indexing and abstracts from over 400 general magazines and the *New York Times.*

Magazine Articles Summaries Select
EBSCO Publishing Inc.
P.O. Box 2250
Peabody, MA 01960-7250
800/653-2726
508/535-8500
Fax: 508/535-8545
Tech. Support: 800/758-5995
Platform: Macintosh, DOS
Grade Level: Senior High School
Curriculum: Reference & Interdisciplinary
Description: 60 magazines full text plus indexing and abstracts from over 400 general magazines and the *New York Times.*

Magill's Survey of Science
EBSCO Publishing Inc.
P.O. Box 2250
Peabody, MA 01960-7250
800/653-2726
508/535-8500
Fax: 508/535-8545
Tech. Support: 800/758-5995
Price: $895
Platform: DOS
Grade Level: Senior High School
Curriculum: Science
Description: Magill's Survey of Science contains the complete text of four print

reference series from Salem Press: Earth Sciences, 1990; Life Science Series, 1991; Physical Science, 1992; and Applied Science Series, 1993. Twenty-three volumes in total are included on the disc. Each volume in the series contains essays by various authors.

Mario's Early Years: Fun with Letters
The Software Toolworks Inc.
60 Leveroni Court
Novato, CA 94949
800/231-3088
415/883-3000
Fax: 415/883-3303
Tech. Support: 415/883-3000
Price: $49.95
Platform: DOS
Grade Level: Primary, Elementary
Curriculum: Language Arts
Description: Children discover the world around them by exploring the elements of that world. Children are introduced to the fundamentals of letters and sounds by way of learning worlds—Vowel, Alphabet, First Letter, Last Letter, Building, Blending and more.

Mars Explorer
Virtual Reality Labs Inc.
2341 Ganador Court
San Luis Obispo, CA 93401
805/545-8515
Fax: 805/781-2259
Tech. Support: 805/545-8515
Price: $69.95
Platform: DOS
Grade Level: Senior High School
Curriculum: Science
Description: A CD-ROM-based program for viewing the surface of Mars, as photographed

by NASA Viking Orbiters. The program can overlay the IAU-approved names of objects of places as well as longitude and latitude lines with labels.

Math Finder
The Learning Team
10 Long Pond Road
Armonk, NY 10504
914/273-2226
Fax: 914/273-2227
Price: $295.99
Platform: Macintosh, DOS
Grade Level: Elementary, Middle, Senior High School
Curriculum: Mathematics
Description: A computer access to curriculum to implement the NCTM Standards. Over 15,000 pages and 1,100 lessons of resources for math teachers to help in the curriculum development process.

Mathematics Vol. 1
Xploratorium
The Renaissance Project
Department of Education
Anglia Polytechnic
Sawyers Hall Lane
Brentwood, England CM15 9BT
Price: Write for information
Platform: Macintosh
Grade Level: Senior High School
Curriculum: Mathematics
Description: Contains five sections (using HyperCard)—Numerical Analysis, Scientific and Graphical Toolkit, HyperTest, Introduction to Calculus, and Mathematical Modeling (Simple Harmonic Motion).

**McGraw-Hill Science and
Technical Reference Set**
McGraw-Hill Inc.
11 W. 19th Street
New York, NY 10011
800/842-3075
Fax: 212/337-4092
Tech. Support: 800/551-2210
Price: $495
Platform: DOS
Grade Level: Senior High School
Curriculum: Science
Description: Two standard references, the
Encyclopedia of Science and Technology,
2nd edition, and the *Dictionary of Scientific
and Technical Terms*, 4th edition.

Mediasource—Historical Library Vol. 1
Applied Optical Media Corporation
1450 Boot Road, Building 400A
West Chester, PA 19380
800/321-7259
610/429-3701
Fax: 610/429-3810
Tech. Support: 800/321-7259
Price: $395
Platform: Macintosh, MPC
Grade Level: Senior High School
Curriculum: Arts & Music
Description: A collection of drawings, col-
ored drawings and black and white photos
of significant events and personalities from
antiquity through WWII with a varied
selection of background music fanfares
and bridges and sound effects.

**Mediasource—
Natural Sciences Library Vol. 1**
Applied Optical Media Corporation
1450 Boot Road, Building 400A
West Chester, PA 19380

800/321-7259
610/429-3701
Fax: 610/429-3810
Tech. Support: 800/321-7259
Price: $395
Platform: Macintosh, MPC
Grade Level: Senior High School
Curriculum: Arts & Music
Description: A collection of full-color
images on topics related to science including agriculture, anatomy, biology, botany,
chemistry and physics, environment science, geology, nutrition, weather and climate and zoology with a varied selection
of background music fanfares.

Middle East Diary
Quanta Press Inc.
1313 Fifth Street, Suite SE 223A
Minneapolis, MN 55414
612/379-3956
Fax: 612/623-4570
Price: $99.95
Platform: Macintosh, DOS
Grade Level: Senior High School
Curriculum: Social Studies
Description: A lengthy review of Middle East
history, personalities and conflicts. Includes
travel, business and political information.

Middle Search
EBSCO Publishing Inc.
P.O. Box 2250
Peabody, MA 01960-7250
800/653-2726
508/535-8500
Fax: 508/535-8545
Tech. Support: 800/758-5995
Price: 10x/yr., $899
Platform: Macintosh, DOS
Grade Level: Middle, Senior High School

Curriculum: Reference & Interdisciplinary
Description: Indexing and abstracts from 125 magazines, with full text from 33 magazines.

Monarch Notes
Bureau for Electronic Publishing
141 New Road
Parsippany, NJ 07054
800/828-4766 (orders)
201/808-2700
Fax: 201/808-2676
Tech. Support: 201/808-2700, Ext. 22
Price: $79
Platform: Macintosh, DOS, MPC
Grade Level: Senior High School
Curriculum: Language Arts
Description: Over 200 different notes and the full text of Simon and Schuster *Monarch Notes*. Also includes author biographies, overviews, character analyses, spoken excerpts, pictures of authors, characters and settings and critical commentaries.

Movie Select
Paramount Interactive
700 Hansen Way
Palo Alto, CA 94304
415/813-8030
Fax: 415/813-8055
Tech. Support: 415/813-8030
Price: $39.95
Platform: Macintosh, MPC
Grade Level: Middle, Senior High School
Curriculum: Arts & Music
Description: A movie recommendation system to over 44,000 movies and videos.

The Multi-Bible 1990 Vol. 1
Innotech Multimedia
2001 Sheppard Avenue E., Suite 118

North York, Ontario, Canada M2J 4Z7
416/492-3838
Fax: 416/492-3843
Tech. Support: 416/492-3838
Price: $98.25
Platform: Macintosh, DOS
Grade Level: Senior High School
Curriculum: Reference & Interdisciplinary
Description: A collection of six Bible databases. Indexes include every word in every version and has been applied to versions in seven languages.

Multimedia Audubon's Birds
Creative Multimedia
514 NW 11th Avenue, Suite 203
Portland, OR 97209
800/262-7668
503/241-4351
Fax: 503/241-4370
Tech. Support: 503/241-1530
Price: $49.99
Platform: Macintosh, DOS
Grade Level: Middle, Senior High School
Curriculum: Science
Description: Full text of James Audubon's seven volume *Birds of America*. Birds of North America are included in 500 color plates, black and white figures and bird calls from Library of Natural Sciences.

Multimedia Audubon's Mammals
Creative Multimedia
514 NW 11th Avenue, Suite 203
Portland, OR 97209
800/262-7668
503/241-4351
Fax: 503/241-4370
Tech. Support: 503/241-1530
Price: $49.99
Platform: Macintosh, DOS

Grade Level: Middle, Senior High School
Curriculum: Science
Description: Contains the complete text of the 1840 first edition of "Octavio" set of John James Audubon's *Quadrupeds of North America.* Over 150 full-color mammal lithographs, full text indexing CD quality sounds for many mammals from Cornell Library of Natural Science.

Multimedia Business Week 1000 on CD-ROM
McGraw-Hill Inc.
11 W. 19th Street
New York, NY 10011
800/842-3075
Fax: 212/337-4092
Tech. Support: 800/551-2210
Price: $99
Platform: MPC
Grade Level: Senior High School
Curriculum: Social Studies
Description: A profile of the *Business Week* 1,000 most valuable companies. Includes Standard and Poor's company data, 25 executives to watch, interviews with 13 top executives and multimedia essay.

Multimedia Encyclopedia of Mammalian Biology
McGraw-Hill Inc.
11 W. 19th Street
New York, NY 10011
800/842-3075
Fax: 212/337-4092
Tech. Support: 800/551-2210
Price: $495
Platform: Windows
Grade Level: Senior High School
Curriculum: Science

Description: The full-text color photographs, artwork and maps of all five volumes of Grzimek's *Encyclopedia of Mammals.* Includes 3,500 full-color images and 500 maps, full glossary of terms, full current bibliography of scientific literature, and movie and sound.

Multimedia Family Bible
Candlelight Publishing
P.O. Box 5213
Mesa, AZ 85211-5213
800/677-3045
Fax: 801/373-2499
Tech. Support: 800/677-3045
Price: $39.95
Platform: Windows
Grade Level: Senior High School
Curriculum: Reference & Interdisciplinary
Description: Combines the classic King James text with 44 animated Bible stories, detailed full-color maps and gazetteer of the Holy Land, more than 100 photos of significant sites in the Holy Land, and a fully-linked Greek and Hebrew lexicon.

Multimedia Music Book: Mozart
Ebook Inc.
32970 Alvarado-Niles Road, Suite 704
Union City, CA 94587
510/429-1331
Fax: 510/429-1394
Tech. Support: 510/713-8904
Price: $24.95
Platform: Macintosh, MPC
Grade Level: Senior High School
Curriculum: Arts & Music
Description: The composer's music and life.

Multimedia World Factbook
Bureau for Electronic Publishing
141 New Road
Parsippany, NJ 07054
800/828-4766 (orders)
201/808-2700
Fax: 201/808-2676
Tech. Support: 201/808-2700, Ext. 22
Price: $29.95
Platform: Macintosh, DOS, MPC
Grade Level: Senior High School
Curriculum: Social Studies
Description: Two-hundred-forty-eight
country profiles from the CIA yearbook,
with added information from the KGB
yearbook, Hammond maps and segments
of national anthems.

My Advanced Label Designer
My Software Company
1259 El Camino Real, Suite 167
Menlo Park, CA 94025
800/325-3508 (orders)
415/325-4222
Price: $59.95
Platform: Macintosh, Windows
Grade Level: Middle, Senior High School
Curriculum: General
Description: Labels are professionally
designed by importing your own com-
pany graphics or select from dozens of
clip art images.

National Parks:
The Multimedia Family Guide
Cambrix Publishing
6269 Variel Avenue, Suite B
Woodland Hills, CA 91367
818/992-8484
Fax: 818/992-8781
Tech. Support: 818/992-8484

Price: $59.95
Platform: Macintosh, MPC
Grade Level: Middle, Senior High School
Curriculum: Reference & Interdisciplinary
Description: A comprehensive interactive
directory of all the National Parks of
America. Includes videos, photographs,
travel planning, and searching park index.

Nautilus
Metatec Corporation
7001 Metatec Boulevard
Dublin, OH 43017
614/761-2000
Fax: 614/761-4258
Tech. Support: 614/766-3150
Price: $137.40, 12 monthly issues;
Backpacs, 6 back issues, $69.95
Platform: Macintosh, Windows
Grade Level: Senior High School
Curriculum: Reference & Interdisciplinary
Description: A multimedia magazine on
CD-ROM that provides information and
software for Macintosh and DOS users.

New Basics Electronic Cookbook
XIPHIAS
8758 Venice Boulevard
Los Angeles, CA 90034
800/421-9194 (sales)
310/841-2790
Fax: 310/841-2559
Price: $69.95
Platform: DOS, MPC
Grade Level: Senior High School
Curriculum: Reference & Interdisciplinary
Description: Created from *Silver Palate
Cookbook* series by the authors Julie Rosso
and Sheila Likins. Includes a library of
over 1,800 recipes, hundreds of color pic-
tures, and cooking hints.

New York Times Ondisc
University Microfilm International
300 North Zeeb Road
Ann Harbor, MI 48106
313/761-4700
Fax: 313/761-1204
Tech. Support: 800/521-0600, Ext. 2513
Price: $2450
Platform: DOS
Grade Level: Senior High School
Curriculum: Reference & Interdisciplinary
Description: Contains all the articles in full text published from 1990 to the present. Updated monthly.

NewsBank CD Junior
NewsBank, Inc.
58 Pine Street
New Canaan, CT 06840-5426
800/762-8182
203/966-1100
Fax: 203/966-6254
Tech. Support: 800/762-8182
Price: $795
Platform: DOS
Grade Level: Middle
Curriculum: Reference & Interdisciplinary
Description: Citations from over 105 magazines with 10 magazines full text, plus articles from 40 newspapers.

NewsBank Index to Periodicals
NewsBank, Inc.
58 Pine Street
New Canaan, CT 06840-5426
800/762-8182
203/966-1100
Fax: 203/966-6254
Tech. Support: 800/762-8182
Platform: DOS
Grade Level: Middle, Senior High School

Curriculum: Reference & Interdisciplinary
Description: Citations from over 200 magazines from 1988 to the present. Includes abstract and full bibliographic data.

Newsweek Interactive—
Unfinished Business
The Software Toolworks Inc.
60 Leveroni Court
Novato, CA 94949
800/231-3088
415/883-3000
Fax: 415/883-3303
Tech. Support: 415/883-3000
Price: $129.95, four editions
Platform: DOS
Grade Level: Senior High School
Curriculum: Social Studies
Description: An interactive disc covering current events through *Newsweek* correspondents.

North American Indians
Quanta Press Inc.
1313 Fifth Street, Suite SE 223A
Minneapolis, MN 55414
612/379-3956
Fax: 612/623-4570
Price: $69.95
Platform: Macintosh, DOS
Grade Level: Senior High School
Curriculum: Social Studies
Description: North American Indians CD includes original information about the American Indian with historical photographs and interpretations.

Peter and the Wolf
Ebook Inc.
32970 Alvarado-Niles Road, Suite 704
Union City, CA 94587

510/429-1331
Fax: 510/429-1394
Tech. Support: 510/713-8904
Price: $34.95
Platform: Macintosh, MPC
Grade Level: Middle
Curriculum: Language Arts
Description: Prokofiev's famous musical piece, narrated by Jack Lemmon, with pictures and musical surprises. Can also be listened to on a standard CD-Audio player.

Peterson's College Database
SilverPlatter Information Inc.
100 River Ridge Drive
Norwood, MA 02062-5026
800/343-0064
617/769-2599
Fax: 617/769-8763
Tech. Support: 800/343-0064
Price: $595, single user; $995, 8 network users
Platform: DOS
Grade Level: Senior High School
Curriculum: Reference & Interdisciplinary
Description: Individual descriptive profiles of 3,300 accredited degree-granting colleges. Includes statistics, expenses, financial aid, majors offered, etc.

Photo Pro
Wayzata Technologies
2515 East Highway 2
Grand Rapids, MI 55744
800/377-7321
218/326-0597
218/326-2939 (bulletin board)
Fax: 218/326-0598
Tech. Support: 800/377-7321
Price: $129
Platform: DOS

Grade Level: Senior High School
Curriculum: Arts & Music
Description: A collection of over 100 photographs of nature scenes taken in the Midwest USA. Format is 24-bit TIFF and PCX. Full reproduction rights for users.

Physician's Desk Reference
Medical Economics Data
5 Paragon Drive
Montvale, NJ 07645
201/358-7200
Fax: 201/573-0867
Price: $595, includes two updates
Platform: DOS
Grade Level: Senior High School
Curriculum: Health
Description: A 2,000 page comprehensive pharmaceutical reference system, which contains a complete collection of prescribing references published by PDR including all product descriptions, *Physician Desk Reference*, *PDR for Ophthalmology*, and *PDR for Nonprescription Drugs*.

Pilgrim Quest
Decision Development Corp.
2680 Bishop Drive, Suite 122
San Ramon, CA 94583
800/835-4332
Fax: 510/830-0830
Tech. Support: 800/835-4332
Price: $99.95; school, $129.95
Platform: DOS
Grade Level: Elementary, Middle, Senior High School
Curriculum: Social Studies
Description: Challenges students with choices and situations like those the Pilgrims faced. School version includes lesson plans, teacher's guide and audio cassette.

Pixel Garden
Quanta Press Inc.
1313 Fifth Street, Suite SE 223A
Minneapolis, MN 55414
612/379-3956
Fax: 612/623-4570
Price: $79.95
Platform: DOS
Grade Level: Senior High School
Curriculum: Arts & Music
Description: Database of 522 ornamental
plants common in U.S. Includes high color
photograph (560 images) and specific
attributes.

Planet Earth: Gaia Library
Xploratorium
The Renaissance Project
Department of Education
Anglia Polytechnic
Sawyers Hall Lane
Brentwood, England CM15 9BT
Platform: Macintosh
Grade Level: Senior High School
Curriculum: Science
Description: Uses James Lovelock's Gaia
Theory, Stella simulations of Daisyworlds,
resources and learning activities to advance
the idea that life on earth is a self-modifying
and self-regulating system. Includes environ-
mental studies, geology and oceanography.

The Plant Doctor
Quanta Press Inc.
1313 Fifth Street, Suite SE 223A
Minneapolis, MN 55414
612/379-3956
Fax: 612/623-4570
Price: $49.95
Platform: Macintosh, DOS
Grade Level: Senior High School

Curriculum: Science
Description: A multimedia database on
trees, turf, flowers, shrubs and other plants
along with plant disorders and cures.

Poem Finder
Roth Publishing Inc.
185 Great Neck Road
Great Neck, NY 11021
800/899-7684
Fax: 516/829-7746
Tech. Support: 800/899-7684
Price: $39.95
Platform: DOS
Grade Level: Senior High School
Curriculum: Language Arts
Description: Indexes 270,000 poems in
1,322 anthologies, 1,300 single author col-
lections and over 100 periodicals.
Keyword searching through all fields,
author, translator, poem, title, book or
periodical title first line. All citations
provide full bibliographical information.

**Prescription Drugs: A
Pharmacist's Guide**
Quanta Press Inc.
1313 Fifth Street, Suite SE 223A
Minneapolis, MN 55414
612/379-3956
Fax: 612/623-4570
Price: $79.95
Platform: Macintosh, DOS, Windows
Grade Level: Senior High School
Curriculum: Health
Description: A pharmacist's guide com-
piling several health professional refer-
ences translated into everyday language.
Most commonly used drugs are referred as
to doses, side effects and how each drug
works in the body.

Primary Search
EBSCO Publishing Inc.
P.O. Box 2250
Peabody, MA 01960-7250
800/653-2726
508/535-8500
Fax: 508/535-8545
Tech. Support: 800/758-5995
Price: 3 discs, $549
Platform: Macintosh, DOS
Grade Level: Elementary, Middle
Curriculum: Reference & Interdisciplinary
Description: Indexing and abstracts from
90 magazines. Full text from 10 maga-
zines. Includes some images and is keyword
searchable.

ProArt
Multi-Ad Services Inc.
1720 W. Detweiler Drive
Peoria, IL 61615-1695
309/692-1530
Fax: 309/692-6566
Price: $32
Platform: Macintosh, DOS
Grade Level: Senior High School
Curriculum: Arts & Music
Description: Over 300 high quality clip art
illustrations which can be imported into
many applications.

Professional Tutor: Learning Windows
Paragon Consultants Inc.
158 Sandy Drive
Boulder, CO 80302
303/442-1613
Fax: 303/939-0209
Tech. Support: 303/465-0195
Price: $39.95
Platform: MPC
Grade Level: Senior High School

Curriculum: General
Description: A step-by-step introduction
to Windows.

Project Gutenberg
Walnut Creek CDROM
1547 Palos Verdes Mall #260
Walnut Creek, CA 94596
800/786-9907
510/674-0783
Price: $39.95
Platform: Macintosh
Grade Level: Senior High School
Curriculum: Language Arts
Description: ISO-9660 ASCII text
CD-ROM. Contains full text of 1991-93
text project, which includes classic litera-
ture, source documents, religious text,
census data, CIA World Fact Book,
almanacs, etc.

Publique Arts
Quanta Press Inc.
1313 Fifth Street, Suite SE 223A
Minneapolis, MN 55414
612/379-3956
Fax: 612/623-4570
Price: $99.95
Platform: Macintosh, DOS
Grade Level: Senior High School
Curriculum: Arts & Music
Description: Image catalog of prints.

Putt-Putt Joins the Parade
Humongous Entertainment
13110 NE 177th Place #180
Woodinville, WA 98072
206/485-1212
Fax: 206/486-9494
Price: $44.95
Platform: Macintosh, DOS

Grade Level: Primary, Elementary
Curriculum: Language Arts
Description: Putt-Putt is a little lavender
car that gets into all kinds of situations and
meets all kinds of creatures—like Rover,
the lunar terrain vehicle.

Quick Art Lite
Wayzata Technologies
2515 East Highway 2
Grand Rapids, MI 55744
800/377-7321
218/326-0597
218/326-2939 (bulletin board)
Fax: 218/326-0598
Tech. Support: 800/377-7321
Price: $119
Platform: Macintosh, DOS
Grade Level: Senior High School
Curriculum: Arts & Music
Description: Professionally drawn, top
quality 300dpi images used for desktop
publishing, brochures, ads, reports and
catalogs. Includes over 3,300 images.

Readers' Guide Abstracts,
Select Edition
H.W. Wilson Company
950 University Avenue
Bronx, NY 10452
800/367-6770
718/588-8400
Fax: 718/590-1617
Tech. Support: 800/367-6770, Ext. 6004
Platform: DOS
Price: 4x/yr., $395; 10x/yr., $695; 12x/yr.,
$995
Grade Level: Middle, Senior High School
Curriculum: Reference & Interdisciplinary
Description: Indexes 240 periodicals and
the *New York Times*, from 1983 to the

present. Includes enhanced titles and
subject headings.

Readers' Guide to Periodical Literature
H.W. Wilson Company
950 University Avenue
Bronx, NY 10452
800/367-6770
718/588-8400
Fax: 718/590-1617
Tech. Support: 800/367-6770, Ext. 6004
Platform: DOS
Price: 12x/yr., $825
Grade Level: Middle, Senior High School
Curriculum: Reference & Interdisciplinary
Description: Indexes 240 periodicals and the
New York Times, from 1983 to the present.
Includes enhanced titles and subject headings.

The Reading Carnival
Digital Theater
5875 Peachtree Industrial Boulevard
Suite 150
Norcross, GA 30092
800/344-8426 (orders)
404/446-3580
Fax: 404/446-9164
Tech. Support: 404/446-3337
Price: $49.95; school, $69.95
Grade Level: Primary, Elementary
Curriculum: Language Arts
Description: Through the use of color and
music, children become involved in read-
ing and learning. Children explore sections
on Animal Facts, Super Hero Stories, and
Fascinating Facts to encourage natural
inquisitiveness.

Resource One Select
University Microfilms International
300 North Zeeb Road

Ann Harbor, MI 48106
313/761-4700
Fax: 313/761-1204
Tech. Support: 800/521-0600. Ext. 2513
Price: $1200
Platform: DOS
Grade Level: Middle
Curriculum: Reference & Interdisciplinary
Description: Indexes 60 magazines with 51 of them full-text, plus one newspaper.

Roger Ebert's Movie Home Companion
Quanta Press Inc.
1313 Fifth Street, Suite SE 223A
Minneapolis, MN 55414
612/379-3956
Fax: 612/623-4570
Price: $79.95
Platform: Macintosh, DOS
Grade Level: Middle, Senior High School
Curriculum: Arts & Music
Description: Contains more than 1,300 reviews, 80 critical reviews, 20 essays and a glossary of movie terms.

Sante
Hopkins Technology
421 Hazel Lane
Hopkins, MN 55343-7116
800/397-9211
Fax: 612/931-9377
Tech. Support: 800/397-9211
Price: $59.95
Platform: DOS
Grade Level: Senior High School
Curriculum: Health
Description: All-in-one cookbook, diet analysis, weight control and exercise program based on 18,000 foods and over 200 exercises. Includes 415 recipes covering over 40 categories.

Science Helper K-8
The Learning Team
10 Long Pond Road
Armonk, NY 10504
914/273-2226
Fax: 914/273-2227
Price: $195
Platform: Macintosh, DOS
Grade Level: Primary, Elementary, Middle
Curriculum: Science
Description: Science helper includes plans for 1,000 hands-on science lessons from six full elementary science programs developed over 15-year period by hundreds of teachers.

Shakespeare
Creative Multimedia
514 NW 11th Avenue, Suite 203
Portland, OR 97209
800/262-7668
503/241-4351
Fax: 503/241-4370
Tech. Support: 503/241-1530
Price: $29.99
Platform: Macintosh, DOS
Grade Level: Senior High School
Curriculum: Language Arts
Description: The complete works of William Shakespeare.

Sherlock Holmes: Consulting Detective Vol. 3
VIACOM New Media Inc.
648 S. Wheeling Road
Wheeling, IL 60090
708/520-4440
Fax: 708/459-7456
Price: $49.95, vol. 1 and 2; $69.95, vol. 3
Platform: Macintosh, DOS
Grade Level: Senior High School
Curriculum: Language Arts

Description: Three full-motion, color video detective stories based on classic Sherlock Holmes cases on each disc. A user can interact with each story, collect clues and help solve the case.

Sherlock Holmes on Disc
Creative Multimedia
514 NW 11th Avenue, Suite 203
Portland, OR 97209
800/262-7668
503/241-4351
Fax: 503/241-4370
Tech. Support: 503/241-1530
Price: $29.99
Platform: Macintosh, DOS
Grade Level: Senior High School
Curriculum: Language Arts
Description: The complete text of all Sherlock Holmes stories by Sir Arthur Conan Doyle as well as *The Medical Casebook* of Dr. Arthur Conan Doyle, *Linoleum Block Prints* by Dr. George Wells, and *Medical Poetry* by Dr. George Bascom.

The Sleeping Beauty
Ebook Inc.
32970 Alvarado-Niles Road, Suite 704
Union City, CA 94587
510/429-1331
Fax: 510/429-1394
Tech. Support: 510/713-8904
Price: $34.95
Platform: MPC
Grade Level: Elementary
Curriculum: Language Arts
Description: A world of make believe kings and queens, princesses, witches and a hundred-year spell. With a combination of animation, art and music, you enjoy a fascinating array of moving pictures.

**The Software Toolworks
Illustrated Encyclopedia**
The Software Toolworks Inc.
60 Leveroni Court
Novato, CA 94949
800/231-3088
415/883-3000
Fax: 415/883-3303
Tech. Support: 415/883-3000
Price: $395
Grade Level: Middle, Senior High School
Curriculum: Reference & Interdisciplinary
Description: More than 33,000 articles, numerous full-color illustrations and photos. CD-Audio capabilities offer high-quality sound, including musical instruments, animal sounds, as well as recordings of historical and political figures.

**The Software Toolworks 20th Century
Video Almanac**
The Software Toolworks Inc.
60 Leveroni Court
Novato, CA 94949
800/231-3088
415/883-3000
Fax: 415/883-3303
Tech. Support: 415/883-3000
Price: $69.95; five-disc set, $199.95
Platform: Macintosh, DOS, Windows
Grade Level: Middle, Senior High School
Curriculum: Social Studies
Description: A multimedia reference work that uses an extensive archive of motion videos to produce a visual encyclopedia of the century. Listen to President Kennedy, attend Woodstock, and land on the moon. Also includes text, audio and photographs.

Sound It Out Land
Conexus Inc.

5252 Balboa Avenue, Suite 605
San Diego, CA 92117
619/268-3380 (orders)
Fax: 619/268-3409
Tech. Support: 619/268-3380
Price: $49.95; $69.95, teacher
Platform: MPC
Grade Level: Primary, Elementary
Curriculum: Language Arts
Description: A colorful musical adventure where children can learn to read on their own by singing and playing games.

Space Adventure
Knowledge Adventure
4502 Dyer Street
La Crescenta, CA 91214
800/542-4240 (orders)
818/248-0166 (bulletin board)
Fax: 818/542-4205
Tech. Support: 818/249-0212
Price: $79.95
Platform: DOS
Grade Level: Middle, Senior High School
Curriculum: Science
Description: A journey into space that takes you past hundreds of breathtaking views, realistic sounds, and musical accompaniment. Simulations with informative note balloons and text will open your mind to the mysteries of space.

Space: A Visual History Of Manned Spaceflight
Sumeria
329 Bryant Street, Suite 3D
San Francisco, CA 94107
415/904-0800
Fax: 415/904-0888
Tech. Support: 415/904-0800
Price: $49.95

Platform: Macintosh, Windows
Grade Level: Middle, Senior High School
Curriculum: Science
Description: Based on NASA film archives, shows all manned space flights from Mercury in 1959 to the present-day shuttle flights. Includes topics on space technology, such as space suits and life in space.

Space Series—Apollo
Quanta Press Inc.
1313 Fifth Street, Suite SE 223A
Minneapolis, MN 55414
612/379-3956
Fax: 612/623-4570
Price: $69.95
Platform: Macintosh, DOS
Grade Level: Senior High School
Curriculum: Science
Description: Over 200 color, black and white photographs and a collection of full-text documents from NASA plus interviews with members of the space program. Chronology from rocket pioneering in 1920 to Apollo 18 splashdown.

Space Time and Art
Wayzata Technologies
2515 East Highway 2
Grand Rapids, MI 55744
800/377-7321
218/326-0597
218/326-2939 (bulletin board)
Fax: 218/326-0598
Tech. Support: 800/377-7321
Price: $199
Platform: Macintosh
Grade Level: Senior High School
Curriculum: Arts & Music
Description: Short demonstration movie clips and animations illustrating recent theories of

creation in the cosmos. Four files discuss various aspects of cosmological theory and how they influence art. Dimensions of space, questions of time, space time and the arts.

Speed
Knowledge Adventure
4502 Dyer Street
La Crescenta, CA 91214
800/542-4240 (orders)
818/248-0166 (bulletin board)
Fax: 818/542-4205
Tech. Support: 818/249-0212
Price: $79.95
Platform: DOS, Windows
Grade Level: Middle, Senior High School
Curriculum: Science
Description: Explore the history and science of speed in this interactive program. Play speed matching games, watch videos featuring IMAX "Speed," or experience a simulation of "the speed of light."

Sports Illustrated CD-ROM
Sports Almanac
Time Warner Interactive Group
2210 West Olive Avenue
Burbank, CA 91506-2626
800/593-6334
818/955-9999
Fax: 818/955-6499
Tech. Support: 800/565-TWIG
Price: $59.99
Platform: Macintosh, DOS
Grade Level: Middle, Senior High School
Curriculum: Sports
Description: Dozens of articles by top sports writers, a chronological listing of 199 sports highlights, profiles of 500 prominent names in sports, and athletic awards from 1931 to the present.

Story Time
Houghton Mifflin
222 Berkeley Street
Boston, MA 02116-3764
617/351-5000
Fax: 617/351-1100
Tech. Support: 800/758-6762
Price: ABC, $95; Level 1, $426; Level 2, $426; 2+, $528; 2+2+, $894; complete set, $1950
Platform: Macintosh
Grade Level: Primary, Elementary
Curriculum: Storybook
Description: A children's reading program centered on themes, each offering three activities centers—reading, writing and story support. Supports English and Spanish.

Super Tom
Information Access Company
362 Lakeside Drive
Foster City, CA 94404
800/227-8431
415/378-5200
Fax: 415/358-4769
Tech. Support: 800/227-8431
Price: N/A
Platform: DOS
Grade Level: Senior High School
Curriculum: Reference & Interdisciplinary
Description: Indexes 180+ magazines, 100 are full-text; includes selected full-text newspaper articles and four reference books.

SuperTom Junior
Information Access Company
362 Lakeside Drive
Foster City, CA 94404
800/227-8431
415/378-5200
Fax: 415/358-4769

Tech. Support: 800/227-8431
Price: N/A
Platform: DOS
Grade Level: Middle
Curriculum: Reference & Interdisciplinary
Description: Indexes 55 magazines, 38 are full-text, plus selected full-text newspaper articles and four reference books.

Survey of Western Art
Ebook Inc.
32970 Alvarado-Niles Road, Suite 704
Union City, CA 94587
510/429-1331
Fax: 510/429-1394
Tech. Support: 510/713-8904
Price: $49.95
Platform: Macintosh, MPC, DOS
Grade Level: Senior High School
Curriculum: Arts & Music
Description: Over 1,000 full-color fine print art images, with accompanying text and explanations.

The Tale of Peter Rabbit
Knowledge Adventure
4502 Dyer Street
La Crescenta, CA 91214
800/542-4240 (orders)
818/248-0166 (bulletin board)
Fax: 818/542-4205
Tech. Support: 818/249-0212
Price: $22.48
Platform: DOS
Grade Level: Primary, Elementary
Curriculum: Language Arts
Description: Taken from the classic Beatrix Potter text with illustrations by L. Johnson to create original water colors for this talking storybook. Characters can be activated on the screen, and children learn to spell and pronounce words.

Talking Classic Tales
New Media Schoolhouse
Box 390, 69 Westchester Avenue
Pound Ridge, NY 10576
800/672-6002
Fax: 914/764-0104
Tech. Support: 800/672-6002
Price: $89
Grade Level: Primary
Curriculum: Storybook
Description: Five classic stories, like Puss-in-Boots and Rumpelstiltskin, to listen to or to read.

Talking Jungle Safari
New Media Schoolhouse
Box 390, 69 Westchester Avenue
Pound Ridge, NY 10576
800/672-6002
Fax: 914/764-0104
Tech. Support: 800/672-6002
Price: $79
Grade Level: Primary, Elementary
Curriculum: Science
Description: Interactive trip through the African jungle; learn about animals, habitats and ecosystems.

Tao of Cow
Quanta Press Inc.
1313 Fifth Street, Suite SE 223A
Minneapolis, MN 55414
612/379-3956
Fax: 612/623-4570
Price: $29.95
Platform: Macintosh, DOS
Grade Level: Middle, Senior High School
Curriculum: Social Studies
Description: Hundreds of black and white and full-color photographs of cows, along with short Zen-like statements about cows.

Terrorist Group Profiles
Quanta Press Inc.
1313 Fifth Street, Suite SE 223A
Minneapolis, MN 55414
612/379-3956
Fax: 612/623-4570
Price: $79.95
Platform: Macintosh, DOS
Grade Level: Senior High School
Curriculum: Social Studies
Description: Details modern terrorist
groups, with background, membership,
leadership, objectives, targets and a
chronology of incidents.

Three-D Dinosaur
Knowledge Adventure
4502 Dyer Street
La Crescenta, CA 91214
800/542-4240 (orders)
818/248-0166 (bulletin board)
Fax: 818/542-4205
Tech. Support: 818/249-0212
Price: $79.98
Platform: DOS, Windows
Grade Level: Elementary, Middle
Curriculum: Science
Description: Don your 3-D glasses to see
dinosaurs come right out of your computer
screen, watch 30 movies, design your own
dino, or check out 150 million years'
worth of paleontological findings.

Time Man of the Year
Compact Publishing Inc.
5141 MacArthur Boulevard NW
Washington, DC 20016
800/964-1518
202/244-6363
Fax: 202/244-6363
Tech. Support: 800/964-1518

Price: $39.95
Platform: MPC, DOS, Windows
Grade Level: Middle, Senior High School
Curriculum: Social Studies
Description: Time magazine summarizes all
the people who have shaped our history for the
past 66 years. Three areas are highlighted—
man of the year articles, in-depth portraits,
and 1992 *Time* magazine issue.

**Time Table of History: Arts and
Entertainment**
XIPHIAS
8758 Venice Boulevard
Los Angeles, CA 90034
800/421-9194 (sales)
310/841-2790
Fax: 310/841-2559
Price: $59.95
Platform: DOS, MPC
Grade Level: Middle, Senior High School
Curriculum: Arts & Music
Description: 4,000 stories linked to effects
including graphics and maps, pictures,
quotes, sounds, music, etc. Also topics
from the first cave paintings to computer
generated choreography.

**Time Table of History:
Business Politics and Media**
XIPHIAS
8758 Venice Boulevard
Los Angeles, CA 90034
800/421-9194 (sales)
310/841-2790
Fax: 310/841-2559
Price: $59.95
Platform: DOS, MPC
Grade Level: Middle, Senior High School
Curriculum: Social Studies
Description: Six thousand stories

enriched by images, maps, sounds and more. From the Trojan horse to Desert Storm, the quest for wealth, power and knowledge is richly illustrated in this interactive environment.

Time Table of History:
Science and Innovation
XIPHIAS
8758 Venice Boulevard
Los Angeles, CA 90034
800/421-9194 (sales)
310/841-2790
Fax: 310/841-2559
Price: $59.95
Platform: DOS, MPC
Grade Level: Middle, Senior High School
Curriculum: Science
Description: The way to learn about man's progress in science and development of technology. Over 6,300 stories linked to special effects, including maps, pictures, sounds, pre-historic timelines, etc. Chronologically from the first stirring of life on the planet to the present world of high technology.

Tom Junior
Information Access Company
362 Lakeside Drive
Foster City, CA 94404
800/227-8431
415/378-5200
Fax: 415/358-4769
Tech. Support: 800/227-8431
Price: $800
Platform: DOS
Grade Level: Middle, Senior High School
Curriculum: Reference & Interdisciplinary
Description: Indexes 55 magazines, 38 are full-text.

Total Baseball
Creative Multimedia
514 NW 11th Avenue, Suite 203
Portland, OR 97209
800/262-7668
503/241-4351
Fax: 503/241-4370
Tech. Support: 503/241-1530
Price: $69.99
Platform: Macintosh, DOS
Grade Level: Middle, Senior High School
Curriculum: Sports
Description: A complete baseball library from 1871 to 1991 World Series. Over 500 images of players, teams and ball parks, 2,600 pages of text, statistics of over 13,000 players, batting, pitching and fielding registers all major league players and more.

Twain's World
Bureau for Electronic Publishing
141 New Road
Parsippany, NJ 07054
800/828-4766 (orders)
201/808-2700
Fax: 201/808-2676
Tech. Support: 201/808-2700, Ext. 22
Price: $39.95
Platform: MPC
Grade Level: Middle, Senior High School
Curriculum: Language Arts
Description: A multimedia program featuring Twain's work and personal life. Includes short stories, essays, speeches, literary criticism and personal letters, period music, drawings and photographs.

Twelfth Night or What You Will
Xploratorium
The Renaissance Project
Department of Education

Anglia Polytechnic
Sawyers Hall Lane
Brentwood, England CM15 9BT
Price: Write for more information.
Platform: Macintosh
Grade Level: Senior High School
Curriculum: Language Arts
Description: Multimedia production of
Shakespeare's play. Uses HyperCard
animations.

UFO

Software Marketing Corp.
9830 South 51st Street, Building A131
Phoenix, AZ 85044
602/893-3377
Fax: 602/893-2042
Tech. Support: 602/893-8481
Price: $59.95
Platform: Windows
Grade Level: Middle, Senior High School
Curriculum: Science
Description: Contains over 1,200 sight-
ings with photographs, full-motion video
and audio. Time span from 1000 B.C. to
present. Search for specific sightings and
UFO events including contact and abduc-
tion reports.

Undersea Adventure

Knowledge Adventure
4502 Dyer Street
La Crescenta, CA 91214
800/542-4240 (orders)
818/248-0166 (bulletin board)
Fax: 818/542-4205
Tech. Support: 818/249-0212
Price: $79.95
Platform: Windows, DOS
Grade Level: Elementary, Middle, Senior
High School

Curriculum: Science
Description: Seven entertaining and educational ways to explore a coral reef, the frigid
waters of the Arctic, or the deepest canyon
on the planet—all within the hundred million
square miles of our planet's ocean.

U.S. History on CD-ROM

Bureau for Electronic Publishing
141 New Road
Parsippany, NJ 07054
800/828-4766 (orders)
201/808-2700
Fax: 201/808-2676
Tech. Support: 201/808-2700, Ext. 22
Price: $395
Platform: Macintosh, DOS
Grade Level: Senior High School
Curriculum: Social Studies
Description: Full text plus illustrations of
100 books covering political, social, eco-
nomic and military perspective of pre-
Revolutionary American history. Source
materials comprise public domain works
published by U.S. Government.

U.S. Presidents

Compton's NewMedia Inc.
2320 Camino Vida Roble
Carlsbad, CA 92009
800/862-2206
800/216-6116 (catalog sales)
619/929-2500
Fax: 619/929-2555
Tech. Support: 619/929-2626
Price: $39.95
Platform: DOS, Windows
Grade Level: Middle, Senior High School
Curriculum: Social Studies
Description: A collection of photographs,
portraits, biographies and statistics of all

presidents. Statistical information is available on all the presidents including some of their wives.

U.S. Presidents
Quanta Press Inc.
1313 Fifth Street, Suite SE 223A
Minneapolis, MN 55414
612/379-3956
Fax: 612/623-4570
Price: $69.95
Platform: Macintosh, DOS
Grade Level: Middle, Senior High School
Curriculum: Social Studies
Description: Biographies, statistics and interesting information on the 41 men who have served as president of the U.S. Includes data on first ladies.

USA State Factbook
Quanta Press Inc.
1313 Fifth Street, Suite SE 223A
Minneapolis, MN 55414
612/379-3956
Fax: 612/623-4570
Price: $49.95
Platform: Macintosh, DOS, Windows
Grade Level: Middle, Senior High School
Curriculum: Social Studies
Description: An almanac of the United States of America.

USA Wars: Civil War
Compton's NewMedia Inc.
2320 Camino Vida Roble
Carlsbad, CA 92009
800/862-2206
800/216-6116 (catalog sales)
619/929-2500
Fax: 619/929-2555
Tech. Support: 619/929-2626

Price: $69.95
Platform: DOS, Windows
Grade Level: Middle, Senior High School
Curriculum: Social Studies
Description: Covering the years 1860-1865, this multimedia Civil War database includes biographies of prominent figures, chronologies, descriptions of campaigns and battles, statistics and photographs.

USA Wars: Civil War
Quanta Press Inc.
1313 Fifth Street, Suite SE 223A
Minneapolis, MN 55414
612/379-3956
Fax: 612/623-4570
Price: $69.95
Platform: Macintosh, DOS
Grade Level: Senior High School
Curriculum: Social Studies
Description: Includes Civil War biographies, statistics, chronology, equipment, campaigns, battles, political figures, photographs, and music from the era played on period instruments.

USA Wars: Desert Storm with Coalition Command
Compton's NewMedia Inc.
2320 Camino Vida Roble
Carlsbad, CA 92009
800/862-2206
800/216-6116 (catalog sales)
619/929-2500
Fax: 619/929-2555
Tech. Support: 619/929-2626
Price: $69.95
Platform: DOS, Windows
Grade Level: Middle, Senior High School
Curriculum: Social Studies
Description: Interact in a sophisticated

strategy level simulation of the command and control activities that took place during military operations in the Middle East. In an actual battle, these rapid decisions are made by analyzing a host of changing variables.

USA Wars: Korea
Quanta Press Inc.
1313 Fifth Street, Suite SE 223A
Minneapolis, MN 55414
612/379-3956
Fax: 612/623-4570
Price: $69.95
Platform: Macintosh, DOS
Grade Level: Senior High School
Curriculum: Social Studies
Description: True American heroes of the Korean War. Compilation of interviews and data collection of actual combat roles during Korean War.

USA Wars: Vietnam
Quanta Press Inc.
1313 Fifth Street, Suite SE 223A
Minneapolis, MN 55414
612/379-3956
Fax: 612/623-4570
Price: $69.95
Platform: Macintosh, DOS
Grade Level: Senior High School
Curriculum: Social Studies
Description: Covers the U.S. involvement in the Vietnam conflict. It contains 61,000 full-text records, order of battle, biographies, major unit histories, order of military rank, medals and awards.

USA Wars: World War II
Quanta Press Inc.
1313 Fifth Street, Suite SE 223A
Minneapolis, MN 55414

612/379-3956
Fax: 612/623-4570
Price: $79.95
Platform: Macintosh, DOS, Windows
Grade Level: Senior High School
Curriculum: Social Studies
Description: United States' involvement in all theaters of operation from 1938 to 1945. Structured to be a photo archive of World War II with biographies, operations, battles and chronologies.

The View from Earth
Time Warner Interactive Group
2210 West Olive Avenue
Burbank, CA 91506-2626
800/593-6334
818/955-9999
Fax: 818/955-6499
Tech. Support: 800/565-TWIG
Price: $79.99
Platform: Macintosh, MPC
Grade Level: Senior High School
Curriculum: Science
Description: Based on the *Voyage Through the Universe* series from Time-Life Books, this interactive documentary details the July 11, 1991 eclipse. It features hundreds of illustrations and photographs, with maps, diagrams and explanatory text.

Visualization of Natural Phenomena
Telos Springer-Verlag Publishers
333 Meadowlands Parkway
Secaucus, NJ 07096
800/777-4643
Fax: 201/348-4505
Price: $59.95
Platform: Macintosh
Grade Level: Senior High School

Curriculum: Science
Description: Resource for advanced work in computer graphics and natural sciences. High-quality text and accompanying multimedia examples on a CD-ROM.

Vital Signs: The Good Health Resource
Texas Caviar Inc.
3933 Steck Avenue, Suite B115
Austin, TX 78759
800/648-1719
Fax: 512/346-1393
Tech. Support: 512/346-7887
Price: $79.95
Platform: Macintosh, Windows
Grade Level: Middle, Senior High School
Curriculum: Health
Description: A personal resource of much health information that can help you understand medical problems.

Vivaldi: The Four Seasons
Ebook Inc.
32970 Alvarado-Niles Road, Suite 704
Union City, CA 94587
510/429-1331
Fax: 510/429-1394
Tech. Support: 510/713-8904
Price: $24.95
Platform: MPC
Grade Level: Senior High School
Curriculum: Arts & Music
Description: This popular classical work is beautifully displayed through pictures and music.

Vocabulearn/ce: French
Penton Overseas Inc.
2470 Impala Drive
Carlsbad, CA 92008-7226
800/748-5804
619/431-0600

Fax: 619/431-8110
Tech. Support: 800/748-5804
Price: $59.95
Platform: Macintosh, MPC
Grade Level: Senior High School
Curriculum: Foreign Language
Description: Interactive foreign language program designed to teach languages. Includes one hour of digitally edited sound with the foreign language software, allowing random access to over 1,500 frequently spoken words and expressions.

Vocabulearn/ce: Spanish
Penton Overseas Inc.
2470 Impala Drive
Carlsbad, CA 92008-7226
800/748-5804
619/431-0600
Fax: 619/431-8110
Tech. Support: 800/748-5804
Price: $59.95
Platform: Macintosh, MPC
Grade Level: Senior High School
Curriculum: Foreign Language
Description: Interactive foreign language program designed to teach languages. Includes one hour of digitally edited sound with the foreign language software, allowing random access to over 1,500 frequently spoken words and expressions.

Vocational Search
EBSCO Publishing, Inc.
P.O. Box 2250
Peabody, MA 01960-7250
800/653-2726
508/535-8500
Fax: 508/535-8545
Tech. Support: 800/758-5995
Price: 4x/yr., $2399; 10x/yr., $2799; 12x/yr., $3199

Platform: Macintosh, DOS
Grade Level: Senior High School
Curriculum: Reference & Interdisciplinary
Description: Includes indexing and
abstracts from 400 trade related magazines, with 80 titles full text. No charge for
on-site networking.

Wayzata World Factbook 1993 Edition
Wayzata Technologies
2515 East Highway 2
Grand Rapids, MI 55744
800/377-7321
218/326-0597
218/326-2939 (bulletin board)
Fax: 218/326-0598
Tech. Support: 800/377-7321
Price: $39
Platform: Macintosh, DOS
Grade Level: Middle, Senior High School
Curriculum: Social Studies
Description: Photos, maps, charts, graphs,
travel advisories and data about countries
around the world.

The Whale of a Tale
Texas Caviar Inc.
3933 Steck Avenue, Suite B115
Austin, TX 78759
800/648-1719
Fax: 512/346-1393
Tech. Support: 512/346-7887
Price: $89.95; home, $39.95
Platform: Macintosh, Windows
Grade Level: Elementary, Middle
Curriculum: Language Arts
Description: A story of a whale that sets
out to learn about electricity amusing
enough in itself for youngsters. Story takes
place during WWI and provides numerous
historic details and music.

The White Horse Child
Ebook Inc.
32970 Alvarado-Niles Road, Suite 704
Union City, CA 94587
510/429-1331
Fax: 510/429-1394
Tech. Support: 510/713-8904
Price: $29.95
Platform: Macintosh, MPC
Grade Level: Middle, Senior High School
Curriculum: Language Arts
Description: Multimedia story, written and
narrated by Greg Bear, explores a young
boy's encounters with his imagination and
censorship in the world around him.

Wild Places—Media Clips
Aris Entertainment
310 Washington Boulevard, Suite 100
Marina del Ray, CA 90292
310/821-0234
Fax: 310/821-6463
Price: $39.95
Platform: Macintosh, DOS, MPC
Grade Level: Senior High School
Curriculum: Arts & Music
Description: Over 100 striking natural
landscapes and close-ups of deserts, rocks,
seascapes and forests. Over 50 sound
tracks, each up to 20 seconds.

World Almanac and Book of Facts
Metatec Corporation
7001 Metatec Boulevard
Dublin, OH 43017
614/761-2000
Fax: 614/761-4258
Tech. Support: 614/766-3150
Price: $59.95
Platform: Macintosh
Grade Level: Middle, Senior High School
Curriculum: Reference & Interdisciplinary

Description: Over one million current facts. Contains full text of print version.

World Library Great Mystery Classics
World Library Inc.
2809 Main Street
Irvine, CA 92714
800/443-0238
714/756-9500
Fax: 714/756-9511
Tech. Support: 714/756-9550
Price: $49.95
Platform: Macintosh, DOS, Windows
Grade Level: Senior High School
Curriculum: Language Arts
Description: Brings you the world of mystery, murder and suspense with 171 classic thrillers. Famous authors such as Doyle, Stevenson and Verne are featured in this collection.

World Library Great Poetry Classics
World Library Inc.
2809 Main Street
Irvine, CA 92714
800/443-0238
714/756-9500
Fax: 714/756-9511
Tech. Support: 714/756-9550
Price: $49.95
Platform: Macintosh, DOS, Windows
Grade Level: Senior High School
Curriculum: Language Arts
Description: Contains over 1,150 poems, sonnets and psalms from Blake to Keats.

World Library Greatest Books Collection
World Library Inc.
2809 Main Street
Irvine, CA 92714
800/443-0238
714/756-9500

Fax: 714/756-9511
Tech. Support: 714/756-9550
Price: $49.95
Platform: Macintosh, DOS, Windows
Grade Level: Senior High School
Curriculum: Language Arts
Description: A collection of over 600 separate books, plays, poems and religious and historical documents.

World Library Shakespeare Study Guide
World Library Inc.
2809 Main Street
Irvine, CA 92714
800/443-0238
714/756-9500
Fax: 714/756-9511
Tech. Support: 714/756-9550
Price: $24.95
Platform: Macintosh, DOS, Windows
Grade Level: Senior High School
Curriculum: Language Arts
Description: Shakespeare's complete works, including 37 plays, five poems, 154 sonnets and features Barron's *Book Notes* study guides for his most popular plays.

World View Media Clips
Aris Entertainment
310 Washington Boulevard, Suite 100
Marina del Ray, CA 90292
310/821-0234
Fax: 310/821-6463
Price: $39.95
Platform: Macintosh, DOS, MPC
Grade Level: Senior High School
Curriculum: Arts & Music
Description: Photographs from NASA archives of the earth from above and of planets and outer space. Also contains originally composed piano and instrumental music.

CHAPTER 8
CD-ROM TITLES BY CURRICULUM AND GRADE LEVEL

This chapter lists all the CD-ROM titles in the Core Collection and Supplementary Title List by curriculum area and grade level.

The curriculum areas are:

Arts & Music
Foreign Language
General
Health
Language Arts
Mathematics

Reference & Interdisciplinary
Science
Social Studies
Sports
Storybook

Within each curriculum area, the list is subdivided by grade level. The grade levels are:

Primary School (pre-kindergarten through second grades)
Elementary School (third through fifth grades)
Middle School (sixth through eighth grades)
Senior High School (ninth through twelfth grades)

Titles that are in the Core Collection in Chapter 6 are marked with a star, and the top ten highly recommended discs are marked with two stars.

ARTS & MUSIC

Elementary School
Lenny's Music Toons
Musical World of Professor Piccolo ★
Orchestra ★

Middle School
Cinemania ★
The Grammy Awards
Jazz: A Multimedia History ★
Microsoft Art Gallery ★
Microsoft Musical Instruments ★★
Movie Select
Musical World of Professor Piccolo ★
Orchestra ★

Roger Ebert's Movie Home Companion
Time Table of History:
    Arts & Entertainment
VideoHound Multimedia ★

Senior High School
Bach and Before ★
Beethoven Symphony #9
Billie Holiday
Cinemania ★
Coate's Art Review: Impressionism
Complete HOUSE
Composer Quest
EPS PRO
EPS PRO 2
Exploring Ancient Architecture ★

Frac Tunes
Freshe Arte
The Grammy Awards
Jazz: A Multimedia History ★
Mediasource—Historical Library, Vol. 1
Mediasource—Natural Sciences Library,
   Vol. 1
Microsoft Art Gallery ★
Microsoft Musical Instruments ★★
Movie Select
Multimedia Music Book: Mozart
Multimedia Beethoven ★
Multimedia Mozart ★
Multimedia Stravinsky ★
Musical World of Professor Piccolo ★
Orchestra ★
Photo Pro
Pixel Garden
ProArt
Publique Arts
Quick Art Lite
Roger Ebert's Movie Home Companion
Space Time and Art
Survey Of Western Art
Time Table of History:
   Arts & Entertainment
VideoHound Multimedia ★
Vivaldi: The Four Seasons
Wild Places Media Clips
World View Media Clips

FOREIGN LANGUAGE

Elementary School
Games in Japanese
Goldilocks and the Three Bears
   in Spanish ★
Language Discovery ★
TriplePlay Spanish ★

Middle School
Discovering French Interactive ★★

Games in Japanese
Goldilocks and the Three Bears
   in Spanish ★
Language Discovery ★
Learn to Speak English
Learn to Speak French
TriplePlay Spanish ★

Senior High School
Discovering French Interactive ★★
Exotic Japan ★
Learn to Speak English
Learn to Speak French
Lingua ROM 3
TriplePlay Spanish ★
Vocabulearn/ce: French
Vocabulearn/ce: Spanish

GENERAL

Middle School
Electronic Eugenean
Mavis Beacon Teaches Typing ★
My Advanced Label Designer

Senior High School
Electronic Dewey
Electronic Eugenean
Federal Grants/ Funding Locator
Mavis Beacon Teaches Typing ★
My Advanced Label Designer
Professional Tutor: Learning Windows

HEALTH

Middle School
Doctor's Book of Home Remedies
The Family Doctor
Heart: The Engine of Life
Vital Signs: The Good Health Resource

Senior High School
Doctor's Book of Home Remedies

The Family Doctor
Food/Analyst PLUS
Heart: The Engine of Life
The Herbalist
Mayo Clinic Family Health Book ★
Mayo Clinic—The Total Heart ★
Physician's Desk Reference
Prescription Drugs: A Pharmacist's Guide
Sante
Vital Signs: The Good Health Resource

LANGUAGE ARTS

Primary School
Animal Alphabet
Annabelle's Dream of Ancient Egypt ★
Busytown
Mario's Early Years: Fun with Letters
Mixed-Up Mother Goose ★
Putt-Putt Joins the Parade
The Reading Carnival
Sound It Out Land
The Tale of Peter Rabbit
Word Tales ★

Elementary School
Advanced Spelling Tricks
Annabelle's Dream of Ancient Egypt ★
Goferwinkel's Adventure
Mario's Early Years: Fun with Letters
Mixed-Up Mother Goose ★
Putt-Putt Joins the Parade
The Reading Carnival
The Sleeping Beauty
Sound It Out Land
The Tale of Peter Rabbit
The Whale of a Tale
Wind in the Willows
    (Talking Storybook Series) ★
Word Tales ★

Middle School
Advanced Spelling Tricks
Beauty and the Beast ★
Beyond the Wall of Stars
Don Quixote
Peter and the Wolf
The Sleeping Beauty
The Tell-Tale Heart ★
The Whale of a Tale
The White Horse Child
Twain's World
Wind in the Willows
    (Talking Storybook Series) ★

Senior High School
Barron's Complete Book Notes
Beauty and the Beast
    (Talking Storybook Series) ★
Beyond the Wall of Stars
Biography and Genealogy—Master Index
CD Coreworks
Columbia Granger's World of Poetry on
    CD-ROM ★
Contemporary Authors
Crossword Cracker and Margana
DiscLit: American Authors ★
DISCovering Authors ★
Don Quixote
Gale's Literary Index
Great Literature Plus
Library of the Future Series
Macbeth ★
Masterplots II CD-ROM ★
Monarch Notes
Poem Finder
Project Gutenberg
Scribner's Writers Series ★
Shakespeare
Sherlock Holmes: Consulting Detective,
    Vol. 3
Sherlock Holmes on Disc

The Tell-Tale Heart ★
Twain's World
Twelfth Night or What You Will
Twenty Thousand Leagues Under the Sea
   (Talking Storybook Series) ★
The White Horse Child
Wind in the Willows
   (Talking Storybook Series) ★
World Library Great Mystery Classics
World Library Great Poetry Classics
World Library Greatest Books Collection
World Library Shakespeare Study Guide

MATHEMATICS

Primary
CountDown ★

Elementary School
CountDown ★
Math Finder

Middle School
Math Finder

Senior High School
CD Calculus
Math Finder
Mathematics, Vol. 1

REFERENCE & INTERDISCIPLINARY

Primary School
Macmillan Dictionary for Children—
   Multimedia Edition ★★

Elementary School
Compton's Interactive Encyclopedia
Compton's Multimedia Encyclopedia ★

Encarta : Multimedia Encyclopedia ★
From Alice To Ocean
Guinness Disc of Records ★
Information Finder Encyclopedia ★
Macmillan Dictionary for Children—
   Multimedia Edition ★★
MACnificent 7.0 Education and Tales
New Grolier Multimedia Encyclopedia ★
Picture Atlas of the World ★★
Primary Search
Random House Unabridged Dictionary ★
Webster's Ninth Collegiate Dictionary ★

Middle School
Adventures
American Vista: The Multimedia U.S.
   Atlas ★
Broadcast News ★
CD NewsBank ★
Compton's Interactive Encyclopedia
Compton's Multimedia Encyclopedia ★
Encarta Multimedia Encyclopedia ★
Everywhere USA Travel Guide
Facts on File News Digest CD-ROM ★
From Alice To Ocean
Guinness Disc of Records ★
Information Finder Encyclopedia ★
MACnificent 7.0 Education and Tales
Magazine Article Summaries ★
Microsoft Bookshelf ★★
Middle Search
National Parks: The Multimedia Family
   Guide
New Grolier Multimedia Encyclopedia ★
NewsBank CD Jr.
NewsBank Index to Periodicals
Picture Atlas of the World ★★
Primary Search
Random House Unabridged Dictionary ★
Readers' Guide Abstracts ★
Readers' Guide Abstracts, Select Edition

Readers' Guide Index to Periodical
  Literature
Resource/One ★
Resource/One Select
SIRS Researcher ★
Small Blue Planet ★
Software Toolworks Illustrated Encyclopedia
Software Toolworks World Atlas ★
Street Atlas ★
SuperTOM Junior
Time Almanac 1993 ★★
TOM General Reference System ★
TOM Junior
Webster's Ninth Collegiate Dictionary ★
World Almanac and Book of Facts

Senior High School
Adventures
American Heritage: Illustrated
  Encyclopedia Dictionary
American Vista: The Multimedia
  U.S. Atlas ★
Books in Print Plus
Broadcast News ★
Canadian Catalog of Media Resources
Career Opportunities
CD NewsBank ★
The College Handbook
Consumer Information
Encarta Multimedia Encyclopedia ★
Everywhere USA Travel Guide
Facts on File News Digest CD-ROM ★
From Alice To Ocean
Guinness Disc of Records ★
Information Finder Encyclopedia ★
John Schumacher's New Prague Hotel
  Cookbook
Magazine Articles Summaries ★
Magazine Articles Summaries Elite
Magazine Articles Summaries Select
Microsoft Bookshelf 1994 ★★

Middle Search
The Multi-Bible 1990, Vol. 1
Multimedia Family Bible
National Parks: The Multimedia
  Family Guide
Nautilus
New Grolier Multimedia Encyclopedia ★
New Basics Electronic Cookbook
New York Times Ondisc
NewsBank Index to Periodicals
Peterson's College Database
Random House Unabridged Dictionary ★
Readers' Guide Abstracts ★
Readers' Guide Abstracts, Select Edition
Readers' Guide Index to Periodical
  Literature
Resource/One ★
SIRS Researcher ★
Small Blue Planet ★
Software Toolworks Illustrated Encyclopedia
Software Toolworks World Atlas ★
Street Atlas ★
SuperTOM
Time Almanac 1993 ★★
TOM General Reference System ★
TOM Junior
Vocational Search
Webster's Ninth Collegiate Dictionary ★
World Almanac and Book of Facts

SCIENCE

Primary School
Animals and How They Grow (Wonders of
  Learning CD-ROM Library) ★
"CELL"EBRATION
The Human Body (Wonders of
  Learning CD-ROM Library) ★
Kid's Zoo
Our Earth (Wonders of Learning CD-ROM
  Library) ★

Science Helper K-8
Talking Jungle Safari
A World of Animals (Wonders of Learning
    CD-ROM Library) ★
A World of Plants (Wonders of Learning
    CD-ROM Library) ★

Elementary School
"CELL"EBRATION
Dinosaur Adventure
Dinosaur Safari
Kid's Zoo
Mammals: A Multimedia Encyclopedia ★
Microsoft Dinosaurs ★
Planetary Taxi ★
San Diego Presents...The Animals! ★★
Science Helper K-8
Simple Machines ★
Talking Jungle Safari
Three-D Dinosaur
Undersea Adventure

Middle School
Butterflies Vol. 1 (ZooGuide Series) ★
Creepy Crawlies
Dictionary of the Living World ★
Dinosaur Adventure
Dinosaur Discovery ★
Dinosaur Safari
Dinosaurs: The Multimedia
    Encyclopedia ★
Encyclopedia of Dinosaurs ★
How Computers Work ★
Illustrated Facts: How Things Work
Mammals of Africa (ZooGuide Series) ★
Mammals: A Multimedia Encyclopedia ★
Microsoft Dangerous Creatures ★
Microsoft Dinosaurs ★
Multimedia Animals Encyclopedia Library,
    Vol. 1 ★
Multimedia Audubon's Birds

Multimedia Audubon's Mammals
Murmurs of Earth: The Voyager
    Interstellar Record ★
Oceans Below ★
Planetary Taxi ★
Prehistoria ★★
Rainforest (ZooGuide Series) ★
San Diego Zoo Presents...
    The Animals! ★★
Science Helper K-8
Seven Natural Wonders ★
Simple Machines ★
Space Adventure
Space Shuttle ★
Space: A Visual History of Manned
    Spaceflight
Speed
Three-D Dinosaur
Time Table of History: Science
    & Innovation
UFO
Undersea Adventure
Whales and Dolphins (ZooGuide Series) ★
Whales & Dolphins ★

Senior High School
A.D.A.M.
Amazing Universe
Animals with Backbones
    (LIFEmap Series) ★
Big Green Disc ★
Biology Digest on CD-ROM
Bodyworks 3.0: An Adventure in
    Anatomy ★
Butterflies, Vol. 1 (ZooGuide Series) ★
Creepy Crawlies
Dictionary of the Living World ★
Dinosaur Discovery ★
Dinosaur Safari
Dinosaurs: The Multimedia

Encyclopedia ★
Distant Suns
Electricity and Magnetism
Encyclopedia of Dinosaurs ★
How Computers Work ★
Illustrated Facts: How Things Work
Introductory Chemistry CD-ROM
LIFEmap Series ★
Magill's Survey of Science
Mammals of Africa (ZooGuide Series) ★
Mars Explorer
McGraw-Hill Multimedia Encyclopedia of
    Science and Technology ★
McGraw-Hill Science and Technical
    Reference Set
Microsoft Dangerous Creatures ★
Microsoft Dinosaurs ★
Multimedia Animals Encyclopedia Library,
    Vol. 1 ★
Multimedia Audubon's Birds
Multimedia Audubon's Mammals
Multimedia Encyclopedia of Mammalian
    Biology
Murmurs of Earth: The Voyager Interstellar
    Record ★
OceanLife: Volume 2—Micronesia ★
Oceans Below ★
Organic Diversity (LIFEmap Series) ★
Planet Earth: Gaia Library
The Plant Doctor
Prehistoria ★★
Rainforest (ZooGuide Series) ★
Seven Natural Wonders ★
Space Adventure
Space Series—Apollo
Space Shuttle ★
Space: A Visual History Of Manned
    Spaceflight
Speed
Time Table of History: Science &
    Innovation

UFO
Undersea Adventure
The View from Earth
Visualization of Natural Phenomena
Whales & Dolphins ★
Whales & Dolphins (ZooGuide Series)★
World Alive ★

SOCIAL STUDIES

Primary School
Our Earth (Wonders of Learning
    CD-ROM Library) ★

Elementary School
about Cows
The Oregon Trail ★
Pilgrim Quest
The Presidents: It All Started With
    George ★

Middle School
about Cows
America Adventure
American Vista ★
Annabelle's Dream of Ancient Egypt ★
Atlas of U.S. Presidents ★
Capitol Hill ★
CIA World Fact Book
Clinton: Portrait of a Victory ★
CNN Newsroom Global View ★★
Ethnic NewsWatch ★
Facts On File News Digest ★
Front Page News—Plus Business
Great Cities of the World, Vol. 1
Great Cities of the World, Vol. 2
Great Wonders of the World, Vol. 1
Great Wonders of the World, Vol. 2
JFK Assassination ★
Let's Go 1993 California & Hawaii
Let's Go 1993 USA

The Oregon Trail ★
Pilgrim Quest
The Presidents: It All Started With
    George ★
Software Toolworks 20th Century
    Video Almanac
Tao of Cow
Time Man of the Year
Time Table of History: Business
    Politics & Media
Time Traveler CD ★
Twelve Roads to Gettysburg ★
U.S. Presidents—Compton's
U.S. Presidents—Quanta
USA State Factbook
USA Wars: Civil War (Compton's)
USA Wars: Desert Storm with Coalition
    Command
Wayzata World Factbook 1993 Edition
World Vista ★

Senior High School
about Cows
African American Experience
America Adventure
The American Indian: A Multimedia
    Encyclopedia
American Vista ★
Atlas of U.S. Presidents ★
Capitol Hill ★
CD Sourcebook of American History ★
CIA World Fact Book
Clinton: Portrait of a Victory ★
CNN Newsroom Global View ★★
Complete Guide to Special Interest Videos
Countries of the World
Desert Storm: The War in the
    Persian Gulf ★
Electronic Encyclopedia of WWII
Enduring Vision ★

Ethnic NewsWatch ★
European Monarchs
Facts On File News Digest ★
Front Page News—Plus Business
Global Explorer ★
Great Cities of the World, Vol. 1
Great Cities of the World, Vol. 2
Great Wonders of the World, Vol. 1
Great Wonders of the World, Vol. 2
History of the World
Illustrated Facts: How the World Works
JFK Assassination ★
KGB World Factbook
Let's Go 1993 California & Hawaii
Let's Go 1993 USA
Middle East Diary
Multimedia Business Week 1000
    on CD-ROM
Multimedia World Factbook
Newsweek Interactive—Unfinished
    Business
North American Indians
The Oregon Trail ★
Pilgrim Quest
The Presidents: It All Started With
    George ★
Seven Days in August ★
Software Toolworks 20th Century
    Video Almanac
Tao of Cow
Terrorist Group Profiles
Time Man of the Year
Time Table of History: Business Politics
    & Media
Time Traveler CD ★
Twelve Roads to Gettysburg ★
U.S. History on CD-ROM
U.S. Presidents—Compton's
U.S. Presidents—Quanta
USA State Factbook
USA Wars: Civil War (Compton's)

USA Wars: Civil War (Quanta)
USA Wars: Desert Storm with Coalition
 Command
USA Wars: Korea
USA Wars: Vietnam
USA Wars: World War II
Wayzata World Factbook 1993 Edition
Who Built America? ★
World Vista ★

SPORTS

Middle and Senior High School
Baseball's Greatest Hits
Sports Illustrated CD-ROM Sports
 Almanac
Sports Illustrated 1994 Multimedia
 CD-ROM Sports Almanac ★
Total Baseball

STORYBOOK

Primary School
Adventures of Pinocchio
 (Talking Storybook Series)★
Aesop's Fables (Discis Books)★
Aesop's Fables
Allie's Playhouse
Amanda Stories
Arthur's Teacher Trouble
 (Living Books) ★★
Beauty & the Beast
 (Talking Storybook Series) ★
Cinderella: The Original Fairy Tale
 (Discis Books)★
Emergent Level One CD-ROM
 (Discis Books) ★
Emergent Level Two CD-ROM
 (Discis Books) ★
Heather Hits Her First Home Run
 (Discis Books) ★

Interactive Storytime, Volumes 1 & 3
Just Grandma And Me (Living Books) ★★
A Long Hard Day at the Ranch
 (Discis Books) ★
Moving Gives Me A Stomach Ache
 (Discis Books) ★
Mud Puddle (Discis Books) ★
The Paper Bag Princess (Discis Books) ★
Scary Poems for Rotten Kids
 (Discis Books) ★
Silly Noisy House ★
Story Time
Tale of Benjamin Bunny (Discis Books) ★
Tale of Peter Rabbit (Discis Books) ★
Talking Classic Tales
Thomas' Snowsuit (Discis Books) ★

Elementary School
Adventures of Pinocchio
 (Talking Storybook Series) ★
Aesop's Fables (Discis Books) ★
Aesop's Fables
Amanda Stories
Arthur's Teacher Trouble
 (Living Books Series) ★★
Beauty & the Beast
 (Talking Storybook Series) ★
Cinderella: The Original Fairy Tale
 (Discis Books) ★
Emergent Level One CD-ROM
 (Discis Books) ★
Emergent Level Two CD-ROM
 (Discis Books) ★
Heather Hits Her First Home Run
 (Discis Books) ★
Interactive Storytime, Volumes 1 & 3
Just Grandma And Me
 (Living Books Series) ★★
A Long Hard Day at the Ranch
 (Discis Books) ★

Moving Gives Me A Stomach Ache
    (Discis Books) ★
Mud Puddle (Discis Books) ★
The Paper Bag Princess (Discis Books) ★
Scary Poems for Rotten Kids
    (Discis Books) ★
Silly Noisy House ★
Story Time
Tale of Benjamin Bunny (Discis Books) ★
Tale of Peter Rabbit (Discis Books) ★
Thomas' Snowsuit (Discis Books) ★

CHAPTER 9

CONTACT INFORMATION:

PUBLISHERS AND DISTRIBUTORS

A.D.A.M. Software
1600 Riveredge Parkway, Suite 800
Atlanta, GA 30328
800/755-ADAM
404/980-0888
Fax: 404/955-3088
Tech. Support: 404/953-2326

Applied Optical Media Corporation
1450 Boot Road, Building 400A
West Chester, PA 19380
800/321-7259
610/429-3701
Fax: 610/429-3810
Tech. Support: 800/321-7259

Aris Entertainment
310 Washington Boulevard, Suite 100
Marina del Ray, CA 90292
310/821-0234
Fax: 310/821-6463

Bowker Electronic Publishing
121 Chanlon Road
New Providence, NJ 07974-1154
800/323-3288

BrightStar
3380 146th Place SE, Suite 300
Bellevue, WA 98007
206/649-9800
Fax: 206/649-0340

Brøderbund (Living Books)
500 Redwood Place

Novato, CA 94948
415/382-4400
Tech. Support: 415/382-4700

Buckmaster Publishing
Route 4 Box 1630
Mineral, VA 23117
800/282-5628
703/894-5777
Fax: 703/894-9141
Tech. Support: 800/282-5628

Bureau for Electronic Publishing
141 New Road
Parsippany, NJ 07054
201/808-2700
Orders: 800/828-4766
Fax: 201/808-2676
Tech. Support: 201/808-2700, Ext. 22

Cambrix Publishing
6269 Variel Avenue, Suite B
Woodland Hills, CA 91367
818/992-8484
Fax: 818/992-8781
Tech. Support: 818/992-8484

Candlelight Publishing
P.O. Box 5213
Mesa, AZ 85211-5213
800/677-3045
Fax: 801/373-2499
Tech. Support: 800/677-3045

CD ROM Inc.
603 Park Point Drive, Suite 110
Golden, CO 80401
303/526-7600
Fax: 303/526-7395

Claris Corporation
5201 Patrick Henry Drive
Santa Clara, CA 95052
800/325-2747
Fax: 408/987-3932

CMC Research
514 NW 11th Avenue, Suite 203
Portland, OR 97209
503/241-4351
Tech Support: 503/241-1530

Columbia University Press
562 West 113th Street
New York, NY 10025
212/666-1000
Orders: 800/944-8648
Fax: 212/316-3100
Tech. Support: 800/767-7843

Compact Disk Products
272 Route 34
Aberdeen, NJ 07747
908/290-0048

Compact Publishing Inc.
5141 MacArthur Boulevard NW
Washington, DC 20016
800/964-1518
202/244-6363
Fax: 202/244-6363
Tech. Support: 800/964-1518

Compton's NewMedia Inc.
2320 Camino Vida Roble

Carlsbad, CA 92009
800/862-2206
619/929-2500
Catalog Sales: 800/216-6116
Fax: 619/929-2555
Tech. Support: 619/929-2626

Conexus Inc.
5252 Balboa Avenue, Suite 605
San Diego, CA 92117
Orders: 619/268-3380
Fax: 619/268-3409
Tech. Support: 619/268-3380

Creative Multimedia
514 NW 11th Avenue, Suite 203
Portland, OR 97209
800/262-7668
503/241-4351
Fax: 503/241-4370
Tech. Support: 503/241-1530

Decision Development Corp
2680 Bishop Drive, Suite 122
San Ramon, CA 94583
800/835-4332
Fax: 510/830-0830
Tech. Support: 800/835-4332

Deep River Publishing
P.O. Box 9715-975
Portland, ME 04104
800/643-5630
207/871-1684
Fax: 207/871-1683
Tech. Support: 207/871-1684

DeLorme Mapping
Lower Main Street, P.O. Box 298
Freeport, ME 04032
800/452-5931
207/865-1234

Fax: 207/865-9291
Tech. Support: 207/865-7098

Digital Theater
5875 Peachtree Industrial Boulevard
Suite 150
Norcross, GA 30092
404/446-3580
Orders: 800/344-8426
Fax: 404/446-9164
Tech. Support: 404/446-3337

Discis Knowledge Research Inc.
45 Sheppard Avenue East, Suite 410
Toronto, Ontario M2N 5W9 Canada
800/567-4321
416/250-6537
Fax: 416/250-6540
Tech. Support: 800/567-4321

Ebook Inc.
32970 Alvarado-Niles Road, Suite 704
Union City, CA 94587
510/429-1331
Fax: 510/429-1394
Tech. Support: 510/713-8904

EBSCO Publishing Inc.
P.O. Box 2250
Peabody, MA 01960-7250
800/653-2726
508/535-8500
Fax: 508/535-8545
Tech. Support: 800/758-5995

Educorp Computer Services
7434 Trade Street
San Diego, CA 92121
800/843-9497
Fax: 619/536-2345

Facts on File Inc.
460 Park Avenue South
New York, NY 10016-7382
800/322-8755
212/683-2244
Fax: 212/683-3633
Tech. Support: 800/322-8755

Falcon Software
P.O. Box 200
Wentworth, NH 03282
603/764-5788
Fax: 603/764-9051
Tech. Support: 617/235-1767

Follett Library Resources
4506 Northwest Highway
Routes 14 & 31
Crystal Lake, IL 60014-7393
815/455-1100
Fax: 815/477-9303

Gale Research Inc.
835 Penobscot Building
Detroit, MI 48226-4094
800/877-GALE
313/961-2242
Fax: 313/961-6083
Tech. Support: 800/877-4253, Ext. 6021

Gazelle Technologies
7434 Trade Street
San Diego, CA 92121
619/693-4030
Orders: 800/843-9497
Fax: 619/536-2345
Tech. Support: 619/536-9999

Globe Fearon Educational Publisher
P.O. Box 2649
Columbus, OH 43216
800/848-9500
Fax: 614/771-7361

Grolier Electronic Publishing, Inc.
Sherman Turnpike
Danbury, CT 06816
800/356-5590
203/797-3530
Fax: 203/797-3130
Tech. Support: 800/356-5590

G.K. Hall & Company
866 Third Avenue, 18th Floor
New York, NY 10022
800/257-5755
212/702-6789
Fax: 212/605-9350
Tech. Support: 617/232-0412

DC Heath and Company
125 Spring Street
Lexington, MA 02173
800/235-3565
800/334-3284 (orders)
Fax: 617/860-1927
Fax orders: 800/824-7390
Tech. Support: 800/235-3656, Ext. 1767

Highlighted Data
6628 Midhill Place
Falls Church, VA 22043
703/533-1939
Fax: 703/533-2039
Tech. Support: 703/516-9211

Hopkins Technology
421 Hazel Lane
Hopkins, MN 55343-7116
800/397-9211
Fax: 612/931-9377
Tech. Support: 800/397-9211

Houghton Mifflin
222 Berkeley Street

Boston, MA 02116-3764
617/351-5000
Fax: 617/351-1100
Tech. Support: 800/758-6762

Humongous Entertainment
13110 NE 177th Place, Suite 180
Woodinville, WA 98072
206/485-1212
Fax: 206/486-9494

HyperGlot Software Co. Inc.
P.O. Box 10746
Knoxville, TN 37939-0746
800/949-4379
615/558-8270
Fax: 615/588-6569
Tech. Support: 800/949-4379

Information Access Company
362 Lakeside Drive
Foster City, CA 94404
800/227-8431
415/378-5200
Fax: 415/358-4769
Tech. Support: 800/227-8431

Innotech Multimedia
2001 Sheppard Avenue E., Suite 118
North York, Ontario, Canada M2J 4Z7
416/492-3838
Fax: 416/492-3843
Tech. Support: 416/492-3838

Interactive Publishing Corporation
300 Airport Executive Park
Spring Valley, NY 10977
914/426-0400
Orders: 800/472-8777
Fax: 914/426-2606
Tech. Support: 914/426-0400

InterOptica Publishing Ltd.
300 Montgomery Street, Suite 201
San Francisco, CA 94104
800/708-7827 (orders)
415/788-8788
Fax: 415/788-8886
Tech. Support: 212/941-2988

IVI Publishing
7500 Flying Cloud Drive
Minneapolis, MN 55344
612/996-6000
Fax: 612/996-6001
Tech. Support: 800/754-1484

Knowledge Adventure
4502 Dyer Street
La Crescenta, CA 91214
Orders: 800/542-4240
BBS: 818/248-0166
Fax: 818/542-4205
Tech. Support: 818/249-0212

Laser Learning Technologies
120 Lakeside Avenue
Seattle, WA 98122
800/722-3505
Fax: 206/322-7421

The Learning Team
10 Long Pond Road
Armonk, NY 10504
914/273-2226
Fax: 914/273-2227

Macmillan New Media
124 Mount Auburn Street
Cambridge, MA 02138
800/342-1338
617/661-2955
Fax: 617/661-2403
Tech. Support: 800/342-1338

Marshall Cavendish Corp.
2415 Jerusalem Avenue, P.O. Box 587
North Bellmore, NY 11710
800/821-9881
Fax: 516/785-8133
Tech. Support: 800/643-4351

McGraw-Hill Inc.
11 W. 19th Street
New York, NY 10011
800/842-3075
Fax: 212/337-4092
Tech. Support: 800/551-2210

MECC
6160 Summit Drive North
Minneapolis, MN 55430-4003
800/685-6322
612/569-1500
Fax: 612/569-1551
Tech. Support: 612/569-1678

Meckler Corporation
11 Ferry Lane West
Westport, CT 06880
203/226-6967
Fax: 203/454-5848

Media Design Interactive
The Old Hop Kiln
1 Long Garden Walk
Farnham, Surrey
GU9 7HP England
011-44-252-737630
Fax: 011-44-252-710948
Tech. Support: 800/654-8802

Medical Economics Data
5 Paragon Drive
Montvale, NJ 07645
201/358-7200
Fax: 201/573-0867

Medio Multimedia Inc.
P.O. Box 2949
Redmond, WA 98073-9964
800/788-3866
Fax: 206/885-4142
Tech. Support: 206/867-5500

Metatec Corporation
7001 Metatec Boulevard
Dublin, OH 43017
614/761-2000
Fax: 614/761-4258
Tech. Support: 614/766-3150

Microsoft Corporation
One Microsoft Way
Redmond, WA 98052
800/426-9400
Fax: 206/936-7329
Tech. Support: 206/635-7172

Multi-Ad Services Inc.
1720 W. Detweiller Drive
Peoria, IL 61615-1695
309/692-1530
Fax: 309/692-6566

My Software Company
1259 El Camino Real, Suite 167
Menlo Park, CA 94025
800/325-3508 (orders)
415/325-4222
Macintosh Customers: 303/522-0815
DOS, Windows Customers: 303/522-3000

National Geographic Society
1145 17th Street NW
Washington, DC 20036
800/368-2728
Fax: 301/921-1575
Tech. Support: 800/342-4460
800/437-4383 (Canada)

New Media Schoolhouse
69 Westchester Avenue, Box 390
Pound Ridge, NY 10576
800/672-6002
Fax: 914/764-0104
Tech. Support: 800/672-6002

New Media Source
3830 Valley Centre Drive, Suite 2153
San Diego, CA 92130-9834
800/344-2621
Fax: 619/438-2330

NewsBank, Inc.
58 Pine Street
New Canaan, CT 06840-5426
800/762-8182
203/966-1100
Fax: 203/966-6254
Tech. Support: 800/762-8182

Nimbus Information Systems
P.O. Box 7427
Charlottesville, VA 22906
804/985-1100
Fax: 804/985-4625

Now What Software
2303 Sacramento Street
San Francisco, CA 94115
800/322-1954
415/885-1689
Fax: 415/922-1265
Tech. Support: 818/992-8484

OCLC Forest Press
6565 Frantz Road
Dublin, OH 43017
614/764-6000
Orders: 800/848-5878
Fax: 614/764-6096
Tech. Support: 800/848-5800

Opcode Systems Inc.
3950 Fabian Way, Suite 100
Palo Alto, CA 94303
415/856-3333
Orders: 800/557-2633
Fax: 415/494-1113
Tech. Support: 415/494-9393

Paragon Consultants Inc.
158 Sandy Drive
Boulder, CO 80302
303/442-1613
Fax: 303/939-0209
Tech. Support: 303/465-0195

Paramount Interactive
700 Hansen Way
Palo Alto, CA 94304
415/813-8030
Fax: 415/813-8055
Tech. Support: 415/813-8030

Pemberton Press
462 Danbury Road
Wilton, CT 06897-2126
800/248-8466
203/761-1466
Fax: 203/761-1444

Penton Overseas Inc.
2470 Impala Drive
Carlsbad, CA 92008-7226
800/748-5804
619/431-0600
Fax: 619/431-8110
Tech. Support: 800/748-5804

Quanta Press Inc.
1313 Fifth Street, Suite SE 223A
Minneapolis, MN 55414
612/379-3956
Fax: 612/623-4570

Random House Publishing
201 East 50th Street, 3rd Floor
New York, NY 10022-7703
212/751-2600
Fax: 212/572-8700
Tech. Support: 801/228-9918 (DOS); 801/
226-9919 (Windows); 801/228-9917 (Mac)

REMedia Inc.
13525 Midland Road
Poway, CA 92064
619/486-5030
Tech. Support: 619/486-5030

Research Publications International
12 Lunar Drive
Woodbridge, CT 06525-9957
800/774-7741
Fax: 203/397-3893
Tech. Support: 800/RPI-RPI-1

Roth Publishing Inc.
185 Great Neck Road
Great Neck, NY 11021
800/899-7684
Fax: 516/829-7746
Tech. Support: 800/899-7684

Salem Press Inc.
131 N. El Molino Avenue, Suite 350
Pasadena, CA 91101
818/584-0106
Fax: 818/584-1525
Tech. Support: 800/221-1826

Science for Kids Inc.
9950 Concord Church Road
Lewisville, NC 27023
910/945-9000
Fax: 910/945-2500
Tech. Support: 910/945-9000

Charles Scribner Sons
866 Third Avenue
New York, NY 10022
212/702-9691
Orders: 800/257-5755
Tech. Support: 800/342-1338

Sierra On-Line Inc.
P.O. Box 53250
Bellevue, WA 08015-3250
800/743-7725
Orders: 800/757-7707
Fax: 209/562-4317
Tech. Support: 209/683-8989

SilverPlatter Information Inc.
100 River Ridge Drive
Norwood, MA 02062-5026
800/343-0064
617/769-2599
Fax: 617/769-8763
Tech. Support: 800/343-0064

SIRS
P.O. Box 2348
Boca Raton, FL 33427-2348
407/994-0079
Fax: 407/994-4704
Tech. Support: 800/426-7477

Softline Information Inc.
65 Broad Street
Stamford, CT 06901
800/524-7922
203/975-8292
Fax: 203/975-8347
Tech. Support: 203/975-8292

Software Marketing Corp.
9830 South 51st Street, Building A131
Phoenix, AZ 85044

602/893-3377
Fax: 602/893-2042
Tech. Support 602/893-8481

The Software Toolworks Inc.
60 Leveroni Court
Novato, CA 94949
800/231-3088
415/883-3000
Fax: 415/883-3303
Tech. Support: 415/883-3000

South Eugene High School
400 E. 19th Avenue
S. Eugene, OR 97401
503/687-3201

Staff Directories Ltd.
P.O. Box 62
Mount Vernon, VA 22121-0062
703/739-0900
Fax: 703/739-0234
Tech. Support: 703/739-0900, Ext. 218

StarPress Multimedia, Inc.
303 Sacramento Street, 2nd Floor
San Francisco, CA 94111
415/274-8383
Tech. Support: 900/555-7827

Sumeria
329 Bryant Street, Suite 3D
San Francisco, CA 94107
415/904-0800
Fax: 415/904-0888
Tech. Support: 415/904-0800

Syracuse Language Systems
719 East Genesee Street
Syracuse, NY 13210
315/478-6729

Fax: 315/478-6902
Tech. Support: 800/688-1937

Telos (Springer-Verlag) Publishers
333 Meadowlands Parkway
Secaucus, NJ 07096
800/777-4643
Fax: 201/348-4505

Texas Caviar Inc.
3933 Steck Avenue, Suite B115
Austin, TX 78759
800/648-1719
Fax: 512/346-1393
Tech. Support: 512/346-7887

Tiger Software
9100 S. Dadeland Boulevard
1 Datran Center, Suite 1500
Miami, FL 33156
305/443-8212
Fax: 305/444-5010

Time Warner Interactive Group
2210 West Olive Avenue
Burbank, CA 91506-2626
800/593-6334
818/955-9999
Fax: 818/955-6499
Tech. Support: 800/565-TWIG

**University Microfilms International
(UMI)**
300 North Zeeb Road
Ann Arbor, MI 48106
313/761-4700
Fax: 313/761-1204
Tech. Support: 800/521-0600, Ext. 2513

Updata Publications Inc.
1736 Westwood Boulevard

Los Angeles, CA 90024
800/882-2844
Fax: 310/474-4095
Tech. Support: 800/882-2844

VIACOM New Media Inc.
648 S. Wheeling Road
Wheeling, IL 60090
708/520-4440
Fax: 708/459-7456

Virtual Reality Labs Inc.
2341 Ganador Court
San Luis Obispo, CA 93401
805/545-8515
Fax: 805/781-2259
Tech. Support: 805/545-8515

Visible Ink Software
835 Penobscot Building
Detroit, MI 48224-0748
800/735-HOUND
Tech. Support: 800/877-4253, Ext. 6021

Voyager
578 Broadway
New York, NY 10012
212/431-5199
Fax: 212/431-5799
1 Bridge Street
Irvington, NY 10533
800/446-2001
Fax: 914/591-6481
Tech. Support: 914/591-5500

Walnut Creek CDROM
1547 Palos Verdes Mall #260
Walnut Creek, CA 94596
800/786-9907
510/674-0783

Wayzata Technologies
2515 East Highway 2
Grand Rapids, MI 55744
800/377-7321
218/326-0597
BBS: 218/326-2939
Fax: 218/326-0598
Tech. Support: 800/377-7321

John Wiley & Sons Inc.
605 Third Avenue
New York, NY 10158
212/850-6172
Fax: 212/850-6799

H.W. Wilson Company
950 University Avenue
Bronx, NY 10452
800/367-6770
718/588-8400
Fax: 718/590-1617
Tech. Support: 800/367-6770, Ext. 6004

World Book Educational Products
101 Northwest Point Boulevard
Elk Grove Village, IL 60007
708/290-5300
Fax: 708/290-5370
Tech. Support: 800/323-6366

World Library Inc.
2809 Main Street
Irvine, CA 92714
800/443-0238
714/756-9500
Fax: 714/756-9511
Tech. Support: 714/756-9550

XIPHIAS
8758 Venice Boulevard
Los Angeles, CA 90034

800/421-9194 (sales)
310/841-2790
Fax: 310/841-2559

Xploratorium
The Renaissance Project
Department of Education
Anglia Polytechnic
Sawyers Hall Lane
Brentwood, England CM15 9BT

Ztek Co.
P.O. Box 1055
Louisville, KY 40201-1055
800/247-1603
Fax: 502/584-9098

CHAPTER 10
A GLOSSARY OF CD-ROM TERMS

AACR2: *Anglo-American Cataloguing Rules*, second edition, 1978. The second edition of AACR1 was published in 1978 in one version for all participating nations.

AACR2R: *Anglo-American Cataloguing Rules*, second edition, 1988 revision. The current standard cataloguing rules.

abstract: The summary of a document that may be read online or printed.

access: Information retrieval from memory or mass storage, such as CD-ROM.

access point: A heading for retrieving a catalog record (includes main and added entries, subject headings, etc.).

access time: The amount of time, measured in milliseconds, between issuing a search command and obtaining the information.

ADC: Analog to Digital Conversion. Converting analog data or signals to digital format for a computer to process.

address: A digital code indicating the location of items on a CD-ROM or in memory.

AI: Artificial Intelligence. AI software programs mimic human responses and problem-solving abilities.

algorithm: A mathematical or text formula used in programming a computer; also a set of instructions.

aliasing: Distortion of digital data that occurs when the sampling rate is too low. Evidenced by jagged edges in images or false tones in audio signals. *See also* **anti-aliasing.**

analog: An infinitely variable or continuous characteristic or signal, such as time or temperature, as opposed to a discreetly variable digital characteristic or signal, such as a pulse or digitized image.

analog video: A video signal that represents an infinite number of smooth gradations between given video levels. By contrast, a digital signal assigns a finite set of levels.

ANSI: American National Standards Institute.

anti-aliasing: Combating jagged edges in images by averaging the pixels along the edges; usually used when putting two images together. *See also* **aliasing.**

application: A word often used with "program" or "software."

architecture: The composition and components of a system described in a way that easily conveys their inter-relationships and functional purpose.

ARCnet: A local area network (LAN) originally developed by Datapoint Corporation in 1977. Uses a token-passing protocol and transmits at 2.5 megabits per second.

ASCII: American Standard Code for Information Interchange. A seven-bit code to represent numbers, letters and control characters.

aspect ratio: The relationship of width and height. Important when transferring an image from one display to another.

audio track: The section of a CD-ROM that contains the sound signal.

audiovisual: Nonprint materials such as films, slides, cassettes, etc.

authoring system: Software designed to help a nonprogrammer develop a multimedia or hypertext application.

AUTOEXEC.BAT: A file executed automatically when a computer is started up. This file will initialize any variables and execute DOS commands to establish the computer's working environment.

average latency: The average amount of time for a CD-ROM drive to find a particular sector of data.

B

backbone network: A network to which several smaller networks are attached.

back up: To make a copy of a software program or data file in case the original is damaged or destroyed.

bandwidth: The range of signal frequencies that audio or video equipment can accept.

barcode: Using bars of different widths and heights to represent numerical data.

baseband: Digital information transmitted across the entire width of a cable.

baud: The number of bits per second transmitted over a communications connection.

beta testing: The second testing level for new software. First level, or "alpha" testing occurs at the development site, and "beta" testing at selected external sites.

bibliographic citation: A precise reference to an original document or source of information. *See also* **full text**.

binary: Composed of two parts.

bit: The smallest unit of computer data, represented by a 1 or 0; shortened form of "binary digit."

bitmap: The arrangement of pixels in rows and columns on a computer monitor to display an image. Each pixel can be black or white, or have up to 32 bits of color.

bitmapped graphics: Pictures created with bitmap software; sometimes called raster graphics.

bit specifications: The number of colors or levels of gray that can be displayed on a computer monitor at one time; ranges from 256 to 16.8 million.

Boolean logic: A logical system of searching for groups of words by combining them with AND, OR, or NOT. Developed by George Boole in the mid-1800s.

boot: To start a computer.

bps: Bits per second. Used to measure speed of data transmission.

branching: Moving nonsequentially from one part of a program to another. *See also* **hypertext**.

bridge: A device that links two physically separate LANs.

broadcast quality: A U.S. standard of 525 lines of video picture information.

brouter: A combination of bridge and router for linking two or more LANs together.

browse: To search online through an index, subject headings, or list of topics.

buffer: A small portion of computer memory allocated to temporarily store data.

built-in: CD-ROM drives mounted internally in a computer, rather than standalone or external. Built-in drives are full-height (3.25" high) or half-height (1.63-1.75" high).

bundling: Selling computer hardware with pre-selected software or peripherals.

burst transmission: Transmitting data intermittently in groups rather than continuously; data is temporarily stored and then released at once at a faster speed.

bus: A pathway between hardware devices, either within a computer or between a computer and external devices.

button: A visible spot on a computer screen that, if touched or clicked, activates a link to another location.

byte: Eight bits that represent one character.

cables: Various lines used to transmit data. Cables used specifically with computers are twisted pair, shielded twisted pair, coaxial, and fiber optic. *See also* **STP** and **twisted pair**.

caching: Temporarily storing CD-ROM data in anticipation of the user's next search request. *See also* **data buffer.**

caddy: The plastic container that holds and protects a CD when the disc is inserted into a CD-ROM player.

CAI: Computer-Assisted (or Aided) Instruction.

carrier: An electric wave or alternating current.

CAV: Constant Angular Velocity. One method of recording and reading data on a disc. Data is recorded in concentric circles of sectors. The disc spins at the same speed all the time, while data is recorded more densely closer to the center of the disc. Not used for recording CD-ROMs. *See also* **CLV.**

CBT: Computer-Based Training.

CCIR 601: A standard resolution for digital television.

CD: Compact Disc. A 12-cm. plastic optical disc used to store large amounts of information. A laser beam reads the digital data, in the form of microscopic pits and lands. Discs may store digitized audio, graphics, video and optical text data.

CD-DA: Compact Disc-Digital Audio. The music disc, first developed by Sony and Philips in 1980.

CD-I: Compact Disc Interactive. A Philips proprietary compact disc format containing prerecorded digital video, audio, and optical text data. The CD-I drive contains its own dedicated computer system.

CD-R: CD-Recordable.

CD-ROM: Compact Disc-Read Only Memory. Information on this disc cannot be erased, altered or added to.

CD-ROM XA: CD-ROM Extended Architecture. The standard for interleaving or alternating audio and graphics or text data. The ability to play an audio track while loading other kinds of data eliminates some of the "wait problems" users have with CD-ROM.

CDTV: Commodore Dynamic Total Vision. A self-contained multimedia system from Commodore.

CD-WORM: *See* **WORM.**

CGA: Color Graphics Adapter. Displays four colors for an IBM-compatible computer.

CGM: Computer Graphics Metafile. A standard format for interchanging images.

classification system: Arranging information according to its subject matter.

client: A node on a network that requests services from another node. Sometimes referred to as a "workstation," as distinguished from a server.

CLV: Constant Linear Velocity. A method of recording and reading data on a disc; used to record CD-ROMs. Data is stored in the same density on one continuous spiral track over the entire disc. Because the data passes over the reading head at the same speed, the disc spins faster or slower according to what sector is being read. The disc's range of speed is 200-500rpm. *See also* **CAV.**

CMYK: Cyan, Magenta, Yellow, and blacK. The colors used in four-color printing.

coaxial cable: A type of cable used for networks. It is well-shielded and insulated, with a central conductor.

command: An instruction to the computer to perform a specified task.

command search: Software that accepts direct commands to the computer to conduct a search for data. *See also* **menu-driven search.**

communications software: Software that can be installed on computers to allow communication or data transmission between them.

compatible: An adjective that describes hardware or software that can be used with a specific computer.

compression: Reducing the size of a data file by removing unused space in the file. *See also* **decompression.**

concentrator: The central hub of a LAN using a star topology. *See also* **topology.**

CONFIG.SYS: A file executed when the computer is started. It allocates memory for certain functions and installs device drivers for peripherals, such as printers and CD-ROM drives.

connectivity: The ability to transmit data from one computer or device to another.

continuous tone: An image, such as a photograph, that uses all of the gray or color values.

contrast: The range between light and dark tones in an image.

controlled vocabulary: Specific terms used to search a database. Similar to a thesaurus.

conventional memory: In the IBM-compatible world, RAM memory from 0 to 1024K.

CPU: Central Processing Unit. The "brains" of a computer.

CRT: Cathode Ray Tube. The computer monitor or display screen.

cursor: A small, flashing symbol which indicates exact location on the computer screen.

DAC: Digital to Analog Conversion.

daisychain: A way of attaching up to seven peripheral devices, such as printers and CD-ROM drives, to a single SCSI port on a computer. Sometimes also refers to a type of computer network.

data: Information. Can be text, video, audio, animation or images.

database: A collection of similar types of information stored as fields and records; often called a file.

data buffer: For CD-ROM, where portions of data are temporarily stored while the drive accesses the next (often assumed) portion. *See also* **caching**.

Data Discman: Hand-held CD-ROM player manufactured by Sony. Uses mini-CDs.

data entry: Adding information to a database or other storage facility using a keyboard, scanner, or other input device.

data export: Sending out images, graphics, video, sound, or text files from one program or computer to another.

data import: Bringing in images, graphics, video, sound, or text files from one program or computer to another.

data preparation: Readying a database for CD-ROM manufacture.

dataware: A collection of data on a CD-ROM or floppy disk only compatible with specific search software.

decompression: Expansion of previously compressed data. *See also* **compression**.

dedicated line: A telephone line reserved for a specific use, such as a modem, fax or network.

dedicated server: A large computer on a network reserved exclusively as the server. Cannot be used as a workstation.

delivery system: Hardware and software required to play back a multimedia presentation; sometimes called the runtime system.

descriptor: Specific word or phrase used to describe or identify something; often listed in a thesaurus. If the list of descriptors is accurate and complete, descriptor searching is fast and efficient. *See also* **free-text**.

device driver: Software that controls the CD-ROM drive; translates operating system commands into commands each brand of drive recognizes.

digital: A discretely variable signal or characteristic such as a pulse, digitized image, or animated video, as opposed to an infinitely variable analog signal or characteristic, such as time, temperature, or movie video.

digital video: A video signal represented in binary format.

digitize: To convert data into a form a computer can recognize and process; also, to convert data from analog to digital.

disc: An optical storage medium.

disk: A magnetic storage medium.

disk caching: Placing frequently used data in RAM for quicker access.

disk drive: Hardware required to access a disk. This may be a hard disk drive or a floppy; either type may be internal or external.

disk server: A big computer that functions as a server on a network; the one or more disk drives on the server are generally very large and fast. *See also* **server**.

display: Information on the computer screen after a search has been executed; also another term for a computer's monitor, terminal, or screen.

DMA: Direct Memory Access. A circuit for transferring data within a computer without using the main microprocessor.

document: A generic term for any file created with an application on a computer, or a journal article, report, book, paper or other item in a database.

documentation: The user's guide, owner's guide, or reference manual that comes with a computer, computer peripheral or software package.

DOS: Disk Operating System. Contains the set of instructions IBM-compatible computers need to function and interact with peripheral devices and software. *See also* **operating system**.

double speed drive: A CD-ROM drive that transfers text and graphics at 300KB/sec, and audio at 150KB/sec.

download: To transfer data from one computer to another. *See also* **upload**.

drive: *See* **disk drive**.

DVI: Digital Video Interactive. Intel's process for compressing full-motion video (FMV) and audio on a CD-ROM (or hard disk) so that it can be played back on IBM multimedia systems. Compression occurs offline and decompression in real-time (as the disc is being used). Seventy-two minutes of FMV can be stored on one DVI disc, whereas only 30 seconds of FMV can be stored on a CD-ROM. It would take an hour to output that video from a CD-ROM.

EGA: Enhanced Graphics Adapter. Displays 16 colors with high resolution on an IBM-compatible computer.

electronic mail: Messages sent between computers connected by a network or by using telephone lines.

e-mail: *See* **electronic mail**.

emulation: Imitation of one device by another.

encode: To convert data into machine-readable format.

end-user: The person who will use information requested; as opposed to an information intermediary who finds information for someone else.

error correction: When an error-correction code is added to each block of data during CD-ROM premastering to ensure error detection *and correction. See also* **error detection**.

error detection: Coding that will find or indicate errors, but not necessarily correct them. *See also* **error correction**.

Ethernet: A baseband LAN developed by XEROX that typically transmits at ten megabits per second.

expanded memory: In the IBM-compatible world, the portion of RAM that must be added or emulated to run some programs, such as WordPerfect and Lotus 2.x and 3.x, most efficiently.

expert system: A program that uses stored information to perform a difficult task usually performed only by a human expert.

extended memory: In the IBM-compatible world, any memory beyond the first megabyte of RAM.

extensions: Programs added to an operating system to give it added capabilities. For example, extensions must be added to DOS for it to recognize files more than 32MB in size, such as those on a CD-ROM.

external drive: *See* **disk drive.**

fax: Common name for facsimile transmission, which uses telephone lines to transmit an image of a document. Sometimes referred to as telecopying.

fiber optic cable: Lines that use light rather than electricity to conduct data.

field: A distinct part of the records in a database that contain similar data. For example, the second field in every record may contain the date the record was created.

file: A single, logical set of data; often a term used interchangeably with "database" or "document."

file server: A node on a LAN that serves as the storage and distribution center for the other nodes on the LAN.

file sharing: More than one node on a LAN accessing a file; the file server maintains shared files.

filter: A computer program written to eliminate irregularities in a database before mastering for a CD-ROM.

fixed disk: *See* **hard disk.**

floppy disk: A removable, portable magnetic storage medium. The current standard is a 3.5-inch disk.

floppy disk drive: *See* **disk drive.**

FMV: Full-Motion Video. Video reproduction at 30 frames-per-second.

font: The complete set of characters for one typeface; includes uppercase and lowercase characters, figures, and punctuation marks.

format: Characteristics of a document; these may include visual (size, orientation, margins, font, etc.), platform (IBM, MPC, Mac, etc.), data (indexing, tables, etc.), and others.

fractals: A type of graphics software that translates the outline of an object into mathematical formulas. These formulas can be used to recreate the object, or modified to create other objects.

frame: One picture or image in video or film.

frame grabber: Computer software or hardware designed to capture and store a single video frame.

frame rate: Video image display speed.

free-text: To search through every word of the documents in a database for the desired text. *See also* **descriptor** and **index searching**.

frequency: The rate at which a signal oscillates, usually measured in hertz (Hz) or kilohertz (KHz).

full text: A document in a database that contains every word of the original. *See also* **bibliographic citation**.

function key: A key on the computer keyboard that activates a specific command when pressed.

gain: To increase (boost) an audio signal.

gateway: A translation device to link two unlike computer functions. This can occur between two LANs or two telecommunications systems.

genlock: Locking two video signals together so they begin at the same time and run at the same rate.

gigabyte: Approximately a thousand megabytes.

gradient: A smooth blend from one color to another, or from black to white.

Graphical User Interface: *See* **GUI**.

graphics: Portrayed information such as maps, charts, graphs, photographs, and pictorial representations.

Green Book: The common name for the set of standards developed for CD-I.

GUI: Graphical User Interface. A visual interface for computers popularized by the Macintosh computer and Windows application.

hardcopy: Paper or print version of machine-readable data.

hard disk: A computer's permanently installed magnetic storage medium.

hardware: The physical components of a computer system such as the monitor, keyboard, disk drives, etc.

HDTV: High Definition Television. A standard for a higher resolution, wider ranged television picture, with digital quality audio.

HFS: Hierarchical File Structure. The design of the operating system used in a Macintosh computer.

high resolution: Better image quality because of more pixels per square inch.

High Sierra: A standardized format for placing files and directories on a CD-ROM. This was amended and became the NISO standard ANS Z39.60-198X (1985).

hit: An item retrieved using a search request.

HSB: Hue, Saturation, Brightness. Allows the definition by percentages of all colors.

hub: The central device in a LAN using a star topology. *See also* **topology**.

hypermedia: Linking text, graphics, audio, and other media together nonsequentially, usually by association.

hypertext: Text linked nonsequentially, with instant access to related parts usually by "point and click" with a mouse. The two most popular hypertext software packages are IBM's Linkway and the Macintosh HyperCard. *See also* **branching**.

icon: A picture that represents a function or feature in a graphical user interface.

ID switches: One or more switches on a CD-ROM drive that assign an ID number to the drive. When more than one peripheral device is attached to the SCSI port, each device must have a unique number.

image: A computerized picture.

image resolution: The measurement of a picture's resolution when it was digitized, measured in Dots Per Inch (DPI).

Imagination Machine: Desktop CD-I player from Philips.

index searching: *See* **descriptor**.

information retrieval: Extracting data from a database, usually according to some search criteria. *See also* **search software** and **online searching**.

initialize: To start for the first time. A floppy or hard disk must be prepared or formatted (initialized) so that the computer can locate stored information.

input: To enter data into the computer; also the entered data itself.

interactive: Software technology that allows users to move through a program according to their own needs and at their own speed; feedback from the program allows choices and branching at many points.

interface: A hardware link between two systems, or the software link between a user and a system.

interlace: Using two vertical scans to display video image; one for the even lines, the other for odd.

interleave: To mix different streams of data, such as audio and graphics, so they can be played back simultaneously.

internal drive: *See* **disk drive**.

interrupt: A command to the computer to stop its current operation, save its location, and start another operation.

I/O: Input/Output.

IPX: Internet Packet Exchange. Novell's Netware communications protocol that routes messages from one node to another.

ISDN: Integrated Services Digital Network. A service provided by telephone companies for transmitting digital data.

ISO: International Standards Organization. Establishes and manages standards for digitizing video, audio, etc. *See also* **NISO**.

ISO 8879: Standard Graphics Markup Language (SGML). Sets the standard for exchange of electronic text. *See also* **SGML**.

ISO 9660: Creates a standard format for files and directories on a CD-ROM; these files can be read on both IBM and Macintosh platforms.

jewel box: Hinged plastic box in which most CDs are packaged.

joystick: An input device like the throttle stick in an airplane. Primarily used for computer games.

jukebox: One single CD-ROM drive mechanism in which four to six discs can be swapped in and out. *See also* **multidrive player**.

KB/sec: Kilobytes per second.

keyword: Any searchable word in a database; distinct from descriptor. Used for full-text searches.

KHz: *See* **kilohertz**.

kilobyte: 1024 bytes.

kilohertz: 1000 cycles per second. Refers to signal frequencies.

KWIC: Keyword In Context. Retrieving a keyword with part of the record in which it appears.

LAN: Local Area Network. A group of computers networked together with cabling and software, all within a small distance.

LAN Manager: Networking software developed by Microsoft and 3Com Corp.

lands: The reflective areas between nonreflective pits on a CD-ROM or audio disc. Together, pits and lands represent binary data.

laser: An acronym for light amplification by stimulated emission of radiation. Optical media is both created and read by a laser beam.

laserdisc: *See* **videodisc.**

latency: The delay when accessing data on a CD-ROM as the disc rotates to the desired position.

LCD: Liquid Crystal Display. A type of display most often used on portable or laptop computers.

leased line: A dedicated telephone line supplied by the telephone company to connect two points; transmission speed is usually fast.

linear: A sequence read from beginning to end. *See also* **hypertext** and **interactive.**

link: A connection between nodes in a hypertext database.

list price: Retail price set by a manufacturer or producer.

local area network: *See* **LAN.**

LocalTalk: A network standard used on Macintosh computers.

logoff: To end a computing session.

logon: To connect to a network, online database, e-mail, bulletin board or other group venture. Usually requires a user name and a password.

machine-readable: Data a computer can "read" electronically.

MARC: Machine-Readable Catalog. MARC records conform to the standard set by the Library of Congress.

master: An original recording of a finished program.

mastering: Producing an original recording mold on a glass disc using a laser to etch pits on the surface of the disc. This master is then used to stamp out multiple optical discs.

MB: *See* **megabyte**.

MCI: Media Control Interface. Microsoft specification for multimedia device control.

megabyte: A measurement of data storage equal to approximately one million bytes.

megahertz: A measurement of the number of cycles per second on a particular frequency that equals one million cycles per second; usually abbreviated MHz. MHz generally measures video bandwidths, while kilohertz (KHz) measures audio bandwidths.

memory: Generally refers to the amount of Random Access Memory (RAM) in any given computer.

menu: A list of available choices of functions provided by the software; pull-down menus are a standard feature of graphical user interfaces.

menu-driven search: Searching for information by choosing functions from a menu. *See also* **command search**.

MHz: *See* **megahertz**.

MIDI: Musical Instrument Digital Interface. The data bus standard for exchanging information between musical instruments, synthesizers, and computers.

MMPC: MultiMedia Portable Computer. Manufactured by Sony.

modeling: Educational software that replicates a real-life situation or process. Variables can be changed to demonstrate cause and effect.

modem: An acronym for modulate-demodulate referring to a device that converts digital signals to analog and analog to digital so that digital data may be sent over telephone lines.

monitor: Video display unit for a computer; also referred to as a terminal, display, or screen.

motion video: A sequence of images displayed fast enough to give the viewer the impression of real motion.

mouse: A hand-operated pointing device used to move the cursor on the computer screen and perform functions by clicking the mouse buttons.

MPC: Multimedia Personal Computer. Developed in 1991 by Tandy and Microsoft. The minimum Level 1 requirements for an MPC are a 386 machine with 2MB of RAM, a hard drive, Windows 3.1, a VGA monitor, a CD-ROM drive and a sound card.

MSCDEX: Microsoft CD-ROM Extensions. Additions to DOS that help the operating system recognize a CD-ROM player and process large files.

MTBF: Mean Time Between Failure. A way to measure hardware's reliability or repair record.

multidrive player: One CD-ROM player with four drive mechanisms. *See also* **jukebox**.

multimedia: The ability to run various kinds of data (text, graphics, sound, motion video, etc.) in one application or for one purpose.

multiplayer: A disc playing system consisting of multiple CD-ROM player units connected to and controlled by a single personal computer.

multisession: The ability of the CD-ROM XA drive to read Kodak Photo CDs that store more than one photographic session. *See also* **single session**.

navigate: To move nonsequentially from node to node in a hypertext or hypermedia database.

NETBIOS: Network Basic Input/Output System. Software developed by IBM to interface LANs, DOS, and applications.

NetWare: Network operating system developed by Novell, Inc.

network: Computers connected by cable and having software that allows them to share programs and peripherals, and to exchange files.

networking: To connect two or more computers or peripherals together.

NIC: Network Interface Card. Must be installed in all computers accessing a LAN.

NISO: National Information Standards Organization. Establishes U.S. national standards for libraries, information sciences, and publishing. *See also* **ISO**.

node: A workstation or terminal on a LAN; an access or entry point in a hypertext or hypermedia database.

NOS: Network Operating System. A set of computer instructions, similar to DOS, for managing LAN resources and activities.

NTSC: National Television Standard Committee. Sets the standard for U.S. color television transmission. The European standard is PAL (Phase Alternation Lines), which is not compatible with the NTSC standard.

OCR: Optical Character Recognition. Software that can translate a scanned bitmap image of text into digital, machine-readable text.

online: Any activity on a computer while it is running, or accessing an electronic database or system using a modem and telephone lines.

online searching: Using a computer and software to access a database on another computer and find the required information. *See also* **information retrieval** and **search software**.

OPA: Optical Publishing Association.

operating system: System software that controls a computer's internal functions. *See also* **DOS**.

optical: Computer systems that use laser technology to record and read data.

optical server: A dedicated server to provide simultaneous users with access to CD-ROM drives.

Orange Book: Sets the standards for CD-ROM WORM (Compact Disc-Write Once Read Many) technology.

overlay: Superimposing text or graphics onto motion video.

packet: A small amount of information in binary digit format transmitted to and from LAN nodes. Treated as single units.

PAL: Phase Alternation Lines. The European standard for color television transmission.

parallel port: A port on the back of a computer through which peripheral devices may be connected and data is passed in parallel rows. *See also* **RS 232C** and **serial port.**

password: A confidential and unique character string or word that restricts user access to databases, LANs, and other group ventures.

PC: Personal Computer. Traditionally refers to the IBM-compatible computers.

PCX: A graphics file format.

peripheral: Assorted and related hardware devices that may be connected to and controlled by a computer, such as a printer, modem or CD-ROM drive.

Photo CD: The CD-ROM standard created by Philips and Kodak for storing and viewing digitized color images from slides and photographs.

PIC: Graphics file format.

PICT: Graphics file format.

pits: The microscopic, nonreflective indentations in a CD's surface. Pits and lands compose the digital data recorded on a CD.

pixel: An acronym for picture element. One single point or dot on a computer display.

polycarbonate: Durable plastic material from which CDs are constructed.

port: A socket in a computer for connecting a peripheral with a cable. Several configurations are available for ports. *See also* **SCSI** and **serial port**.

premastering: Preparing information for mastering and pressing into optical discs. The stages for producing CD-ROMs are data preparation, premastering, mastering and disc replication.

printer: A device for making a paper copy of a computer file; attached to the computer by cable.

printout: A paper record of a computer file, online search or database listing.

program: A set of instructions for accomplishing a specific task; can also be called "software" or "application."

prompt: An indication from the computer that it is waiting for the user to take action; usually the prompt is a simple flashing character, but it may take the form of a dialog box.

protocol: A set of rules that governs transmission of data between various hardware devices.

proximity search: An online search that specifies the physical relationship of the keywords by indicating "next to," "near," "within," "adjacent to," and so on.

public domain: Material not copyrighted.

QuickTime: Apple's Macintosh system software that integrates video, sound and animation across all applications.

RAM: Random Access Memory. Data storage in a computer that permits rapid and nonsequential access. All data in RAM disappears when the computer is turned off.

raster: A pattern of scanning an image from left to right and top to bottom.

raster graphics: *See* **bitmapped graphics.**

read: Retrieving data from a computer storage medium.

real-time: Processing data immediately; no storage or offline processing occurs.

recall: The number of records retrieved from a database.

record: A collection of information related to one item or subject; in a database, one record has multiple fields, with each field containing similar information.

Red Book: Standard creating CD-Audio discs.

relevance: The ratio of the number of relevant records retrieved during a database search as related to the number of relevant records actually present in the database.

repeater: A device to boost signal transmission; can be used to extend a network's geographic limitations.

replication: Producing multiple copies of a CD-ROM master disc.

resolution: The number of pixels in a given area. The higher the number of pixels, the higher the resolution and the clearer the graphic image.

retrieval program: *See* **search software.**

RGB: Red, Green, Blue. Refers to a type of computer monitor with separately controlled color output; generally high resolution.

ring: A network topology in which nodes are connected in a closed loop. Data is transmitted in one circular direction.

Rock Ridge Group: Promoters of UNIX-based 9660 standards with new features for UNIX.

ROM: Read Only Memory. Internal memory used by the computer for its own purposes.

router: A device that selects the best path for transmitting data between two LANs.

RS 232C: A standard serial port on the back of the computer for connecting peripheral devices. *See also* **parallel port** and **serial port**.

runtime system: *See* **delivery system**.

sampling: Measuring the value of an analog signal at intervals, then encoding those values to create a corresponding digital signal; especially used with music.

scanner: A hardware device that converts information on paper to a bitmapped graphic on a computer.

SCSI: Small Computer System Interface. An eight-bit parallel bus interface for connecting a peripheral to a computer. SCSI-2 specifications contain standardized audio commands for CD-ROM drives; also has faster transfer speeds. *See also* **port** and **serial port**.

search engine: *See* **search software**.

search software: Software programs specifically written to search and extract information from electronic databases. *See also* **information retrieval** and **online searchware**.

SECAM: *Sequential Coleur Avec Memoire*. The French standard for color television transmission.

sector: The smallest addressable unit of a disc's track.

seek time: The actual amount of time it takes for the CD-ROM drive's optical beam to move from reading one location to the next location. A major part of the access time.

SEGA CD: CD peripheral for a 16-bit Genesis system; docks with a Genesis game console.

serial port: A standard port on the back of the computer for attaching peripheral devices. Data is transmitted in a single file. *See also* **parallel port, port, RS 232C,** and **SCSI**.

server: A large computer that controls a network and provides shared access to resources and files. *See also* **disk server**.

SGML: Standard Graphics Markup Language. *See also* **ISO 8879**.

shareware: Software available for trial from software groups or large bulletin boards. Shareware deemed worth keeping generally requires a small fee payable to its producer.

shielded twisted pair: *See* **STP**.

shielding: Protecting transmission hardware to prevent interference.

single session: A Photo CD with only one set of digitized images. *See also* **multisession**.

software: Specific instructions written in computer code that computers use to perform certain tasks.

software driver: Hardware that helps a computer communicate directly and efficiently with a peripheral device.

sound board: A hardware component that helps IBM-compatible computers broadcast quality sound from digitized sources such as a CD-ROM.

spin-up time: The amount of time a CD-ROM drive at rest takes to get up to speed.

standalone: A self-contained CD-ROM player external to the computer.

standards: Rules for software production, format or access so that products will be available to users across many different platforms.

star: A LAN topology in which all the network nodes are connected directly to a central hub.

STP: Shielded Twisted-Pair cable. Provides some protection against interference. *See also* **cables** and **twisted pair**.

surge protector: A device used to protect a computer against sudden electrical surges.

SVGA: Super VGA. Improved resolution and increased number of colors for IBM-compatible display. *See also* **VGA**.

telecopying: *See* **fax.**

terminal: A computer output device from which the user receives information; also called a monitor, screen, or display.

text: Legible character strings usually stored and transmitted in ASCII form.

thesaurus: A list of designated words or descriptors, to help when searching a specific database.

TIFF: A graphics file format.

token ring: A LAN topology in which data is transmitted only when a flag or "token" is present; data collisions are, therefore, prevented.

topology: The physical and logical characteristics of a LAN such as star, ring or bus. *See also* **concentrator** and **hub.**

tower: A hardware peripheral with multiple internal CD-ROM drives.

track: A continuous segment on a CD.

transceiver: An interface device in Ethernet installations.

transfer rate: Speed at which a CD-ROM player displays accessed information on the screen.

TSR: Terminate and Stay Resident. Software that loads into memory before other programs can be executed.

turnkey system: A complete system purchased from one vendor that contains every element needed to "turn the key" and start working.

twisted-pair: Cable with two main wires twisted along its entire length; primarily used for telephone wiring. *See also* **cables** and **STP**.

Ultimedia: IBM's standard for a multimedia computer; runs on a PS/2 computer and supports CD-ROM XA and DVI.

UNIX: An operating system developed by Bell Labs.

update: To bring a database up-to-date by adding the latest information, or a new version of a software package.

upload: To transfer data from a local computer to a distant computer. *See also* **download**.

VGA: Video Graphics Array. Monitor used by IBM-compatible computers for multimedia applications. *See also* **SVGA**.

VHS: Video Home System. The industry standard for consumer videotape.

video capture: *See* **frame grabber**.

videodisc: An optically-encoded disc containing up to 54,000 analog images or 30 minutes of full-motion video.

virtual reality: A computer-generated alternative world in which the user can interact with objects and initiate actions.

VIS: Video Information System. A CD-ROM system from Tandy that connects to a television.

window: A defined area on the screen containing specific information.

Windows: A graphical interface for an IBM-compatible computer featuring pull-down menus, icons, and use of a mouse.

workgroup: People with similar work-related needs and who require access to similar resources.

workstation: An individual terminal or computer on a LAN.

WORM: Write Once Read Many. An optical system used to create a custom database where data is written once to a blank disc and can then be retrieved many times.

write: Writing or recording data to a computer storage medium.

XGA: Extended Graphics Adapter. IBM graphics standard that includes VGA and a higher resolution.

Yellow Book: The common name for the set of standards developed for CD-ROM.

INDEX

....

Notes

Notes